Praise for

OLD WHITE MAN WRITING

"Joshua Gidding, the Pessoa of his own disquiet, is a master of tonal nuance, working to nail the least discrepancy between his language and the truth of what he feels. He is onto himself, and onto himself being onto himself—a regress that exposes, chastens, and, for the reader, delights."

> **—SVEN BIRKERTS,** critic, editor, and author of *The Miró Worm and the Mysteries of Writing* (forthcoming) and many other books

"In *Old White Man Writing*, Joshua Gidding takes an unflinching look at seventy years of life—ideas, learning and teaching, love, joy, regret, privilege, sorrow, pain, hate, guilt, friendship, parenthood, writing, shame, and even the act of self-examination—with a view to a verdict. This is memoir as blood sport."

> **—THOMAS PERRY,** author of *Hero, The Old Man* (now a series streaming on Hulu), the Jane Whitefield collection, and many other bestselling novels

"Gidding proves to be 'old' only literally. His memoir is replete with a bracing, meta modernity—sometimes deeply funny, sometimes deeply rueful—and has the uncompromising, at times self-flagellating energy of a much younger man trying to figure out his place in the universe. With the help of his impish, sardonic (and hilarious) alter ego Joßche, he recounts the stages and experiences of a long life that have made him the young old man before us: a writer determined to reveal himself with an honesty that is both breathtaking and rare."

> **—HOWARD FRANKLIN,** writer and director, *Quick Change* and *The Public Eye*

"Joshua Gidding enables the reader to understand the process and meaning of memoir writing in ways we never imagined. Under the sometimes unwelcome light of 'biographization,' the people he has wronged and cherished are showcased in an extraordinary manner that rekindles the embers of lives that might otherwise be lost. This is an extraordinary book that invites us to join as participants, not voyeurs. The journey is worth it. You'll see your world differently (and perhaps more fully) after visiting here. I promise."

—**MURRAY SINCLAIR,** author of the Ben Crandel mystery trilogy and the novel *F. Scott Fitzgerald: American Spy*

"Howard Jacobson said that 'art is made ... in the language of the dispossessed ... by those who consider themselves to have failed at whatever isn't art.' Joshua Gidding, who titled his previous memoir *Failure,* is a connoisseur of his own malfunctions and he interrogates them again here—his deep loves, betrayals, abysmal grief, his incompleteness, his wit, his inwardness, self-consciousness, blindness, ungenerousness and expansiveness, via his art—his own alive, discursive, crude, poetic, erudite, funny, brave, joyful, heartbreaking and ultimately liberating 'language of the dispossessed.'"

—**JO PERRY,** author of *The World Entire, Pure,* and the *Dead* series

"This is vintage Josh Gidding—honest, unflinching, unflattering, *hopeful,* and oh so refreshingly real. With a keen eye and sharp intellect, Gidding excavates his own life, searching for important truths about race and privilege, holding them to the light, inspecting them, refusing the shade and comfort of triteness, preferring instead to keep himself in the harsh light. In doing so, he has articulated something essentially human: the need to be heard, whoever we are. Gidding's exploration is as meaningful—and necessary—as it is uncomfortable. But that's the point. We squirm because he's telling us the parts that normally get swept under the rug. This book is a spring cleaning of dirty secrets, and contributes a valuable voice to an important conversation."

—**GREG NOVEMBER,** Jack Straw Fellow (2021) and author of "The Business of Killing Tony" (*Boulevard*)

"*Old White Man Writing* pits a first-person narrative that custom leads us to identify with the biographical author, Joshua Gidding, against his invented opposing self, Joßche, who exposes the contortions and distortions of the first-person narrator as he fails to meet the expectations his privileged white position has generated. The book gives us charged exchanges between these two narrators, vivid in themselves, that also make clear that experience is always our shaping of experience, and that this shaping is always tinged, consciously or unconsciously, by our motives, even as we have been shaped by our whole history. For those of us who have read Gidding's *Failure: An Autobiography*, his new memoir is an occasion to discover depths at which we had only guessed, or hadn't even guessed."

—**PETER MANNING,** Professor of English, Emeritus, Stony Brook University, and author of *Byron and His Fictions* and *Reading Romantics: Texts and Contexts*

"A friend of mine wanted to know why some relatives swept dust into the room instead of out the door. She found out that her Jewish family got swept out of Spain in 1492, and that it was considered sacrilegious to sweep the dust out past the mezuzah on the front doorframe. Now look at this passage from *Old White Man Writing*: 'I thought of bundling my books together and naming them "Out from under the Rug." The idea being that the stuff I was writing about—failure, and loss, and shame—is the stuff that, in America, gets swept under the rug. And I was the guy to sweep it back out again.' Well, it's all here. He's a brilliant confessional American with top skills in the comedic self-deprecation department. The sacred in his work is literature, authors, and the making of story from searing loss. A great book is the best imaginary friend, and readers will delight in the parasocial completion that comes from listening in to Gidding's storytelling."

—**JOHN WHALEN-BRIDGE,** author (*Political Fiction and the American Self* and *Tibet on Fire*), editor (*The Emergence of Buddhist American Literature* and *Writing as Enlightenment*), authorized biographer of Maxine Hong Kingston (forthcoming), and Associate Professor of English, National University of Singapore

"Josh Gidding takes an unsparing look at his own life as a self-described liberal white man of privilege. The result is a sharp, provocative, and brutally honest account that lays bare the complexities and contradictions of being an 'old white man writing' about race in today's world."

—**STEPHANIE STAAL,** author of *Reading Women: How the Great Books of Feminism Changed My Life* and *The Love They Lost: Living with the Legacy of Our Parents' Divorce*

"Think you have a firm handle on the political, cultural, and institutional changes in the last couple of decades? Well, you're wrong. Joshua Gidding's *Old White Man Writing* delightfully and warmly upsets those blubby certainties, not to embarrass us but to delight us with a wonderful play on our deep (and shallow) certainties."

—**JAMES R. KINCAID,** Aerol Arnold Professor of English, Emeritus, University of Southern California, and author of the novels *Lost* and *A History of the African American People (Proposed), by Strom Thurmond* (with Percival Everett), and many books of literary and cultural criticism

OLD WHITE MAN WRITING

OLD WHITE MAN WRITING

BY JOSHUA GIDDING

MASCOT® BOOKS

an imprint of Amplify Publishing Group

www.mascotbooks.com

Old White Man Writing

Cover illustration by Marco Primo

For more information, please contact:
Mascot Books, an imprint of Amplify Publishing Group
620 Herndon Parkway, Suite 220
Herndon, VA 20170
info@mascotbooks.com

Grateful acknowledgment is made to the following for permission to quote from song lyrics:
Alfred Publishing, LLC, for "Play That Funky Music," written by Robert Parissi, © 1976.
Alfred Publishing, LLC, and Chris-n-Jen Music, for "Don't Let Me Be Misunderstood," written by Bennie Benjamin, Gloria Caldwell and Sol Marcus, © 1964, 1992.
Hal Leonard, LLC, for "In My Life," written by John Lennon and Paul McCartney, © 1965, Sony/ATV Music Publishing.

Library of Congress Control Number: 2023923973
CPSIA Code: PRV1024A
ISBN-13: 979-8-89138-091-2

Printed in the United States

for Allen and Kirby

and for Julie,

"…namque tu solebas
meas esse aliquid putare nugas."

"I'm just a soul whose intentions are good.
Oh Lord, please don't let me be misunderstood."

—Eric Burdon and the Animals (1965)

OLD WHITE MAN WRITING

CONTENTS

PART I

PART I

Many years ago, in the early '90s, when I was in graduate school at USC and our son Zack was in preschool and then kindergarten, I used to take him to play at a small neighborhood park in Pacific Palisades, where I grew up. At the time, my parents were still alive and living in the Palisades, but Diane, my first wife (who was then very much alive, and not even sick yet), and Zack and I were living in much-less-tony East Hollywood, near the corner of Normandie and Sunset. One day at the park, while Zack was playing on the grass, I got to talking with a guy around my age, late thirties—maybe a little younger—who was there for a picnic with his girlfriend. (At least I assumed she was his girlfriend, since she looked considerably younger—mid-twenties, I would say.) He was outfitted in a French cycling shirt, shorts, and cap—the whole nine yards. A real go-getter. And sure enough, not long after we'd started chatting, he let it be known he worked in real estate and lived in the Palisades. He asked me what I did and where I lived, and I told him, also mentioning that I'd grown up in the Palisades and my parents still lived there. He asked me if I owned or rented. I told him we rented.

"Yeah, it's gotten really crazy on the West Side," he said. "I'm really glad I bought when I did. No way could I afford a house here now."

"Tell me about it," I said, perhaps affecting more regret than I actually felt. For Diane and I liked our ethnically diverse neighborhood, which was largely Armenian and Hispanic, though there'd been a more recent influx of Thai and Vietnamese immigrants as well. And as the bullish realtor went on about matters of interest to him—rising property values on the West Side, and the seller's market—my reflexive agreement began to seem somewhat disingenuous to me. What knew I, after all, of such worldly matters? I was a high-minded graduate student, studying the British Romantics and their literary interrelations.

As we talked, I began to be aware of being sized up and categorized by my interlocutor as something of a cautionary tale—a sense that soon became explicit when he declared, "Yeah, I was lucky to get in when I did—just under the wire." He paused for a moment's reflection. "I mean, I wouldn't want to have happen to me what happened to you."

"Really?" I replied. "What happened to me?"

The strange-sounding, not-quite-innocent question hung in the air for a beat, and then he grew flustered and mumbled something I couldn't entirely make out, though I did catch the phrase " … got priced out of the market."

With nothing more to be said on either end of the conversation, I went to check up on Zack, and soon after, the realtor and his girlfriend packed up their stuff and left.

It pleased me to see this guy hoist on his own petard, and I have retold the story a number of times, to much amusement. I repeat it here, though, for a different reason—not to look serenely victorious in the face of another guy's jerkitude, but because now, these many years later, my question has acquired a different resonance—not that of an apt and well-deserved put-down but of a genuine quandary: What *did* happen to me?

I am reminded here of something my father once said to my grandmother in the last year or two of her life. He had brought her to Los Angeles from New York, her native city—and from the brownstone on the Upper East Side she'd lived in for almost sixty years—and installed her in a Jewish nursing home on La Brea Ave. We had gone together one afternoon to visit her. She was in a very low state, as she usually was in that place: depressed and confused, but still lucid enough to frame a reasonable question, which she posed quizzically to both of us.

"How did this happen to me?" she asked. "How did I get here?"

My father replied, impatiently and rather brutally, "You got old, Ma."

I have never forgotten this brief exchange, not only because it was so harsh and heartbreaking, but even more, I think, because of the tone of my father's blunt answer, which was spoken without any apparent compassion or understanding for her confusion—if confusion it was, and not just frank wonder—or any apparent regret, either, for this inevitable (or maybe not so inevitable) turn of events. Rather, he sounded angry. Angry at her for getting old, and apparently not being able to see that, and maybe also angry at himself for the part he'd played in her denouement. What happened to me, at that small park in the Palisades and since, was undoubtedly different from what happened to Grandma Cissie; but our questions have since assumed, to my ears, some of the same baffled plangency. The answer I will attempt to give here is certainly longer and more elaborated than my father's, and with none of his anger or impatience (two qualities that he, with his writer's Hemingwayesque disbelief in psychotherapy—he thought it would interfere with his imagination—was never quite able to get a handle on). Still, it's a fair question, and deserves a fair set of answers.

The first answer is the same as my father's, if not in tone, then at least in substance: I, too, have gotten old—not nearly as old, yet, as my grandmother, but certainly well on the way. The second is that I've gotten more conservative—not politically (at seventy, I'm still a registered Democrat, and always will be, though of a merely liberal rather than progressive stamp, which I guess would count as conservative in some people's eyes) or socially—I embrace the browning of America, even if it passes me by (yet if it didn't pass me by, what would I have to write about?)—but rather culturally. I listen to mostly classical music now, and read books by mostly dead white European males. (I mean that most of the writers I read tend to be dead white European males, not that they are only partly alive. Zombies aren't my thing. Another generational marker that dates me.) And I guess in a sense I've gotten more male, and more white, too. Of course, I have always been male and white; what I mean is, I just never realized it before—at least not in the way I am coming to realize it now.

And just how is that? In being white and male, and straight, and privileged (I grew up in the Palisades, after all, even if I did get priced out of the market), I find myself identified with a group that many literary editors these days don't seem much interested in hearing from. It's the "OK, Boomer" syndrome, but one that includes the categories of race and gender as well. So culturally superannuated am I, in fact (with a nod here to the endearing Charles Lamb, another one of the defunct crew I like to read), that it makes me a little uncomfortable to use the terms "race and gender" unironically. They are not terms I was brought up with, and they sound a little disingenuous on my tongue. (Yet another strike against me, this time a linguistic one.) I feel I have no right to this kind of language; it's the diction of the young, the progressive, the diverse, the—OK, I'll just say it: the morally more enlightened and therefore superior.

I am being only partly ironic here. The irony comes from age and experience, though not in the sense that these qualities give me access to any greater knowledge or wisdom. They just give me a different perspective, which sometimes gets me in trouble with my progressive son, now thirty-seven and a lawyer. He tends to be impatient with my irony, and I think I understand why. He sees it as a defense—the defensiveness of a privileged older man (bordering on just plain old), who feels his ideals, his liberal but not progressive ideals, have become slightly tarnished with age. On balance, though, I would rather be scolded and corrected by the young than dismissive of them. If their moral enlightenment and superiority strike me sometimes as a little self-righteous, I recognize it is the same self-righteousness I once wore.

What bothers me is not envy at the finer moral instincts of the young, or the sense that they may after all be right in matters of race, gender, etc. It's the idea, coming not only from Zack, but from my second wife Julie as well, who is two years younger and also more progressive than I, that certain topics—race, gender, and so on—are off-limits for oldsters like me to consider in a more critical light. I resist this idea for a number of reasons. It hampers my freedom. It dismisses my qualifications, such as they are. (Even though I recognize that those qualifications—products of my privilege—could be seen as symptoms of the very problem I represent.) It disenfranchises me. It denies me a chance to explain myself, on the grounds that this explanation would be not only irrelevant, but slightly offensive as well. It muzzles me; and, like any dog—even one that's had its day—I resist the muzzle.

I recognize that this resistance is partly just another aspect of my privilege as an older straight white male. I have always been accorded a place at the table; indeed, it has always been *my* table. At my ultra-privileged prep school, the Phillips Exeter Academy, we all sat around oval oaken seminar tables called "Harkness Tables," which were part of the "Harkness System"—the result of an opulent 1930 endowment by the philanthropist (and oil tycoon) Edward Harkness, which stipulated that there be, at least ideally, no more than twelve students in a class, all of them sitting around a Harkness Table. The endowment also entailed the hiring of enough faculty to reach a schoolwide twelve-to-one student-faculty ratio. Around the Harkness Table, we few—we happy few!—were encouraged to express ourselves, to add thoughtfully to the ongoing discussion. There was no hiding at the Harkness Table. We all had a voice, and it was inconceivable that we would ever be prevented from using it.

I know all of this reeks of privilege. But to me, in all honesty, its smell is similar to what one experiences sitting on the toilet, where one recognizes that one's own product, which would stink to anyone else, has a scent that is perhaps not quite so bad—that is even, as La Rochefoucauld might have said, "not entirely displeasing to us." Now, my trace of pleasure at the Rochefoucauldian stink of my privilege—let us call it the Toilet Effect—is certainly not anything to boast of; though not to acknowledge it at the outset would only make me guilty of further disingenuousness. I am ashamed of my privilege; yet certain of its products I am rather proud of. For example: my classical education (BA in classics from Berkeley, preceded by a Classical Diploma from Exeter—one of only a handful in the class); my tastes in art, music, and literature; even my prose style. Yes, they all stink to high heaven of privilege; yet I continue to entertain the hope that the aroma may not be displeasing to the gods.

Which gods are those? The literary gods. The gods who hold sway over the editors and readers at the literary journals and publishing houses who continue to reject my submissions. And why do they continue to do this? Because of their reek, no doubt. (The submissions', not the editors', or their readers'!) So why don't I get rid of this reek? Well, the Toilet Effect. Besides, to try to do so would be—once again— disingenuous. It would be to try to change who I am. I am, willy-nilly, a creature of privilege, who had his chance and blew it. Which is to say, I failed to take advantage of all the advantages I had. For example, I didn't get into Harvard from Exeter, and then I didn't get in again, when I tried to transfer from Berkeley. *(Oh boo-hoo! You can't be serious! You call that a failure?* Yes I am, and I do.) I published my first novel at age twenty-six, but it bombed, and there was no second novel. (Several attempts, but no second novel.) I went to a second-rate graduate school (at least it was at the time I went to it), and then got a job at a fourth-rate private college on Long Island. (Literally fourth-rate; it was ranked consistently in the fourth—that is, the bottom—tier of American colleges and universities by *US News & World Report*.) I taught there for nineteen years, until the school (unsurprisingly) went bankrupt and had to close its doors. Now I am a part-time adjunct instructor at a community college just south of Seattle.

I mention all of this not to garner sympathy (though more likely the reader's response will be one of contempt and dismissal, perhaps with a bit of *Schadenfreude* mixed in; you see, Joßche, I am already throwing you a bone. *Yes, I see.*), but only to establish the facts behind my abiding sense of failure, of having blown it. And this sense of failure, in turn, occasions a sense of double-guilt: the guilt of being privileged, and the guilt of knowing that I blew my privilege. Granted, this double-guilt is also self-contradictory, in that it involves two fundamentally different, even opposed, kinds of guilt. And it is also true that this second kind of guilt—the guilt of failure—is more self-perceived than real. My achievements, such as they are, are certainly not failures in any objective sense. But we are not really talking about objectivity here; we are talking about subjective feelings, and so my sense of failure trumps the reality. I have not produced nearly enough to justify my privilege. It seems to me I have produced very little, in fact—certainly less than was hoped for.

OK, Boomer—as you Americans say. The problem is, nobody wants to hear this shit. Save it for your private journal. Not your blog, because you don't even have a blog. Some of your colleagues do, but you are so superannuated that you don't. Print is still the only form of publication that is real to you. So save it for your private, handwritten journal, never to be published, never to be printed. Never to be validated or even acknowledged. You had your chance—your many chances—your too many chances—and you blew it. Your time is over, Boomer, and your kind is over, too. Make way for the new.

I recognize that this opinion, voiced by my nemesis Joßche (more—all-too-much—of him anon), while uncharitable, is not unjustified. I have—as my other nemesis, the realtor guy, might have said—aged out of the market. I am writing this knowing it will probably be dismissed out of hand by the young editors' readers to whose publishing houses I will be submitting it *(if you ever will be submitting it)*. So who, then, am I writing it for? Well, it's beginning to look like it's for none other than myself, which is to say, basically, for no one. (Remember that old Beatles song?) And what does that mean, to be writing for no one? And isn't this claim more than a little disingenuous as well? Do I really believe I am writing for no one? Well, no, not completely. I have hopes that someday—more likely after my death than before, but not very likely even then—I will have readers. It is a frail and distant hope, but a hope nonetheless. A hope little more substantial, perhaps, than throwing a penny into the fountain. Almost nothing, but not quite. Gestures. But gestures merit some attention, too. They are not exactly nothing. Gestures are a kind of degraded or inchoate action. An action that stops short—way short—of commitment. But still. Gestures are indicative of a wish (closer to a velleity, perhaps), or a hope. The hope that my writing may, after all is said and written, be received and heard by someone other than just myself. Call my hope, then, the penny-in-the-fountain kind. A disposition of the soul, tending toward the forestallment of despair. A gesture that keeps me from despairing. (More of despair too, anon.) That keeps me writing—writing in the face of despair. (My writing is also a way of avoiding despair, the despair brought on by my failed efforts to have it published. And so we go round the merry-go-round!) I am writing in the face of my better knowledge that current market conditions (as my real-estate nemesis would say) are trending against me and my kind, not only now but into the foreseeable future. Maybe my writing amounts to a kind of wager that there may be those in the future—the harvesters of the pennies in the fountain, so to speak—who may find something for themselves in what I have to say. And the hope of those future harvesters serves as a kind of counterbalance to the realtor guy.

I realize the title I have chosen for this confession is problematic. It could be an instant turn-off, both in all of its separate parts and taken as a whole. It does not strike a sympathetic note at the outset. Or maybe it does, depending on where your sympathies lie. Or maybe, even, the phrase appeals both to your sympathies and your antipathies. If so, then you are my ideal reader. And it is at you, Ideal Reader—sympathetic/antipathetic reader, who is both attracted and repulsed by the notion of an Old White Man Writing—that I am aiming. I do not really expect to find you, but I have my hopes. They, the literary powers that be, have not taken those away.

And what of those hopes, those pennies in the fountain? What exactly are the hopes of an Old White Man Writing? What could he possibly have to hope for at this late stage of the game? That there might be someone listening? Someone who cares, or might care, about his situation? Someone who is not so turned off by the problematic identity of the writer—"Old White Man"—that they automatically dismiss him and his writing out of hand? Or misidentify him as reactionary? A resentful Republican complaining about the changing of the guard, the passing away of the literary ancien régime?

Because actually, Old White Man Writing, as already indicated, is none of those things. He is a liberal Democrat, who shares, if he cannot fully embrace, some progressive positions: a sympathy for Democratic socialism (and a respect for Bernie, although he could not back him for president; he voted for Hillary and then Biden); support for, and maybe even an embrace of, demographic change in the USA, which is historically and biologically inevitable, and even to be wished for (because white people are kind of a drag, aren't they?); and speaking of history, an acceptance of the course of history, and a belief that its arc bends toward justice (though with some tragic kinks along the way); an abiding respect for science, scholarship, academics (the field, not so much the people—though he is an academic himself, and it is perhaps because of this very fact that he does not so much respect the people in the field), and learning in general. These are some of the salient values of Old White Man Writing.

So now that I have trotted out his liberal credentials—the beliefs that will permit me, I hope, to use the phrase "Old White Man Writing" in a way that will not be taken invidiously—let us return to the other hopes in which Old White Man Writing continues to write. The hopes, the pennies in the fountain, that allow him to write and that constitute the grounds of his writing, if not exactly the matter of it. Or maybe they are the matter of it; maybe hope itself is the very essence of his writing. Because to write the kind of stuff Old White Man Writing writes is to hope to be listened to, perhaps even to be heard. This kind of writing, you could say, is a sign of hope, or at least a signaling of it. *Scribo, ergo spero.* I write, therefore I hope. I hope you can hear me. See me. Please see the dried-out old white dust bunny in the corner.

Is there, perhaps, just the tiniest bit of thematic resemblance here—irony of ironies!—to the opening pages of *Invisible Man*? Or is that just an outrageous travesty, whereby I forfeit the right to be taken seriously? Still, is there even the slightest echo—*mutatis mutandis*—of Ellison's novel? Though surely there are many *mutandis* here that need to be *mutatis*—perhaps too many to permit the analogy, which in any case will offend some people. I thought of deleting this whole section but finally decided to keep it. I figure there is no point in trying to make myself look better than I am. In that regard, should I add insult to injury here and claim literary kinship with Rousseau as well? No, better leave that one alone.

But I digress. I do tend to digress. *Caveat lector.* I also tend to throw around Latin—an occupational hazard for a former classics major. And I realize the Latin, plus the digressions, can also be a turn-off, unless you are that particular brand of ideal reader—my sympathetic/antipathetic reader—who has a taste for that kind of thing. But I cannot presume on that, and will do my best to keep the digressions and Latinisms under control. (Though I already know I will not always be able to restrain myself. As I say, *caveat lector.* But also, *gaudeat optimus lector*! Let the Ideal Reader rejoice! And better *optimus lector* than Hannibal Lecter!)

So, Old White Man Writing. Look at him go. He writes, he hopes. He drinks tea (lots of it); then he writes some more. He's been at it now for what, forty-six years? At least. Started writing his first (and only) novel in the summer of '78, when he was twenty-four. Published it two years later. To no acclaim. Panned in *People* magazine. But that story has already been told (in *Failure: An Autobiography*, 2007) and will not be repeated here. By a more generous estimate, he has been writing since 1965–66, when his sixth-grade teacher, Mrs. Latta, first encouraged his efforts. And after that Miss Compton, in eighth grade. Senior year at Exeter he took creative writing, and again as a sophomore in college. Four years after he graduated, *The Old Girl* (1980) was published. It wasn't that good. Terribly overwritten. (And he still has a tendency, maybe more than a tendency, in that direction.) So how did it even get published? Well, he happened to know an editor at a major trade publisher, an old college friend of his father's, who then became a friend of his, too. Good Old White Boy Network. (Yet another strike against him.) And then, after that first publication, zip for twenty-seven years, except for one short story in a small and short-lived literary journal; one essay-length memoir in an anthology published by his high school—I mean, prep school (*Say it again!* OK, Exeter. *There, that wasn't so bad, was it?* Well, maybe.); and three scholarly articles. Dissertation unpublished.

His publication history since 2007 has been similarly undistinguished: a handful of personal essays in literary journals, mostly online, and a number of book reviews, all online. The two book-length memoirs he wrote after *Failure* also unpublished, though not for lack of trying. Query letters sent out to around two hundred agents and independent publishers. A few requests for full manuscripts, but no dice. Yet Old White Man continues to write, and not without some small (though, frankly, diminishing) hope. Look at him still go.

The Old White Man, of course, is me. I am seventy years old, teaching part time at a community college just south of Seattle. I was a full-time professor for nineteen years at an obscure four-year private college on Long Island; but that college, seriously underfunded and mismanaged (*and seriously bad, too, a terrible school! Near the bottom of the fourth tier in* US News & World Report. *Shouldn't you tell them that, too?* I just did, Fritz. See above, and read my lips.), finally went bankrupt in 2016. Now drawing a decent Social Security income and monthly annuity payments from a TIAA account. Our mortgage is all paid off, and Julie just inherited a serious chunk of change from her deceased aunt. Materially speaking, I've got it pretty good. Very good, actually. I certainly cannot complain. Though I am sort of complaining, aren't I? And if there's anything more of a turn-off than Old White Man Writing, it's Old White Man Complaining. So my writing career hasn't exactly turned out to be a smashing success? So what? Maybe I'm just … not that good a writer.

This reminds me of a story my late brother-in-law (Diane's brother) told of a fancy meal he once had at an expensive resort in the Caribbean. The food was not that good. He told this to a waiter, who smiled, winked, and replied, "I know." And I'm wondering … Am I sort of that waiter? Do I secretly know that my product, the writing I am serving up here, is not that good? Then again, am I in any position to be a fair judge of the matter? Though shouldn't I be, after doing it seriously (more or less) for forty-six years? But I just said "more or less seriously," and maybe, by putting it that way, I am showing that I am, like the smiling, winking waiter, in on the joke. Maybe I am, when all is said and done, just not that serious a writer. In addition to being not that good a writer, I am also not that serious a writer. Old White Man Writing—but not all that well, and not all that seriously. So fuck him. Fuck me.

Harsh, I know. Is this really where I stand on the matter? Or am I what they call an "unreliable narrator"? Do I even trust myself? Admittedly, I have never had much self-confidence. And I wonder: Does this make me more, or less, trustworthy? Or does self-confidence really have nothing to do with trustworthiness? And who even cares? Does anyone care about the case of Old White Man Writing? Do I? Maybe I am writing this to find out.

Grammatical note: The phrase "old white man writing" is ambiguous. It can be construed as either a participial phrase or a gerund phrase. One of the courses I taught for years at the bad college that went bankrupt was English grammar. It was one of my two favorite courses to teach. The other was Chaucer—in the original (though I am not a medievalist). I am, or was, a generalist, but trained as a Romanticist. Now, however, I just teach composition part time at a community college. But I still love teaching grammar, and as a composition instructor I have ample opportunity to do that. So the phrase "old white man writing" could mean either "there is an old white man who is writing" or "this is writing of the 'old white man' variety." But in the latter case, you should really put hyphens between the adjectives: "old-white-man writing." And which case is it here? I guess it is both. Mostly the former, but sometimes the latter. I am an old white man, writing (about an old white man writing); and the kind of writing being done here is undeniably of the "old white man" variety. God, I love grammar. But only the descriptive, linguistically informed kind. I am not a prescriptivist. No Grammar Police for me. Usage determines correctness. So say the linguists, and so say I. (But I am not a linguist, either.)

As an OWMW (pronounced "OW-mow"), I have come to feel my day is over. And I am certainly not the only one to feel that way. *(No, you're certainly not.)* It seems to be a truth universally acknowledged—or, if not universally acknowledged, at least generally sensed by the literati, among whom I count myself, or aspire to count myself—that the day of the straight white male writer, and a fortiori the old straight white male writer, is over. Even if white male writers are still a force in the publishing world—and there are varying opinions on this—the emergent consensus seems to be that their previous dominance is now on the wane. And a good thing for it, too, the feeling runs. (At least so runs the feeling in Seattle, where I live now. And I tend to agree. As I say, white people are kind of a drag.) The title of a 2015 article in the *New Republic* seems a fair assessment (and foretelling) of the situation today: "White Male Writers: No Longer the Default, and Not Terribly Interesting." In the words of that conniving waiter: *I know.* My ilk is perceived as less than interesting, less than sexy, and with a message less than urgent. Pack it in, OWMW. You are a dog who's had his day. Yield to the young lionesses, panthers, and jaguars. (Not to mention the cougars! Go cougars!) All the cool cats of our future literature. OK, Boomer—haven't you heard? It's over.

Back when I was at Exeter (1969–72. Do I date myself? Very well then, I date myself; I contain multitudes of oldsters), my friend Mike Ward—a bona fide alumnus of Woodstock Nation, who had hair down to his waist until the powers that were, a week or two after school started, made him cut it (after which it was only down to his shoulders)—used to say, only half-jokingly, "I hate hippies." I knew what he meant. At the time, Mike aspired to be a blues musician. (And has now realized that ambition. As Michael "Mudcat" Ward, he is a big deal in blues circles, and the recipient of several national blues awards for Best Acoustic Bassist.) His masters were the bluesmen of the Mississippi Delta and South Chicago traditions: Mississippi John Hurt, Mississippi Fred McDowell, Sonny Boy Williamson II (a.k.a. Rice Miller), Muddy Waters, Little Walter, Junior Wells, Buddy Guy. He liked to quote McDowell: "I don't play no rock 'n' roll—jus' the nat'chul blues." Mike had no time for hippies. Hippies were bland, middle class, and white. They lacked edge and soul. He had bigger catfish to fry, Mike did. Mind you, he was well aware of being perceived as a hippie himself; and that ironic self-awareness was part of the appeal of his declaration. And so I say, in a similar vein, "I hate old white men." Even if they are writers. Especially if they are writers. We are kind of a drag. (Remember that song? The Buckinghams, 1967. I loved the organ riff.) Our time is past; we are perceived as having nothing new to say. Enough already. Let someone else have a chance. And let that someone else be a young lesbian of color, an Asian trans man, a nonbinary Indigenous person (I believe they call them "Two-Spirit")—someone of a different flavor, with a fresh new story to tell: a message of urgency and relevance. Move over, OWMW. In fact, to the back of the bus with you. Feel the pain, for a change; you have earned it.

I have to admit, though, that the writer in me bridles at the appeal to stereotypes. They are not the stuff of good writing. (*Pace* my late brother-in-law's conniving Caribbean waiter, and his secret knowledge, I still like to think of myself as a good writer.) Show me the story, not the storyteller, the message, not the medium. Good writing is good writing. Yet surely the identity of the writer is also important, and constitutes part of their material? The stardust of which we are made may all be the same, but the molds are different. And those different molds are what is important and interesting. And white and male, to say nothing of old—Boomer-old, anyway; Greatest Generation-old, whatever is left of them, is another matter entirely—are just "not terribly interesting." I get it.

And yet, I write. *Eppur' si scrive*, to paraphrase Galileo. The earth revolves around the sun, and the writer writes. It is important, though—it is of the essence—to have a story to tell. Does the OWMW have a story? And if so, is it a story anyone wants to hear? Does anyone want to hear from, and about, the dried-out, pale old dust bunny in the corner? Or should it just be swept up and dumped and flushed, no questions asked?

I referred earlier to a couple of unpublished, book-length memoirs I wrote after *Failure: An Autobiography*. They were titled *The Widower: An Afterlife* and *Shame: A Transgression*. I thought of bundling them together with *Failure* as a trilogy and naming it *Out from under the Rug*. The idea being that the stuff I was writing about—failure, and loss, and shame—is the stuff that, in America, gets swept under the rug. And I was the guy to sweep it back out again. The unsightly, unseemly detritus of our days. It deserves to be examined, too. It is part of us. (Hair, finger-nails, skin flakes, dried-out boogers—whatever composes those dust bunnies in the corner. I don't really want to think about it. And yet here I am, writing about it!)

But perhaps examining the unsightly and unseemly is a fool's errand. It's sort of like painting a turd. Who wants to see that shit? It goes against human nature to invite people to look closely at this stuff. And therein lies the rub: my project goes against human nature, and I am on a fool's errand in pursuit of it. On the other hand, isn't it also human nature to be a bit curious about the unsightly and unseemly? Maybe. But we don't like smelling other people's shit, do we? No, but don't we sometimes sort of like the smell of our own shit? Don't we find it not always exactly distasteful (as La Rochefoucauld might have put it)? The Toilet Effect (q.v.)? Or have I stepped over the line once again, as I am all too prone to do? Well, "You never know what is enough unless you know what is more than enough" (Blake). *But the appeal to literary authorities here is beside the point. And you already mentioned the La Rochefoucauld thing, anyway. The disgusting remains disgusting. Sometimes a cigar is just a cigar, Schatzi.* He's probably right. Who he? Joßche. We'll get to him in a little bit; I just don't want to deal with him right now.

I mentioned a couple of failures of mine: the failure of my first (and only published) novel, and the failure of my two subsequent book manuscripts after *Failure* to find a publisher (or even an agent). But I failed to mention that *Failure* itself was already dead upon release (DUR, a first cousin of DOA), because the publisher went bankrupt immediately after its publication. (Bankruptcy seems to be a theme here; I have already noted that the college I taught at for nineteen years finally went belly-up in 2016, after years of mismanagement.) And there is also a more recent failure, unfolding even as I write: the failure of my incipient novel, tentatively entitled *Dark White*, to advance itself. It has now been aborted in manuscript after about two hundred pages, in favor of the project you are presently reading. (If indeed you are reading anything at all; that of course depends on whether it ever sees the light of day, which I am preemptively, defensively assuming it won't. Though that will hardly keep me from writing it, if only as a kind of thumbing-of-the-nose at the publishing world, as well as an instance of that peculiar hope delineated above.) I suppose I should say a little more about the aborted novel, since certain aspects of it touch upon the current project.

Curiously, *Old White Man Writing* bears the same relation to *Dark White* that *Failure* bore to a previous (also unpublished) novel, *The Bohemian Period*. After I completed the manuscript of the latter—twenty-two years ago now, in the late summer of 2002—I sent it out to a couple of agents. *(Only two agents? Poor little lamb! What did you know, back in the day?)* One of them rejected it, but the other expressed interest in taking it on as a young-adult novel. I immediately dismissed this idea. I had written it as a novel for adults, not young adults, and the thought of it as matter for juveniles seemed an insult, both to my abilities and my intentions. (I later came to rue my foolish arrogance, but such was my thinking at the time.) And so I determined to go no farther with any efforts to promote *Bohemian,* but instead to begin a new project. I said to Diane that I'd had it with writing autobiographical novels; my next book would be straight autobiography. "What will you call it?" she asked. "*Failure: An Autobiography,*" I immediately replied, and she laughed. Her laughter was the genesis of the book.

I bring up this incident because of a perceived correlation (or at least I perceive it) between the two failed novels, *Bohemian* and *Dark White*, and the respective autobiographical projects that came out of them, *Failure* and *Old White Man Writing*: failed autobiographical fiction giving way to autobiographies whose subject is failure. But the correlation here turns out to be even closer and more interwoven than I thought, because *Dark White* itself—both the two hundred pages already written (now aborted) and the plans for the remaining two-thirds of the novel—is also, or rather was intended to be, an outgrowth of (and sequel to) *Bohemian*. The subject of *Dark White* was to be race—specifically, the relationship between the white protagonist, eleven-year-old Jeff Gerber (same initials as mine—get it?) and his Black friend Tecumseh Robinson, fourteen, whom he is later estranged from, through an act of betrayal on Jeff's part, but finally reunited with at novel's end. I nixed *Dark White* because I found myself, approximately one-third of the way in, unable to invent Tecumseh's parents and, consequently, unable to imagine Tecumseh himself as a full-fledged character. I see this as a failure of the fictional imagination, just as I see, now, my failure to follow through with *Bohemian* also as a failure of the fictional imagination: in the latter case, the failure to imagine, or rather reimagine, as a young-adult novel, a story originally cast, and written, as a novel for adults. Out of both failures—*The Bohemian Period* and *Dark White*—I sought to salvage (or, in the case of *Old White Man Writing*, am seeking to salvage) a viable work of autobiography. In both failures there is the hope of a redemption of sorts: out of abortion, completion; out of failure, success.

Which is ironic, really, because on the face of it, at least where failure is concerned, I claim not to believe in redemption. I don't subscribe to the standard belief that out of failure comes eventual success, if only one is persistent and determined enough. Though perhaps it would be more accurate to say that, while I can certainly see the truth in this belief, I don't agree that the only value of failure lies in its contribution to eventual success. I reject the "stepping stone" theory of failure. I see failure as having an absolute value in and of itself, as an experience of spiritual, emotional, and moral worth and meaning. Failure builds character—or so runs the conventional wisdom. And I actually do believe this (in many ways I am quite conventional), and would take it one step further. The experience of failure deepens and grows you. Failure entails suffering, and suffering has spiritual value. Failure is strictly necessary in order to become fully human. It is not a stepping stone to anything else; it has absolute value, and is self-sufficient.

Now I know I may be misguided in this belief, or at least in the extent to which I take it. I may be romanticizing suffering, and mythologizing my own suffering, in the sense that I conceive of it as feeding into a personal myth: the myth of the suffering person as a "deep" person or, at any rate, a deeper person—deeper than the person who celebrates success. For example, when I watch pennant races or world series on TV, my interest and allegiance are always in and with the losers. Yes, I can appreciate the joy and transport of the winners, but they do not interest or move me. My heart is with the losers. The losers are reflective, thoughtful, mindful, soulful. The winners are caught up in the bodily exultation of the moment—the animal thoughtlessness of triumph. Sure, there are genuine excitement and joy in victory; but there are thought and reflection in defeat. And it is finally with thought and reflection that I cast my lot. ("It is better to go to the house of mourning than to the house of mirth.")

But why, you ask, must one choose between the two states? Why not celebrate with the winners at the same time that you are commiserating with the losers? Well, the both/and state is certainly good work if you can get it; I just never have been able to get it.

This resistance to happiness is a familiar thing; it has been with me since childhood. My awareness, as a child, that I was happy was sometimes accompanied by a kind of self-conscious embarrassment, an inhibition of instinctual feeling. A sense—no, more than a sense: a sensation, a physical damper, a veil of disruption—that came over me, interposing itself between me and the pleasure I was experiencing. The scrim, if you will, of an unwelcome awareness. It was as though there were some kind of "killjoy genie," some imp of the perverse, that came unbottled in order to interfere with my unmediated high spirits.

  I remember something like the Killjoy Genie first appearing at Tocaloma Boys' Club, where I spent two afternoons a week after school—Tuesdays and Thursdays, from third through sixth grade—playing kickball, softball, flag football, capture the flag and basketball at Stoner Park (*sic*) in West LA. The Killjoy Genie would arrive during moments of minor triumph, when my better genie was cheering me on: "You did it! You got a *hit*, you bastard! Now run! Slide, if you have to, but get on base! Take the acclaim, accept the praise, embarrassing as it is. Suck it up! Suck up that good stuff! Take it in. Don't run away from it. Go, guy!" But in the midst of my small victory, another silent voice would intervene, as a kind of foil to the better genie's encouragement: the Killjoy Genie, interfering with things, breaking up the play, attempting to poison the moment, whispering doubt and denial. The KJG, as I experienced it then, was perhaps the child's imaginary version of what I would learn years later was the *servus publicus*, the "public slave"—a designated state functionary who would ride next to the victor in ancient Roman triumphal processions, whispering in his ear, as a corrective to the adulation of the crowd: "Look behind you, and remember you are only a man." ("*Respice post te, hominem memento.*") To be sure, as a child it was never a question of triumph or adulation that I had to be recalled from, but only simple happiness. Happiness was my triumph—though of course I never thought of it in those terms at the time. But I knew, even back then, that happiness made me a little uneasy. Why? Because I sensed it was only temporary? Because I felt it wasn't deserved? Or because it felt, my happiness, somehow external to me, something gratuitous and out of place? Did I feel unworthy of it? Or was the problem something else? Was it that the reality of other people, in whose presence, and because of whose praise, recognition, affection, perhaps even love, I was feeling the happiness—parents, friends, classmates, the other boys at Tocaloma—pressed so closely upon me that my happiness was constrained by my palpable sense of their feelings and expectations? Was that it?

Maybe it was just that my happiness, even as a child, was never unmixed, because of an almost oppressive sense of the other people in whose presence I was feeling that happiness. Those other people, whoever they were, always made me feel self-conscious. And that self-consciousness (perhaps my greatest curse, now that I think about it) served as a counterweight to the happiness; served as its *servus publicus* and prevented it from ever soaring. My self-consciousness, by definition, was nothing more (and nothing less) than my inhibitory sense of myself: who I was, who I had been yesterday, how I was perceived, who—other than my parents—genuinely liked me, and whom I genuinely cared about. These irreducible particularities, these quiddities of my being, weighed on me; I felt their specific gravity, as it were, which seemed like a check, a bafflement, to my euphoria. Matter and spirit, you might say—the matter of other people, the spirit of joy—were in conflict. I knew the weight of others, their perceptions and expectations, and it pressed down upon me.

The KJG was nothing like an auditory hallucination. (My mental illness is Bipolar II, not schizophrenia.) Indeed, it may have been an early manifestation of the depression part of my Bipolar II. The KJG would sometimes arise in the midst of games, parties, or celebrations to inform me that I wasn't really enjoying myself but just pretending to, that I would rather be by myself, at home, with Mom. The KJG was perhaps nothing more than a perverse (because half-voluntary) expression of self-consciousness, the kind of self-consciousness that always made me more of an observer than a participant in the action. I see now that there was something compulsive about the

KJG. It was at least partly, if not wholly, within my control. So in a sense, even though it made me uncomfortable, I deliberately sought to invoke it—or at least to have it "standing by," so to speak, as a possibility. *(You to the KJG: "Stand back, and stand by."* Hahaha, Joßche. That's a good one, I have to admit.) The KJG was always an option I could exercise. Though exactly why I would ever want to exercise it remains unclear.

I once had a student who, when he got the right answer in class, would make an electronic-sounding noise with his mouth. It was annoying and distracting, and I spoke to him about it. He said his therapist identified it as "voluntary Tourette's syndrome." I pooh-poohed the idea at the time (my understanding was that Tourette's syndrome is always involuntary), but now I think maybe I was wrong. Perhaps the KJG is a kind of silent version of voluntary Tourette's syndrome.

Why was it, and why is it still, so hard, and so fraught with ambivalence, for me to receive compliments? What is it that does not like to see gratified my hidden hunger for praise, for deserved acknowledgment by my peers? What is it in me that will not believe it? What is this perverse thing that wants me to retreat into a kind of virtual burrow, to go back nostalgically in memory to the quiet hours of anonymity, when life was simpler and somehow purer?

There is an added twist to this internal Imp of the Perverse. The voice of the KJG doesn't just tell me that I am unworthy of the happy feeling—and don't we all have our own versions of that voice? Isn't it familiar to all of us, in all its manifold, individual registers? It tells me something else as well, something stranger and even more discomfiting. It tells me that those who are patting me on the back, cheering me on, giving me praise and compliments, are wrong. They are mistaken, perhaps even deluded. And because I feel they are, I feel sorry for them. My first reaction to praise for a recognized achievement is to feel sorry for the person, or people, who are congratulating me. And it has been ever thus. My peers, my congratulators, are misguided. They've got the wrong guy. They are on the wrong track. And because I am grateful to them, despite their error—because I owe them a debt of gratitude despite their mistake—I feel sorry for them. They seem vulnerable to me, and my feeling sorry for them registers that sense of vulnerability. Out there in the wide-open, exposed spaces of my success, I see how vulnerable they are, those mistaken cheerleaders of my fraudulent accomplishments. And I wish they would "stop it," in the words of Waymarsh to Strether in *The Ambassadors*. I wish they would stop making me feel embarrassed for them. Their open faces seem particularly vulnerable. It is enough to make me long for the private solace of my burrow. And I am already, in my mind at least, back there. I am not here, in the light of recognition and success. I am back there, down in the comforting, subdued light of my burrow.

I suppose I should say something more about that, too.

There are a number of things about success that scare me. First of all, it brings pressure—the pressure to follow up, to keep succeeding—and I have never been very good at handling pressure and follow-up: I tend to choke in the clutch, going back to the days of Tocaloma softball and the emergence of the KJG. It's not just the pressure of the follow-up that spooks me; it's also the sheer effort required. (That's where my constitutional laziness kicks in.) Then there's my romantic belief, acquired no doubt from my Irish Catholic mother from Scranton, PA, that success is somehow corrupting, whereas failure—certain kinds of failure, anyway—are ennobling. This notion is no doubt connected to another characteristic of mine: the strong desire to retain a personal sense of purity and innocence. (You could call this my own brand of purism. More on that in a moment.)

Success also produces a condition of exposure, in at least a couple of senses: exposure for the fraud I suspect myself of being (you probably know the drill: "If I should ever achieve success, it will automatically be fraudulent and counterfeit, by virtue of the fact that I am the one achieving it"), but also exposure of a more physical and elemental (albeit idiosyncratic) sort: a laying open of the individual self to the "natural elements" of social life. No more retreating into my private, comfortable, comforting burrow. (See Kafka here—the beginning of "The Burrow," perhaps my favorite of his stories: "I have completed the construction of my burrow and it seems to be successful.") For success, you see, has nowhere to hide; it is, or can be, a very public spectacle, whereas the digestion of failure is a private affair. (And perhaps the comforting quality of its privacy is one of the things that attracts me to it.) Success, at least in the public form I am conceiving of it here, is not at all comforting, but rather the opposite: it is exigent and demanding, rigorous and unforgiving. ("A more severe, more harassing master," as Wallace Stevens puts it. He is another of my masters.) It does not allow of retreat into the burrow. Success creates a glare, an open exposure to bright, harsh light. And I do not like bright, harsh light. I am the creature of more diffuse, crepuscular emanations: the light, say, of late summer afternoons and evenings. I seek a more forgiving illumination for my being. I would like to inhabit a painting by one of the Hudson River School of painters.

I think my interest in failure—in its phenomenology, if you will, its mysteries of consciousness, the depth and variety of emotion connected with it—has something to do with my elective affinity for depth in general, for deep states of emotion and sensibility, as if the lighter sides of life and experience had little merit at all, or at least none worth exploring. But maybe here I am just playing it safe, exploring the details of my burrow, of what I am familiar with, the light and limited terrain I am so well adapted to, rather than thinking about why I am so comfortable in that burrow to begin with, and looking at the fears that are keeping me inside of it.

But what about the environment outside the burrow, the wide-open landscape of success: its exposure, expectations, rigors and demands? Its freedom! Well, those things are frightening to me. The world of action, activity, achievement is frightening to me. It produces, among the other effects already mentioned, performance anxiety. Will I choke in the clutch again? Will I fail to cut it? Will I disappoint?

It's funny how you can be afraid of what you want—or think you want. *It's called ambivalence, Schatzi, and it shouldn't come as a surprise to any conscious person, let alone any writer.* I know. And I guess I've been mystifying and romanticizing my relationship to failure, rather than seeing it as a by-product of my fear of success. An attraction to failure just always seemed so much more interesting, romantic, ennobling—and plain *unusual*—than a fear of success. And I have always had an exceptionalistic predilection for the unusual. The untrodden way has always held a great—all-too-great!—mystique for me. How I love that epigram of Spinoza: "All things excellent are as difficult as they are rare." (And let us have it in the original Latin, while we are at it: "*Omnia praeclara tam difficilia quam rara sunt.*") Sing it, most excellent Amsterdam Sephardic Jew! Sing the song of the chosen few!

Now, if the idea of success is perceived as somehow ignoble and corrupting (as it was in my Irish Catholic mother's value system, which I absorbed practically with her milk), then for me to become successful also means losing my innocence and purity, the innocence and purity that come from anonymity. Because remember, according to Hildegarde Therese Colligan Gidding, my master teacher in these matters, the losers are better people than the winners. As well as sadder. But their sadness is a badge of honor. And my own default condition, as I believe I mentioned, has always been a slight sadness: a habitual, baseline depression. Nothing so severe as clinical depression (except perhaps once; this will be discussed in due course), but rather an environmental, ambient depression. Mild depression is the sea I swim in, the water that floats me. My depression, my failure, are my virginity, you might even say. My purity. And success threatens to violate that purity. To become successful would be to lose my defining sadness—and therefore my virtue.

The comparison to virginity was not an idle one, because the prospect of losing my sadness is not so unlike how the prospect of having sex was for me the first time around, at seventeen. (I didn't actually go through with it until I was eighteen.) Apparently, I was not all that eager to do it. Actually, that's putting it mildly. I was scared. I was scared of losing my virginity, which would mean losing the last part of my childhood innocence. I figured as long as I retained my virginity, I could feel that aspect of my childhood, and its innocence, was still intact. This "willed innocence" was also not unlike my "Santa Claus Syndrome," whereby I could tell myself that I still believed in Santa Claus by paying lip service to him, even though I had really stopped believing by fourth grade. In this way, the wish to believe could stand for the belief itself. The desire to still be innocent was great enough that it could crowd out, at least for another year or two, my common-sense knowledge of the fictionality of Santa Claus or, later, the "carnal knowledge" of my inevitable sexual destiny. In the case of the latter, the preservation of my virginity was like a pledge, a token, of the status quo of my childhood, a reassurance that I was the "same person" I had always been. The safe burrow—the burrow here of my innocence, rather than of my failure—was still there and could be repaired to. And insofar as my innocence, my "status quo," was associated with my baseline mild depression, the avoidance of any kind of success, acclaim, or recognition was an assertion of the status quo, a preservation of my childhood identity. Just as I had been afraid of losing my belief in Santa Claus and, later, losing the innocence of my virginity, just so, on into adulthood today (nay, early old age), I am afraid of losing my sadness. And insofar, too, as success might mean an end to my sadness, I am afraid of success as well.

The prescription of an anti-depressant (Zoloft) twenty-eight years ago, which I am still taking, has hugely lessened my baseline sadness, and also enabled me to handle pressure much better. But the imprint of the baseline sadness remains—if only as a memory of the status quo, and a reminder of my temperamental inclination. And I would have it no other way. I set much store by the memory of my burrow (and my mother. Shades of *The Runaway Bunny*? Sing it, Margaret Wise Brown.). It is a kind of token of identity, a touchstone of who I am. I am the guy who used to be the kid who was usually just a little bit sad. And when he wasn't—when he became happy in the glow of a recognized achievement and was congratulated by others—the KJG would emerge from the bottle of his mind to make him feel sorry for his cheerleaders in their delusion, and remind him of the way it had been in the burrow, and might be again. Remind him of the solace of anonymity and the baseline sadness.

I'd like to touch upon a couple more aspects of the KJG before putting him back in the bottle. I noted before that the appearance of the KJG was partly voluntary, a kind of "voluntary Tourette's," compulsively invoked as a retarding agent to dampen my enjoyment. But there are two other iterations of the KJG that are entirely voluntary. One is a character named Joßche, who, you may have noticed, has been interrupting me for some time now. *(Hello, Reader—or not!)* He will be dealt with presently. The other came to be known (by me, anyway) as the Friday Night Syndrome.

When I was nine or ten, and perhaps a little older, too, I used to like to pretend it wasn't really Friday night when it was. I remember one Friday night in particular. I was out to dinner with my parents at the old Hamburger Hamlet (of sacred memory; the staff of this staple of my childhood were preponderantly, if not entirely, Black) on San Vicente Blvd. in Brentwood. I was feeling very happy as I looked forward to the weekend in store—so happy, in fact, that I began trying to make myself believe that it was not in fact Friday night at all, but rather Sunday night, that worst of all nights, the end of all mirth and hope, the repository of all woe, the graveyard of our great expectations and lookings-forward-to. The asshole of the week, not to put too fine a point on it. (On Monday and Tuesday nights, you see, one is already "in it," so to speak. The week is already undeniably happening. One can admit the reality and deal with it and begin to look forward to the weekend again. But Sunday night somehow always arrives unexpectedly; its insuperable gloom takes one by surprise. And this never changes as one gets older, except in summer, if you're a teacher. Then, summer Sundays are a liberation—like having two Saturdays in a row. The phenomenological economy of the week in summer is totally different from the rest of the year.)

The purpose of this strange behavior, I think, was to create a future surprise for myself, to insure a kind of golden nugget of expectational treasure that lay in store. A sort of booster shot to paradoxically add to the pleasure I was already feeling in contemplation of the weekend ahead by temporarily cancelling it. The happiness of Friday night could somehow be truly appreciated and "contemplated about" (I idiosyncratically use the intransitive locution, rather than the customary transitive one— "contemplated"—because it seems dreamier, more indirect, and thus more descriptive of what I do and how I do it) only by being made to contrast with the despair of Sunday; and this needed to be accomplished not just theoretically, but viscerally as well. I felt I had to make myself more fully experience the happiness of Friday night by inhabiting, if only temporarily, in my mind, the misery of Sunday evening. By nipping pleasure in the bud and trampling it underfoot, I could then recover it and so enjoy an enhanced version of it. The way of true gratification lay through denial. (Similarly, sometimes when I got a new toy that I had especially wanted, I would deliberately not play with it for a while, and even hide it and pretend that I had never gotten it.) And in this I was not wrong. Kind of insane, perhaps, but not really wrong; only supremely perverse in feeling I needed to manufacture that denial myself, not knowing—not having any way to know, at that young age—that life itself would inevitably provide the denial I sought.

You will have noticed that there is something quite childish—and even, once again, rather virginal—about all of this: an inability to handle the full-strength, adult intercourse of the emotions. This perverseness is probably not unrelated to the grimace I used to make when Diane and I were embracing (she could feel me grimacing over her shoulder, and would say, patiently and gently, "Stop grimacing"), and that I still sometimes make when Julie and I embrace. Giving in to pleasure is like giving in to an embrace; I cannot take it "uncut," cannot tolerate it without administering the antagonist agent—the grimace, the Friday Night Syndrome—of a deliberately-engineered disbelief.

In this way, the FNS was the calendrical version of the KJG, just as the spousal grimace was—and still is—its matrimonial version.

At the outset of this account, I mentioned the famous opening of *Invisible Man* and suggested a possible resemblance between our two protagonists. That suggestion was no doubt totally out of line. *You can say that again.* Yet if there is really no comparison to be made, there is certainly one glaring difference that is very much on the mind, and to the purpose, of the Old White Man Writing: which is that he is not Black. Does he wish he were? Not really, apart from the occasional fantasy. *But you, Senator, are no Rachel Dolezal.* Nice, Joßche. I'll give you that one. Though I do believe—and here I am probably going to be out of line again—that some advantages might accrue to me as a writer seeking publication if I were Black. And also if I were forty years younger, and female—or, better yet, an LGBTQ POC. *Here we go again with the stereotypes.* I know. They don't do anyone any good, perhaps least of all yours truly. But if I don't really wish I were any of the above, I do sometimes wish I wasn't white. And not just because white people are kind of a drag.

It was probably some combination of such sentiments that led me—along with Julie (though she had her own reasons, too, and I can't really speak for her)—to join a Whiteness Awareness Study Group a few summers ago. Of course we did! I mean, what else were we going to do? As well-intentioned white people living in Seattle, what else were we going to do with our white guilt? Anything more proactive would have been out of character for me. I know I'm not cut out to be a Social Justice Warrior. I mean, I marched in a local BLM demonstration after George Floyd was murdered in 2020 (pale shades of my father, who, in a much more substantial and meaningful show of alliance, flew to Alabama for the Selma march in the spring of 1965); but that, and joining a Whiteness Awareness Study Group, was about as far as I could go in the direction of any kind of racial activism.

Our group of six met once a week at the Ballard apartment of one of the members. The discussion leader was a middle-aged woman I'll call Suzette. She had a withered arm from polio she had contracted as a little girl. Joßche noticed it immediately. *So did you!* Yeah, but you noticed it first. It was only slightly withered—but withered enough for Joßche. He didn't like her at all. I think she set off something in him. *Speak for yourself, Schatzi. You are totally projecting here. You're the one with the cripple thing, not me. Remember your beloved Paul?* Don't you dare even mention him, especially not that way. Never talk again.

OK, before we go any farther with this, I should explain about Joßche. (Paul can wait.) I noted previously, in passing, that Joßche was one of the iterations of the Killjoy Genie, though they are certainly not the same. The KJG preceded Joßche by many decades, but they could be said to run on the same principle. These entities—Joßche, the KJG, the Friday Night Syndrome—all exist to baffle my pleasure. (*Grammar alert*: I use "baffle" here in its nominal sense: "something that balks, checks, or deflects; an artificial obstruction for checking or deflecting the flow of gases [*Hahaha! Indeed!*] … sounds … light … etc.") But Joßche is different from these other baffles in that he is a textual artifact. *So say you.* He is, in fact, an artifact exclusive to this text. I've never encountered him anywhere else. He will interrupt us from time to time. I apologize in advance for this. I will do my best to silence him, but unfortunately this will not always be possible. Because, you see, Joßche is my alter-ego. We are very, very different, but we are also connected, as alter-egos tend to be. Joßche is my creation—though he would, and will, pretend otherwise, and claim I am *his* creation. Which is actually quite understandable, when you think about it, because Joßche is a biographer. A German biographer. A progressive German-Catholic literary biographer, with a titanium membrane implanted in his skull (the result of a serious childhood bicycle accident). *Too much information, Schatzi. And that last bit was not yours to divulge.* No, I think they have a right to know, especially since you just called Paul a "cripple." You, with a titanium membrane in your head! Anyway, Reader, Joßche is an associate professor of German at Cal State LA, and is currently working on a biography of Thomas Mann in Pacific Palisades—which, as previously noted, is the suburb of Los Angeles where I grew up. Despite all our differences, we have certain things in common, Joßche and I, such as an interest in Thomas Mann and literary biography, a sometimes questionable sense of humor, and a deliberately mischievous resistance to political correctness (even though he identifies as a progressive). And for the time being, that is all the background I will give on him.

Anyway, Suzette set off something in him. I restrained him—but I almost didn't. Now what was it about Suzette that bugged me? Was it her earnestness? Not exactly. More like her political correctness. (Though they went very well together.) She started off the first meeting by acknowledging the Indian—*Watch it!*—sorry, Native American land we were on, the land of the Duwamish people. Now why was that so annoying? Because it seemed so reflexive, so obligatory? But surely it's a good thing to be aware of atrocities and genocide? These things really were done to human beings, by human beings, and other human beings—including the OWMW—greatly benefited from them. What matters my petty annoyance in the light of such suffering? How dare I be annoyed? But I was. Not at being reminded of history and all its horrors, though. I guess it was just the reflexive, obligatory quality of Suzette's reminder—the sense of paying lip-service to political correctness—that annoyed me. *Well, sometimes the political correctors are right. Even the registered moderate Democrat in you has to acknowledge that.* To hell with the registered moderate Democrat! How about the feeling human being? Doesn't the feeling human being have to acknowledge the correctness of the political correctors? *Yes, but then the feeling human being encounters certain obstacles within himself.* Yes. Obstacles such as Joßche. I mean, such as you. Sad but true. The obstacle of the Joßche Factor. *"Der Joßchenfaktor."* As should be obvious by now, my German is only approximate, if that. *(You can say that again.)* I really have no German at all. Never studied it. Now, if I'd gone to grad school in classics—as I once, as an undergraduate, thought I might—instead of English, I'd no doubt have had to study German, because so much of the great classical scholarship of the nineteenth century, and on into the twentieth (before you-know-what), was written in German. Joßche often gives me a hard time about this. He had a classical education at the *Gymnasium.*

But just what is the difference, you may ask, between Joßche and the Joßche Factor? Is there any difference? Perhaps it's already time to dispense with the fiction of Joßche as a separate entity? *No! I need to be separate from you.* I realize that, but what you need really doesn't matter. You don't get to call the shots here. Remember, you are a figment of my imagination, not the other way around. *I wouldn't be so sure of that.* But OK, let's just say, for argument's sake, that you *are* separate from me—at least partly separate—and that it is my choice, not yours, to keep you separate. Why then? Why would I want to keep Joßche separate? So I can fob things off on him? But wouldn't it be more accurate to say that I need what he represents? *And what is that?* I suppose another name for it, in KJG fashion, would be the Imp of the Perverse. Joßche is my Imp of the Perverse. A figment, yes, but one who feels so real. A part of me. My "opposing self." The term is Lionel Trilling's—the title of his fourth book. Trilling is another one of my masters, my critical master *par excellence.* A rather severe moralist, he was. The title of his selected essays is so telling: *The Moral Obligation to Be Intelligent.* That pretty much says it right there, doesn't it? His moralism is probably the main thing that makes him so untimely. *Unzeitgemässe Betrachtungen*! (Joßche is big on Nietzsche.) The untimely meditator, Trilling is. A throwback—and therefore all the more admirable and appealing.

But the subject was Suzette, not Lionel Trilling (or Nietzsche). How did I get onto them, anyway? Oh yeah, *The Opposing Self.* How Joßche is my opposing self, and Suzette and her political correctness pissed him off. But what did we expect when we (Julie and I) joined a Whiteness Awareness Study Group in Seattle? It was almost as if I joined it to prove something to myself. What? That I'm not a bigot? *(Or that you are?)* But didn't I already know that? I guess not. I mean, yeah, I knew I wasn't a Trumpian bigot, in the sense that I knew I wasn't like the people at the rallies. All those complacent, gleeful, untroubled white faces—so untroubledly white. And what about all the hate and anger, and the acting out? But it's the complacency, and the glee, and the untroubledness, especially—the untroubled whiteness—that make the most impact on me. Of course the Trumpians are troubled, too—but not by what they *should* be troubled by: their own malign deplorableness. (I think Hillary was right-on there.) All that anger and hatred against "the liberals" and "the swamp." Even more hate and anger at "the liberals," I think, than against Black and Brown people. (I remember once, when Trump was still president, seeing a photo in the *New York Times* of a guy at a Trump rally wearing a jacket that said, "Make Liberals Cry Again." Joßche had to laugh at that, in spite of myself.) Because, according to the Trumpians, it's "the liberals," the white liberals, who are the betrayers—the privileged, elitist betrayers of the "white race." But the hate and anger aren't even what make the strongest impression when I see their faces in the news. It's the complacency, the untroubled certainty. "The best lack all conviction, while the worst / Are full of passionate intensity." Sing it, WB. Gives me a chill to think of what the world was on the brink of then, when Yeats wrote that, and then to think of what we might be on the brink of now ... *Might* be? Who am I kidding?

I think that what bothered me more than anything else about Suzette—*But I thought you were going to ease up on her!* Yes I am. Eventually. All in good time. Sit tight, Fritz. (And suck my *Jägermeister* while you're at it.) I recognized she was not a bad person. She just bugged me. And the thing that bugged me the most about her was her humorlessness, and her lack of irony. (As if she should have been more like me—humorous and ironic.) I know, I know—how narcissistic can you get! I mean, it's not like I joined the Whiteness Awareness Study Group to meet more people like me. *So why did you join?* Good question.

I said before that I wanted to prove something to myself about bigotry—my bigotry. That I wasn't bigoted, and maybe also that I was. But "prove" isn't quite right. I wanted to face the bigotry—if that's what it was; and maybe bigotry is too strong a word; let's just call it my unexamined racial assumptions, then. I wanted to face my unexamined racial assumptions, and deal with them, and figure out what they were all about. Figure out how a nice half-Jewish boy (but the wrong half, and so not really Jewish at all, by some accounts) from Pacific Palisades—and maybe that's part of the problem right there: the lily-white, candy-ass Palisades. What real writer grows up in such a place? I mean, Roth grew up in Newark; Bellow grew up in Chicago, and was born in Montreal; Updike grew up in Shillington, PA. (Wherever the hell that is.) But Pacific Palisades? Yeah, I know; Thomas Mann and Henry Miller both lived there at different times; but they sure didn't grow up there. Anyway, I guess I wanted to know how a nice half-Jewish boy from Pacific Palisades, with liberal parents (I told you my father marched in Selma, when I was in fifth grade, right? That was a big deal for me.), could be worried that he might be a mild racist in some ways. Could sometimes have—that is, discover in himself—certain attitudes and thoughts and emotions that were out of character with who and what he had been raised to be.

But just what attitudes and thoughts and emotions are we talking about here? That Black people are different from white people? *Duh!* With their history and experience in this country how could they not be?

Yes, but to be too conscious of those differences—those physical and cultural differences—is not good, is it? It must say something about you that is not what you want to hear and know. OK, fair enough. And what is that? That I am somehow not, I don't know, "pure of heart"? What does that even mean? And was that ever even a serious goal of mine—to be pure of heart? Well, I suppose actually, yes, it was. Viz., wanting to maintain my innocence and virtue. Kierkegaard said, "Purity of heart is to will one thing." If that is true, then I am *so not* pure of heart. Because I think all sorts of things, contradictory things, at the same time, all the time. Joßche—the Joßche Factor, the Joßche Function, the Joßche Effect, whatever you want to call it—is only one example of this.

But wait a minute, Chester. Ouch. That hurt. As you knew it would. And we haven't gotten there yet. I think you know what I'm talking about. *Yes I do. The Black ventriloquist doll. OK, I withdraw that last comment. But my point is, that's not exactly what Kierkegaard meant, or even wrote. Read the quote again and then what you wrote just after it. He said, "Purity of heart is to will one thing." "Thinking all sorts of things" isn't the same as "willing one thing." One of your problems is that you don't will anything—much less one thing.*

Ouch again. Though he's right this time. I mean, you're right. But that's a huge subject, and I'm not going to get into it at the moment. *No, of course not. Just sweep it under the rug. Out of sight, out of mind.* That's just not true, Joßche. You know me better than that. If anything, I sweep stuff back *out* from under the rug, as I explained earlier. Yet and still, you are not wrong about the will thing—the matter of my "weak will," and my disinclination to action. *The Hamlet Effect.* Yes. But I don't want to get into that right now, either. Right now we're on the subject of Suzette.

I think another thing that pissed me off about Suzette, besides the political correctness and the humorlessness and lack of irony, was her physical plainness. I'm ashamed to admit this, but it's true. She was a plain-looking, middle-aged woman. She wasn't attractive. And she knew it, of course. And I think this made her defensive. She made a sarcastic reference, in her opening remarks at our first meeting, to how being "pretty" was one of the things—like being white, and male, and straight, and a parent—that give you automatic, unspoken, but very real entrée and privilege and legitimacy in our society, and that some people—many people, actually—were subtly (and maybe not so subtly) penalized for not being. Suzette wrote a list of these things, social advantages and disadvantages, on her large, butcher-paper writing tablet, set on an easel that she carried with her (in her good arm) for that first meeting, and "pretty" was one of them. And I noticed the contrast between Suzette and another woman in the group, whom I'll call Natalie, who was very pretty, and was married to an African American man. One of the reasons she'd joined the group, she said, was to get a different perspective on her husband's experience and problems in white Seattle. Julie and I agreed that Natalie should have been the group leader, not Suzette, because Natalie just seemed like a natural leader, and in fact was some sort of group leader or director at T-Mobile, where she worked. Anyway, Suzette was ill-suited for the job, because she seemed uncomfortable in the role, and had some baggage she was bringing with her.

Then again, who doesn't have baggage? I certainly have a heavy load myself. I mentioned that it shames me to admit I resented Suzette for not being good-looking. Actually resented it, as if it were a personal affront. And that wasn't even the first time I had had this feeling, either. There was a woman I became friends with on the lot at Warner Bros. in the early '80s, when I was working there as a script-reader, who was very homely. I once remarked to her, in passing—and in irritation, I'm sorry to say; I forget the exact context of the remark, and I wonder now what it could have been—that she wasn't going to win any beauty contests. And she later called me on it. And I apologized profusely. But never enough to suit my conscience. In that way, it reminds me of something I'll call the Herb McCarthy's Incident (we'll get to that in the next section), because it revealed to me, actually, one of the mysteries of my being. (Not to sound too grandly Heideggerian or anything, but it's true.) Or maybe it wasn't such a mystery after all. Just another sign that I can occasionally be a pig, and sometimes a shit. *Watch it with the dumping on yourself.* Yes, he's right again. I'll explain about that, too. All in good time.

Yeah, there were all sorts of messed-up things going on with me in that Whiteness Awareness Study Group. Things connected not only with my whiteness but with my maleness, too—as just illustrated. (I was the only man in the group. Maybe that had something to do with it.) And I wonder. Was I maybe doing penance for these things by joining WAGS in the first place? (I know the acronym should be WASG, not WAGS, but WAGS sounds better. More eager to please.) I think maybe I was. Doing penance, that is, for the sometimes ungenerous thoughts about Black and Brown people, primarily. But also, in submitting to Suzette's leadership, I think I was doing penance for the woman at Warner Bros. But it was even more than that. I think I was also doing penance for my privilege, for having grown up the son of a screenwriter in candy-ass Pacific Palisades. For having gone to private schools all my life, until Berkeley, where I wasted my freshman year (at least it sometimes seems that way, when I look back on it) trying to transfer to Harvard, where my father had gone, and which had already rejected me the year before. (And was to reject me again that year.) Penance, too, for having gone to Exeter (also like my father), where I took Latin and Greek and graduated with a Classical Diploma and felt oh so superior for my classical pedigree. (I also majored in classics at Berkeley. *You already told us that.* Be quiet.) Penance for all that stuff. So it seemed only fair and just that I should have to suffer through Suzette and WAGS and the book we read, Robin DiAngelo's *What Does It Mean to Be White? Developing White Racial Literacy.* I had read her *White Fragility* earlier, with equally mixed feelings. Was that penance, too? No doubt. Talk about political correctness! Though I have to admit, I basically agreed with just about everything she said in both books. It was just her sociologist's way of saying it that bugged me. No humor, no irony. Sound familiar?

But it wasn't only the need to do penance that brought me to WAGS. I was also curious. Curious, in part, about my lack of curiosity about things Black. *Even African American literature?* Maybe *especially* African American literature. Big on the classics, and the Jews, but bad on Blacks and women. Jesus, that sounds really bad, I know. *Well, it is.* I know it is—but you're even worse! You're a German-Catholic Nietzschean, for Christ's sake! *But the subject isn't me, Schatzi.* Ah, I sometimes wonder...

Anyway, I mentioned this in group – the Black part, not the women part, since all the others in the group were women – and Suzette gave me an "assignment," which was to compile a list of African American writers I wanted to read. And of course, I didn't do the assignment. Not only because it was Suzette who gave it to me, but also—more importantly, I think, and more badly—because I didn't want to do it. I mean, why should I read African American writers when I could be reading my crew (Roth et al.)? *Well, how about because you are ignorant about African American literature, and you don't like being ignorant about anything?*

Actually, Joßche is wrong about that. It's not really true that I'm ignorant about African American literature. I've read *Invisible Man*, obviously. Actually, I even taught it in grad school, as a TA. And I've read slave narratives—well, at least Douglass and Jacobs—and various anthologized pieces for the American lit. surveys I've taught: Washington, Du Bois, Hughes, Baldwin, Walker, Morrison *(Hey, two women! And two Black women, no less! Double credit!)*, Ellison, Wright, and Coates. I really liked Coates. *So what! You want to be congratulated on this? This is just virtue-signaling! You want to be given credit for this, and maybe even some extra credit while you're at it, Professor?* Alright, point taken. The truth is, I'm just not that *curious* about African American literature on the whole. Not ignorant, but not curious, either. Zack gave me the new Coates novel for Christmas, but I know I probably won't read it, because Julie read it and was disappointed. It makes me feel bad to admit all this, though not really for the reasons it should, including that I should feel like I'm missing out on something. I feel bad primarily because it makes me feel sorry for my son for giving me a book I probably won't read. That really gets to me. Feeling sorry for people is a big thing with me. And I know that's also bad. It's condescending, sentimental, useless, and inept, to name just a few. But I can't help it. I've always been that way. I think it's probably somehow related to feeling embarrassed for people, which is also a problem for me, as explained earlier. And those people include myself. I feel embarrassed for myself for some of the things I'm writing here. And I am pretty sure you feel embarrassed for me too, Reader. And I wonder—is that a fatal flaw in a book, for the reader to feel embarrassed for the writer? I mean, it's OK for the reader to feel embarrassed for a character in a book, but for the *writer*? Does it make any difference if the writer is also embarrassed for himself and makes that clear? *(In der Tat, allzuklar!)* Does this kind of textual self-awareness make the embarrassment—on both the reader's and the writer's part—better or worse? *Actually, these are interesting questions.* Thanks, Joßche. (Sometimes he can be semi-decent.) And what if the writer is also a character in the book? What then? And what if the writer is actually *two* characters in the book—Josh and Joßche? Or am I just confusing the writer and the persona of the narrator here? But I make no pretense that the writer—me, Josh Gidding—is to be differentiated from the narrator, Josh Gidding. Though he *is* to be differentiated from the persona of his alter-ego, Joßche. *Is that what you think I am, just a persona and/or an alter-ego? I think you are once again being "disingenuous" here. (One of your favorite words, apparently. And you overuse it.) I am more than an artificial, contrived persona. I am also a part of you. That is to say, there is a part of me that is a part of you, and a part of me that is separate from you. And the part that we share is just the part of you that you don't want to "cop" to, as you Americans say, so you just try to distance yourself by labeling me a fictive persona.*

Well, he does have a point there. Joßche is a literary device, sure, but he is more than just a device. He is my own "counter-voice," if you will. Now you can see the reason, or one of the reasons, why Philip Roth is one of my masters. *And you, Senator, are no Philip Roth.* Well played, Joßche. I'll give you that one, too.

Where were we? Oh yeah—poor Suzette (see, I feel sorry for her, too!) and the WAGS. And my penance and lack of curiosity. And doing penance for my lack of curiosity. On that note, I mentioned something else to the group that I think is relevant here. When I was growing up, in you-know-where, the candy-ass capital of the world, we had a Black gardener from Mississippi. Willie. Willie Dillard. And one time—I guess it must have been the summer after we graduated from Exeter—my friend Mike (whom I mentioned earlier; he was my roommate for two years) came to LA to stay for a few days. (He was on his way to Santa Cruz to play with a blues band in a club on the Boardwalk there.) And one day, when Willie was working in the garden, Mike started talking to him. I guess they talked for about fifteen minutes or so. Maybe longer. But it was fifteen minutes longer than I'd ever talked to Willie in my life, who at that point must have been working for us for about thirteen years—since we'd moved into the house in 1959. And Mike found out that Willie played guitar. Who knew? Certainly not yours truly. But Mike found this out by actually talking to the guy. Who, by the way, was missing one of his fingers (so more power to him for playing guitar; was he maybe even an unsung Django Reinhardt? I guess we'll never know), which you could tell even when he was wearing gardening gloves, because one of the fingers was floppy. (That made me feel sorry for him, of course. *Of course.*) Now, how did that accident happen? I have no idea. You would have actually had to talk to him to find that out. I should ask Mike; he probably knows.

Mike knows a lot of things. I admire him greatly, which I guess is obvious by now. He is, in a way, my moral compass. One of them, anyway, especially in the matter of Blackness. His relationship to Blackness (he is a white Jewish boy from Lewiston, ME; not too many of those) is one of the things I most admire about him. He seems to feel it—Blackness—in his bones, somehow, and has as long as I've known him. We were roommates our sophomore and senior years at Exeter, and even then, blues was basically his life. He was always playing the records of the old Delta blues guitarists and the Chicago blues harp players that I mentioned before. Senior year, Mike began a correspondence with the legendary ragtime composer and pianist Eubie Blake, then brought him up to Exeter from Brooklyn to give a concert on campus. That was a big deal. Mike also did an American history term paper on Fats Waller, and included a full discography. (That was more of a big deal back in 1972.) He introduced me to music I probably never would have known otherwise. With Mike, there was no affectation of connoisseurship, as there was never any affectation of any sort; there was, to the contrary, a kind of ingenuousness I called his "innocence," which would clearly embarrass him when I mentioned it, and which he would claim not to understand: "If I'm innocent, then you're guilty!" he would thunder, in mock anger. But he just really, really loved that music, and it showed in his shining, soulful eyes whenever he played it.

How did this happen to a Jewish boy (fully Jewish) from the old factory town of Lewiston? His father, who owned a jewelry store and various other businesses in Lewiston, played piano and had a large collection of old jazz records that Mike had grown up with. But that hardly could fully explain what seemed his natural, almost inborn affinity for Black bluesmen. If I were a believer in metaphysical things, I would point to his past life in the Mississippi Delta to explain this inveterate attraction. But Mike would have none of such stuff; and besides, I prefer the mystery of the thing. As mysterious as him finding out more about Willie Dillard (the moniker of a Delta bluesman if there ever was one; all that's missing is the "Blind") in fifteen minutes than I ever managed to ascertain in thirteen years.

And I'll tell you something else. The Herb McCarthy's Incident would never have happened to Mike.

In the summer of '67—the Summer of Love in San Francisco, and the Summer of Riots in Philip Roth's Newark, as well as in Detroit, Boston, Atlanta et al.—I was thirteen. And for part of that summer, I was with my parents in Hampton Bays on Long Island, where they had a cottage dating back to the days before they had me. We used to go to a restaurant in Southampton called Herb McCarthy's (long since defunct). My dad knew Herb McCarthy from Exeter. (Yes, my father went to Exeter, too—*You already told us that as well.* Be quiet again.—and so did his brother, my Uncle Tiger—so I guess that makes me a double-legacy. Whoopee.) Anyway, we had gone out to dinner at Herb McCarthy's with a couple of my parents' friends. We were sitting at a table outside, and across the way was a biracial family: Black father, white mother and their children. And I was staring at them, the father in particular. I knew at the time that it was not polite to stare, and I also knew something more important: that it was wrong, very wrong, for me to be staring at this particular family. I knew—or at least at thirteen I sensed, I had an undeveloped, instinctive feeling—that this biracial family was part of what my father had gone to Selma to march for: freedom, equality, the brotherhood of man. And that there were people who hated this family and would kill them if they got the chance. Lynch them. Bomb them. Burn them alive. Beat them to a pulp and then bury them in a gravel pit, as they'd done to those three civil rights workers in Mississippi a few years earlier. Maybe I was thinking of these things as I was staring at them. But honestly, I'm not exactly sure what I was thinking. Maybe I was just absentmindedly dreaming and not completely aware of what I was doing, which was (at the very least) being extremely rude. But here I am giving myself the benefit of the doubt, and maybe also being disingenuous. *(Verdammt! What is it with you and the disingenuousness? Is this part of your unreliable narrator thing?* Be quiet once again.) Because although I may not have been completely aware of what I was doing, I was partly aware of it. And yet I kept doing it; I deliberately kept on doing it. I kept staring at them. It became a kind of game. A game concocted out of boredom—but not a benign one. A game sort of like the one I sometimes played in second grade, when I would decapitate ants with my fingernail. Something I told myself was harmless, but I knew wasn't.

But why? Why was I playing this game? Was I just trying to piss off my parents? But they weren't paying any attention to me; they were talking with their friends. Was I trying to get back at them then for ignoring me? For dragging me out to dinner at this fancy place, when what I wanted to do was to stay home and listen to my new records, The Jimi Hendrix Experience (*Are You Experienced?*) and Cream (*Fresh Cream*). (I had taken up the guitar a few years before, and in ninth grade would play in a band that did covers of a bunch of Cream songs. That was already pushing it for me as a guitarist, though, and I knew well enough to leave Hendrix alone. Senator, I was no Jimi Hendrix. Nor Clapton, for that matter. But now that I think of it, how could I be a racist if I liked Jimi Hendrix? *Are you kidding?* Yes. That was a joke. Lighten up, Fritz.) Maybe my interest in the family was just curiosity—idle curiosity. *(Curious about a biracial family, but not about African American literature?* Jesus Christ, I was only thirteen! Besides, I wasn't a big reader yet. Cut me some slack!) As I was saying, idle curiosity—but not benign. Like the ants.

I wasn't just curious, though; it was more than that. Because it wasn't like I'd never seen a biracial family before. Growing up, I'd been to several parties with Harry Belafonte and his family—his second wife, Julie, and their son David. My father had written a movie, *Odds Against Tomorrow* (which had a racial theme, as it happened), directed by his friend Robert Wise, that starred Harry Belafonte, and Belafonte and his family used to come to parties at Bob Wise's beach house. David Belafonte was about my age. Julie, his mother, had dark skin, but my mother told me that was because she dyed it; she was actually white. Jewish, in fact. So David was sort of like me—half-Jewish. (Actually, he was more Jewish than me, because his mother was Jewish, and mine wasn't.)

Of course, one could point out here that to adduce Harry Belafonte in this way—in the way of "acclimating" yourself to biracialism—is the worst kind of tokenism. Yes, I would have to agree. So perhaps I, and my parents, and Bob Wise—may they all rest in peace—should hang on the hook of tokenism for a while, too. (If it is possible for them to hang on the hook while also resting in peace.)

But what was perhaps most interesting about the HMI was that I was pretending to be more curious about the biracial family than I actually was. I was pretending to be curious so that I could have my curiosity be a cover for something else. For what? I think for the game I was playing, which was to piss off not my parents, but the father—the Black father. I was being deliberately rude and provocative to him and his family, to see what kind of reaction I would get. To see what, if anything, he would do. Because if he did something, that would show that I had power, some kind of power. The power to get a reaction out of a perfect stranger, who had done me no harm. The power to make a stranger mad, for no reason at all. The power—OK, yes—of a white person over a Black person. The power of a child—for if I wasn't exactly a child in age anymore, I was still a child in mentality—over a grown-up. The power of a *white* child over a *Black* grown-up. That was it. It was all about power, racial power. Black power? Of course not. *White* power. The power of the bad guys. The power of the racists. The power, ultimately, of the slave owners. Of the Confederacy. The power of evil. My evil. Me as the Bad Seed.

I think this is taking it a bit too far, don't you? I mean—slave own-ers? Confederacy? The Bad Seed? Come on, Schatzi, you were just a punk kid—a privileged, bored punk kid who was experimenting with being an asshole. A total asshole.

OK, point taken once again. I withdraw those last remarks. It was, in any case, a lot to accomplish for a child of thirteen, just out to dinner with his parents. And it worked. At some point during our dinner, the father got up and came over to our table. The experiment blew up—as I had known it would. I wanted it to blow up. It was designed to blow up. I wanted to destroy something, as with the ants. I wanted to have that power, and to show I had it. The Black father came over to our table and said to my father something like, "I think you should know that your son has been very rude. He's been staring at me and my family the entire time we've been sitting here, as if we don't have a right to be here. Your son should know that this is a free country, and if he doesn't know it already, he should learn it. He should know better. He is old enough to know better. And he should be ashamed of himself."

And I was. I was red in the face, which felt hot and large, and my ears were ringing. So what did I do? I pretended not to know what he was talking about. I continued my performance—this time, in the role of innocent. My performance of racism had gotten me into trouble, as I knew it would, so now I played the part of the innocent child. And my parents fell for it. Though my father automatically apologized to the man. I'd been half-hoping he'd say something like, "Hey listen, buddy, you've got the wrong guy. I marched in Selma." But of course he didn't say that. *Apparently your father was not under the control of your juvenile fantasies.* No, apparently not. He apologized for me, as I was pretending surprise and incredulity—butter wouldn't have melted in my mouth. But after the man left, my parents agreed that he must be an angry person with a chip on his shoulder. And I let them believe that.

Did they believe it, though? And did they really believe my protestations of innocence? Or did they just pretend to? Were they really, secretly, as ashamed of my behavior as I was? No, I don't think so. I don't think they really knew what I had been doing. Because if they had known, they would have made a much bigger deal out of it afterwards than they did. The fact that they didn't must have been because they were either clueless—which they weren't—or just deliberately refusing to deal with it, pretending I hadn't been staring at all (or just putting it out of their minds). At any rate, I never mentioned anything to my mother about the game I had been playing. I, who always told her everything, never told her this. I never told her what I'd really been up to. I never told her about the performance, or the experiment, or the white power thing. I kept the whole lousy thing to myself, for over fifty years.

Until I told it to the WAGS, who decided it was a power thing and not really a racist thing. But I'm not so sure. *Neither am I.* Shut up, this is serious. *I am serious. And I have a serious question for you. Didn't your parents ever talk to you afterward about what happened? You say they thought he had a chip on his shoulder. And that was it? They didn't say anything else to you? They didn't ask you what you were doing and why?* Like I just said, they thought the guy had a chip on his shoulder. *But you also said you wondered if they really believed that, and if they really believed you were as innocent as you maintained. It just seems odd to me that your parents—and especially your father, Selma-marcher that he was, which apparently left a strong impression on you—would not have pursued the matter. It seems like it could have been an important "teaching moment," as they say. It also seems odd that no one in the WAGS picked up on this, either.* Picked up on what? *On the fact that everybody in the family—your family—just swept the whole thing under the rug (if you'll pardon the expression). Especially since you make such a point of telling us that your project is to deliberately sweep things back* out *from under the rug, for all to see.* That's true—but that's now. This was then. I didn't have that project then. I was thirteen. *A hypersensitive thirteen, to hear you tell it—and with a hypersensitive mother, too. It's very strange that neither the civil rights crusader nor the empath should have seen fit to have a talk with you after such a fraught encounter. Don't you think?* Now that you mention it, I suppose so, yes. I guess they dropped the ball on that one. *And that never occurred to you before?* Why should it have? This is my cross to bear, not theirs. *Sounds like punishment to me—the "Hairshirt Principle", with a vengeance.* Let it alone, Fritz. Let's change the subject. *Very well. I can see I've touched a nerve.*

My mother, as Joßche mentioned, was an empath, and also—not surprisingly—a great reader of Proust. That was another thing we shared, in later years. She was also a big fan of the Beatles. And one of Mom's favorite Beatles songs was "In My Life." "There are places I'll remember / All my li-i-i-ife, though some have changed. / Some forever, not for better; / Some have go-o-o-one, and some remain. / All these places had their moments ... ," *und so weiter.* One of the things that makes that song so great is its universality—the fact that everybody has those places and moments. They don't have to be special, or in any way unusual, except to the people they are special to. But they can contain whole worlds of feeling and meaning. My favorite movie is *My Dinner with André (oh, I thought you were going to say* Guess Who's Coming to Dinner. Shut up.), and one of my favorite scenes in that movie—though actually, the whole movie is basically just one scene, right? So my favorite part of that one scene is when Wally, in response to André's stories detailing his extraordinary travels and adventures in Poland and Scotland, talks about the cigar shop on the corner. Wally says that if you truly knew everything that went down in the cigar shop on the corner, it would blow your mind. And I believe that. Because if you go deep enough, there is no such thing as an *un*extraordinary life story; everyone's life, if looked at closely and deeply enough by the right person, can be seen as exceptional. (Willie's story, which Mike learned more about in fifteen minutes than I did in almost fifteen years, would be one example of this.) And this reminds me of Garrison Keillor's famous line about all the children of Lake Wobegon being above average. It's funny, and wise, because it's so true. We all want our children to be above average, and every life is unique to the person living it (and to those who love them). A life doesn't need to be extraordinary to be interesting. Every person has a story to tell—especially today, in what seems to be the Golden Age of Memoir. And if everyone has a story to tell, then it follows—at least according to the little theory I'm about to put forth—that everyone also has a story *to be told*, if not by the subject themselves, then by somebody else in a position to tell it. Much follows from this, I think.

I can trace the origin of my theory—part of it, anyway—to the fall of 1978. November 1978, to be exact. I was browsing in a bookstore in

Westwood—Westwood Books, also now defunct—scanning the shelves
for books by or about Henry James. I found and bought, on the promise
of the title alone, a book called something like *Stories of the Major
Period* or *Tales from the Major Phase*. I no longer have the book (how
is this possible?), but I well remember the immediate throb of response
I had to the title. That one could have—and even better, be *seen* to
have—a Major Period! This seemed to me, at the time (and still does),
an achievement of no small note. I toyed around with the possibility of
applying this idea to myself, to my own life and writing. I had just sold
my first (and only) novel—at the time only half-written—to the editor
I mentioned earlier, and frankly was feeling pretty good about myself.
I was now officially in the community of "real" writers, was I not?
Poor little lamb! I won't dispute you on that, Joßche. I mean, who was
I to even think about having such a thing as a "Major Period"? Henry
James's claim—not his own, but his critics' and biographers'—was
based on his writing, his art. I had (and still have) achieved little
enough of either. *You can say that again.* But the idea fascinated and
continues to fascinate—as if there were time yet to turn things around,
produce a body of work, and have it divided up by future critics and
biographers into "Major" and "Minor Periods." This will almost certainly never happen for me *(but notice he cannot quite bring himself to
entirely give up the hope, either!)*, and so I have created instead a classification based not on what I have written, or ever will write, but merely
on what I have lived so far: my life with and without Diane, and my
new life now with Julie. (Classified, respectively, as the Major, Minor,
and Julistic Periods.)

    The possibilities of such classifications—of a life so felt and per-
ceived, as the "Master" James himself might have put it (and, not so
incidentally, *The Master* is the title of the final volume of Leon Edel's
five-volume, magisterial and definitive biography of Henry James. Oh,
how gratifying are the descriptors "magisterial and definitive," especially when applied to biography! How one longs, in fantasy, to have

them conferred upon one's own work!)—such classifications are not without their appeal. It is not really the appeal of fame, which does not much interest me, but of a life put in order, which does, since mine seems such a mess: so improvised, so haphazard, and with such a gaping hole (Diane's death) at the center. To have—or at any rate to be perceived as having—"Major" and "Minor Periods" is to have attained to a certain coherence, purposefulness, progress, and direction in one's life. Such a system of classification suggests that others—critics, biographers, scholars, those who *know*—have sifted through the evidence, judiciously and objectively (yet also sympathetically), and have concluded that you, your life, your work, are worth the effort. You *matter*. And more: you have, in a sense, *prevailed*. Exceptions are to be made in your case, by those in a position to make them. Your flaws are perceived, by some at least, as virtues. You are excused, forgiven, and vindicated. You are understood implicitly by those with the highest professional credentials: the scholars and critics, the biographers and historians, the editors, introducers, forewordsers and afterworders. Your life and work have been justified—nay, canonized—by the full panoply of critical apparatuses. ("The Armamentarium," I call it.) You have, in a word, been validated.

Thus were sown, many years ago now in Westwood Books, the early seeds of my penchant for what I call "biographization": the tendency to imagine my ongoing life retrospectively, as though it were already the subject of a later (probably posthumous) biography—as though the germ of a later fulfillment were already present in it. To "biographize" is to imagine your life and writing (or whatever work it is you do; the work itself doesn't really matter), and the relation between the two, as if from the point of view of a future biographer, editor or critic. No doubt it is my predilection for reading literary biography that has shaped—or even created, in the Wordsworthian sense (" ... every Author, as far as he is great and at the same time *original*, has had the task of *creating* the taste by which he is to be enjoyed.... " [emphasis is the author's])—my own taste for looking at one's life and writing in this way. But I don't think I am alone in this. I believe many of us do the same thing, if not in the form of an imagined future biography, then perhaps as an imagined film or miniseries or long-format series, in which we are the stars, and the story is our life (or certain choice scenes therefrom). We all feel the need to give shape, structure, and meaning to our experience; we all hope to discover a fictional order—and biographical order is always, to some degree, fictional—in the random disorder of our lives.

But "biographization" does more than just satisfy our particular vanities; it shows us that we all, in our different ways, seek forgiveness for our "weakness" and "uncertainty" through the exercise of our biographical imaginations. The words in quotes are those of Proust, my Supreme Master (as you may already have divined). He wrote, in a 1908 letter to his close friend Geneviève Straus, " ... only that which carries the stamp of our choice, our taste, our uncertainty, our desire and our weakness can be beautiful." Sing it, Marcel. We seek forgiveness, and perhaps even vindication, in the eyes and judgments of others (preeminently, biographers), for what might have only appeared, at the time, to be our errors, vanities, and failures—but which are seen, in biographical retrospect, to be our hidden virtues. We desire the kind of disinterested understanding that it is the business of biographers and critics to confer. (For "biographers" here, you can also read "therapists," "clergy," or "filmmakers".) We want our work in this life—and I mean "work" in its widest sense, not restricted to works of art or craft or undertakings of note, but including also the everyday work we do to earn a living and provide for our family—we want our work to be acknowledged and understood by someone who not only cares, but has the qualifications and has earned the right to be able to assess our accomplishments in the light of critical standards of judgment. We want the work of our days (or, in Proust's case, nights) to be weighed in the balance, and valued according to its merits, and found worthy.

This is all highly dubious. Take it from me, as a professional biographer. Please stop now, and never talk again. Well played once again.

Joßche is alluding to something my son Zack once experienced in high school. He was in a bullshit session with a group of his buddies, and one of them said something extremely stupid. Out-of-the-ordinary stupid. Someone else put his finger to his lips and said simply, "Ssh. Never talk again." However, with all due respect to that high-school wag, I will go on.

The idea of biographization entails the wish for—and indeed, the imagined future achievement of—"biographical vindication," the conferral of a kind of biographical validity through a retrospective authority (say, a biographer), whose job it is to discern intimations of one's future achievements in one's early beginnings. (Thus the biographical need to link "The Early Years" with "The Major Phase.") To chart, in other words, one's development as an artist (or, indeed, practitioner of whatever work it is that one does). Now according to such a scenario—the "biographizational scenario," let us call it—one receives posthumous recognition not only for one's achievements but (even more importantly) for one's errors, which will be seen, in the future, to have been formative. (*Grammatical note*: The future perfect tense—"will be seen ... to have been"—is the natural verb tense of biographization, because the future perfect envisions a future potential as already accomplished. A done deal-to-be. It is, if you will, the most gratifying of the verb tenses, and—unsurprisingly—my favorite.) One is "allowed," "permitted" one's mistakes by the generous eye of future critico-biographical judgment. One's mistakes are even necessary, because formative; for how was one to have developed precisely as one did without them? Of course, you could say that everyone's mistakes are formative, but the writer's, the artist's mistakes are sanctioned by the authority of said critico-biographical judgment. One is allowed one's self-indulgences not only through the special operation of artistic license, but also through the process of biographical examination and vindication. One receives the "biographical imprimatur."

So the fantasy goes—or so, at any rate, went mine, first concocted of an autumn's night in that bookstore in Westwood when I was twenty-four.

Another aspect of biographization that I've touched on briefly *(Ver-dammt! Nothing about you is brief!)* but want to say more about is "periodization": the idea that one's life can be divided into various periods: Major, Minor, pre-Major, post-Minor (the latter being, in my case, the Julistic Period). The idea of periodization also goes back a ways—not as far as 1978, but rather to 1987, when Zack was born, and then the years following—up to when he was in first or second grade. The origins of periodization—at least my particular version of it; the general idea of course is a long-established historiographic one, with special applications also in art history, musicology and literary history—came largely from photos of Zack as an infant, toddler, and child. More specifically, from the whimsical urge to classify the hun-dreds of photos Diane took of Zack from the ages of newborn to around six. I devised a way of categorizing these photos based mostly on Zack's facial features in them. This taxonomic scheme (a feature of "The Taxonomic Imagination"; but that's another story. *I'm sure it is!)* broke roughly into four "periods": minor Minor (infancy), major Minor (babyhood), minor Major (toddlerhood), and major Major (childhood and beyond). I really got into it. Diane and I would have long discussions—which could grow quite detailed, and sometimes heated—about the niceties of classification. Transitional periods were especially fraught. For instance, was the photo of Zack with Meme Bear (his first—but not dearest—stuffed animal, and spelled that way [and pronounced in two syllables] so as not to be confused in name with his grandmother Mimi, Diane's mother; the dearest would have to be Voo, a dog, who was lost in a hotel room in Milan during Zack's Fulbright Fellowship year; yes, Zack kept a stuffed dog with him all through college, but that's yet another story. *Oh for God's sake!)*— was the photo of Zack with Meme from the major Minor or minor

Major Period? (As I recall, that was the trickiest transition—major Minor to minor Major.) Diane tended to see these distinctions as merely academic; but I resisted that characterization. The work I was doing in graduate school was merely academic, but the classification of Zack's periods was more important than that. It entailed the way in which a system that had originally been merely photographic had evolved into a schema that became biographical, based not only on visuals but also on actual events: e.g., the birthday-cake-all-over-the-face birthday party (one year old—still minor Minor but on the cusp of being major Minor), as opposed to the robot birthday party (five or six, can't be sure—but indisputably major Major).

And if Zack's childhood could have such a classificatory scheme, why couldn't other children's as well? And why limit periodization just to children? Hadn't this system already been applied, for some time (albeit in a different context), to writers and artists and musicians? Picasso's Blue and Pink Periods are canonical; so are Beethoven's Late Quartets. The American composer Morton Feldman once put out a record entitled *The Early Years.* And I have mentioned already the curious (and possibly life-changing) thrill-cum-revelation I experienced in Westwood Books in the fall of 1978, when I happened upon an edition of Henry James's short stories entitled *Tales from the Major Phase.* Oh my God! To be able to be said to have had a "Major Phase"! How gratifying is that? What a consummation devoutly to be wished!

But why, I further came to ask myself, limit the idea of periodization to children, writers, artists, and musicians? Why couldn't, say, our gardener Willie Dillard have a Major Period, too? It seemed to me—and still does—that everyone is entitled to a Major Period (as well as a Minor Phase and Early Years). Of course, in the commonly understood sense, we all have our "early years"; but the designation of "Early Years," in my system of classification, has a different ring, meaning, and implication. In biographization, the denomination "Early Years" suggests other years of productive (nay, consummatory) maturity yet to come. If someone has a Minor Phase, it can only be in light of there already being (or better yet, of *there already having been*—or, best of all, *there already having been about to be*) a Major Period, coming either before or after the Minor Phase. We will leave out *(Promise? Please? Pretty please?)*, for the time being, as an aspect of periodization, a discussion of the difference between a Phase and a Period, though the distinction is probably self-evident: a Phase is shorter than a Period, and less definitive (and perhaps also less clearly demarcated, though not necessarily), and can be contained within the latter. For example, the Major Period—the twenty-three and a half years of my life with Diane—contained the Pre-Zack and Worcester Phases; the Julistic Period—the period in which I met, married, and am coming to know Julie—includes The Interregnum (the time after I met Julie but before we began living together), which was also a Phase. (The study of Julie, by the way, is known as Julistics—just as the field of German Studies is also known as Germanistics. *[Ach Du lieber!]* The "-istics" suffix is somehow deeply pleasing to me, betokening as it does a scientistic approach that I find both dubious and beckoning. *You are insane.)*

And finally—to begin to lay this long excursus to rest *(Gott sei Dank!)*—what if we all became, or at least tried to become, each other's biographizers, if only in imagination? What if we all felt responsible for telling the story of another person's life, as it was actually lived? Its works and days? What would that do to the way we looked at the lives of others? And how would it change the way we looked at and understood our own? To believe that everyone's life was at least capable of biographization might even, in a way, change the world. Or am I just indeed, as Joßche thinks, being insane? *You are just being insane.*

Speaking for myself (if I can ever do that around here, with this guy breathing his beer-, sauerkraut-, sausage-, and Jägermeister-reeking breath down my neck), *The Life of Willie Dillard* would be a book I would be interested in reading. The thing is, there is something in me—a big something—that would rather read about Willie's life than actually talk to him about it. Talking to him would make (or would have made) me feel self-conscious, and in "bad faith," because I would have known there was a hidden agenda behind my interest. My motives—unlike Mike's—would not have been pure. Nevertheless, if I were to talk to Willie about his life (which is of course impossible, as he surely must be dead by now—unless he is over one hundred, which I very much doubt; though I suppose it is remotely possible), the knowledge that there were biographizing motives behind my impulse would cause me to see his life differently. It would then be the subject of a notional biography (and, incidentally, that's not a bad thumbnail definition of biographization: "notional biography"), and so would receive a kind of "validation" it would probably not otherwise possess. It would have "biographical validity." It would have the heft of biographical authority behind it. It would in that sense be "authorized." The status and effects of the biographizational function would elevate it (as a high tide raises all boats), and this also would please me greatly.

I've been talking quite a lot about Willie—who, as noted, I hardly ever spoke to in real life—and neglecting someone else (also African American) who worked for us, and whom I knew much better than Willie. Her name was Aline. Aline Jackson. I suppose if I were ever to attempt to biographize another person, my first subject would not be Willie, but Aline.

Aline Jackson was our maid for thirty years. I was always told by my mother to call her our "housekeeper," but I think it's time to scrap that euphemism. She was our maid. And yes, I suppose you could say she was another "servant." Like Willie. And like Paul. *Oh yes, the crippled German manservant you've already mentioned. Are we to get a "biographization" of him, too?* All good things come to those who wait, asshole. Just hold your horses, as Jack Holt might have said. *Who's Jack Holt?* You'll see when we get to Paul. Right now we're with Aline, whom—like Paul—I loved.

But did I *really* love her? Because if I had, would I have done the things I did?

Aline grew up on a small, hardscrabble dirt farm in East Texas, out-side Houston, in the '40s and '50s. She moved to LA I'm not exactly sure when *(blame this ignorance on her biographizer!)*, and came to work for us in 1965. Which would mean she was already working for us at the time the Herb McCarthy Incident occurred. I actually hadn't thought about this before. Does that make the HMI even worse, considering that we'd had a Black woman working for us for two years, and yet I was still intent on performing my hateful experiment at the restaurant in '67? And is it "dumping on myself" again (as a Facebook friend once said I was doing when, a few years after the publication of *Failure*, I posted the title page of an unpublished manuscript I had just completed entitled "Shame: A Transgression") to say that it was hateful—or is it just the truth? (Because, I have to say, what others see as self-denigration I tend to see as just being honest, and reporting the truth as it appears to me.) Was Aline also work-ing for us during the Watts riots of '65? I believe she was. I seem to remember Mom emphasizing that Aline was safe during the riots, because she lived in Compton, not Watts—a distinction that is still lost on me but seemed important at the time, if only because it seemed important to Mom: our *housekeeper*, who lived in *Compton*. I had no idea then where Compton was—indeed, I had no real idea where Watts was either, except that it was nowhere near the Palisades.

Aline worked for us on Mondays, Tuesdays, Wednesdays, and Fridays. On Thursdays she worked for a Mrs. Ross, who always held a fixed yet vague place in my imagination as the person who "interrupted" Aline's week with us and must therefore hold a certain importance to be able to do so. The fact that I was never to lay eyes on Mrs. Ross only served to increase her status and significance in my mind—that, and the facts that Aline had started working for her before she'd started working for us, and that her once-a-week slot in Aline's schedule was not to be preempted by anything having to do with us. Then again, why should it be?

For some years—from '65 to at least '72—Aline and Willie overlapped in our employ, and Mom liked to tell the story of what Willie said to Aline when she was arriving for work one day. As Aline was walking down the driveway, past where Willie was working in the front garden, he stopped her and said (probably with his trademark high-pitched, cackling laugh; I can still hear that laugh, and the fact that I now recognize in it the inflections of a certain Jim Crow complaisance—marked by the desire not to offend, and to appear harmless, which he'd probably brought with him from Mississippi—only makes it all the more resonant and indelible in my mind's ear), "You sure do smell good. You been gettin' into Miss Anne's perfume?" Mom then explained to me who the proverbial "Miss Anne" was: the lady of the plantation.

In the event, Aline was deeply offended by Willie's remark, on at least a couple of counts (as I see it now): by the allusion to the dead hand of slavery and Jim Crow, and the suggestion that they were still in some ways living in that world, at least as far as Willie was concerned; and even more by the suggestion that she was stealing, and couldn't afford to buy her own perfume. The thought that Willie might see himself and Aline as not all that different from slaves on the plantation was close enough to the truth, as my imagination figured it, to really get to me then, and stick with me still. After all, didn't they do our dirty work? Didn't Willie sometimes pick up our dogs' dried turds from the backyard? Wasn't it undeniable that Aline cleaned my toilet? I saw irrefutable evidence of this in the blue-colored toilet-bowl cleaner that was sometimes still present when I returned home from school, and which I then immediately, out of guilt, tried to unsee. And didn't she wash the sheets that were soaked nightly with my urine until almost the end of seventh grade, when I finally stopped wetting the bed? So sad and deplorable, on all counts; and so true.

My passive guilt as far as Aline was concerned was bad enough; added to it was the active guilt of my behavior to her, which was worse than my guilt about Willie because with Aline, my sins were those of commission, not just omission. (Here I feel my Catholic side kicking in.) A few shameful incidents stand out.

THE FART

I once audibly passed gas in Aline's presence, and she said, in her high, gentle voice, but with a frown, which she did not often wear, "*Josh*. That's very rude." I blushed, but I think I also laughed, and I am pretty sure I did not apologize. After all, what was the big deal? She cleaned our toilets, didn't she? What was a mere fart compared to that? (Though, as mentioned just above, I often also tried to ignore the fact of her cleaning my toilet—to just put it out of my mind, pretend it wasn't happening; and so the bad faith of the "Fart Rationalization" seems all the more egregious now.) I would like to think this incident happened when I was still in elementary school, or junior high at the latest, but I'm afraid that is far from the truth. I believe I was either in high school or college at the time. What could I have been thinking? The easiest (and most transparently disingenuous *here we go again*) interpretation would be that I considered Aline "a member of the family", and so did not feel the need to behave any differently around her than I would around my parents. And there might even be a grain of truth in that rationalization; but I don't really believe it, and can't accept it. The likelier explanation is a more hateful and damning one: Aline was just our Black maid. Case closed. I may have been careful to refer to her, as per Mom's instructions, as our "housekeeper" around others; but as far as my own behavior around her was concerned, she was just our Black maid. I was fond of her, and even, in my own way, loved her; and I sensed—or at least wanted to believe—she reciprocated those feelings. But she was still, and always, our Black maid. To pretend to myself that my thinking ran substantially otherwise would be simply to add an unnecessary element of more bad faith to my already-sufficient casual racism. I farted in her presence because she was, for all my intents and purposes, not even there.

THE PSYCHOTIC BLACK CHEF

This incident, unlike The Fart, can be precisely dated: it was early in the fall of ninth grade—1968. So a little more than a year after the HMI and the Newark Riots. I had spent the weekend at my friend Charlie's family's cabin in Wrightwood, in the San Gabriel Mountains. Charlie's parents were from Virginia. One of their guests at the cabin that weekend—I believe he was a relative, perhaps an older cousin of Charlie's—told a tall tale, a scary "campfire story," featuring a psychotic Black chef on the loose, terrorizing the good (i.e., white) folks of the community. Especially scary—which is to say, meant to be especially scary—was the narration of the way the Black chef's white chef's uniform, his white teeth, and the whites of his madly bulging eyes shone in the moonlight as he ran amuck in the neighborhood, brandishing a butcher knife.

Now as it happened, my parents were having a dinner party the evening I got back from the cabin. It was a Sunday, and Aline had come to help with the party. And for some unfathomable reason *(well, perhaps not all that unfathomable, Schatzi; see end of previous incident),* I saw fit to repeat the tale of the Black chef to the company that night. At the time, Aline was in the kitchen, which directly adjoined the dining room. There was a Dutch door between the dining room and kitchen, but it was always open, and there was also a wide communicating space above the low partition between the stove in the kitchen and the sideboard in the dining room. This open space made it easy for anyone in the kitchen to hear whatever was being said in the dining room. During dinner parties at which she was working, Aline always sat on a stool in the kitchen to eat. As soon as I began my story, before I'd even begun to describe the chef, my mother intuited danger and tried to cut me off at the pass; but I was undeterred, and proceeded to recount everything in the unremitting, minstrel-show detail in which it had been narrated up at the cabin, down to the grisly finish of the psychotic rampage.

The story, of course, was met with mortified silence at the dinner table. It was clear that Aline, in the kitchen, could hear everything. I'm sure that Mom apologized profusely to her on my behalf later that evening; and I'm just as sure that I didn't. As with the HMI—not to mention The Fart—I pretended I had done nothing wrong; though even halfway through the story, which I sort of didn't want to continue but somehow couldn't stop, my face was hot with shame. There is a line from Proust that describes one aspect of the situation perfectly: "I had gone too far along the road that led to the realization of this desire to be able to turn back." But exactly what that desire was, and why it needed to be realized at that particular moment—or any moment—I had no clear idea, and still don't.

Just out of curiosity, did your mother or father speak to you afterward about this incident either? I don't know. I don't think so, but I really don't remember. Though I guess I would remember it if they had. *I see. So in that way, too, it really was almost an exact parallel to the HMI.* Maybe, yes. I guess they dropped the ball there, too. *I guess so. Not exactly Selma-worthy either, was it?* No comment. *I see. Let the record show that the author has no comment.*

CHESTER

My mother had often mentioned an old English movie from the 1940s—one of her favorites—called *Dead of Night*, composed of a series of interconnected horror vignettes, one of which concerned a ventriloquist's dummy that took on a life of its own. Shopping for a Christmas present for her one year (again, I was not nearly as young as I would like to believe; this was either when I was in college or after, when I was living in New York and visiting my parents for the holidays), I found a ventriloquist's dummy that seemed just the thing: capable of producing exactly the right combination of fear and campiness that would recall for Mom the movie she'd so loved to be terrified by long ago. And to top it off, the dummy was Black. What luck! To placate whatever inner doubts I may have had about it, I told myself that Aline would laugh along with us at this object, too; for surely she would appreciate its outrageous grotesquery.

But Mom didn't quite see it that way. The doll, who I'd decided would be named "Chester" even before I gave it to her *(and hence your previous touchiness regarding that name)*, went directly from sitting under the tree on Christmas Eve to sitting at the very back of Mom's closet on Christmas Day, before Aline could have a chance to see it (or so Mom hoped). And Chester never emerged from the closet. But that didn't mean that Aline didn't see him. Of course she did. Because I showed him to her, probably subconsciously hoping to preempt whatever disaster was in the making by bringing her in on the joke. And what was her reaction? As I recall, she had no reaction at all—or, more likely, just kept it to herself. After all, we were her employers. She relied on us for four-fifths of her income. What was she going to do—call me out for being a racist and quit? No doubt if it had come to that, I would have also, like my mother in the Black Chef Incident, apologized profusely and begged her to stay—we all would have, including my Selma-marching father. But it never came to that, and her silence when confronted with Chester spoke volumes. With the result that I still carry this shit around with me, and always will. Which, I do not doubt, is exactly as it should be.

Play that funky music white boy
Play that funky music right
Play that funky music white boy
Lay down that boogie and play that funky music
Till you die. Till you die.

THE PHOTO/PICTURE

Aline was very heavy, and quite short; and the contrast between her squat girth and the soft delicacy of her voice (and also the shyness of her manner) had the paradoxical effect of making her words, and the impression they made, all the stronger. But her weight, which only increased over the years, led to serious diabetes and subsequent vision problems. In later years, her eyesight got so bad that even with her glasses on, she needed a magnifying glass to read the paper. One evening, when she was reading an article about a show at the LA County Art Museum, she asked me a question I have never forgotten.

"Josh," she said in her soft, shy voice, "what the difference between a photo and a picture?"

"What do you mean, Aline?"

She showed me the article she was reading, which had a photo of a painting. "Is that a photo or a picture?"

I realized that by "picture" she meant painting. "Oh, I see. It's a photo of a painting—a photo of a picture."

"So what the difference?"

I thought that because of her poor vision she was having trouble seeing the photo clearly; but it was soon evident that wasn't really the problem. It turned out she'd never seen an actual painting. At first I didn't believe this could be true, so I pointed out that LACMA, like all art museums, had lots of paintings. But she'd never been to LACMA—or any art museum; in fact, she'd never been to a museum at all. The more we talked, the softer her voice became, until it was barely above a whisper.

"Well then," I concluded heartily, "we should go to the museum sometime." She nodded, but we never did.

THE COKE-BOTTLE DOLL

As I've said, Aline grew up on a dirt farm some miles outside Houston. She once told Diane a story I have never forgotten—and neither did Diane. *(Interesting that she told it to Diane and not to you. What do you make of that?* Another good question. Let me think about it. *You mean you never thought about it before?* I don't think so, no. *Well, I have a few ideas.* I'm sure you do. But please stop interrupting.) Actually, what she told Diane wasn't even technically a story, just a bit of personal history. But resonant all the same. It can be briefly told. *(And then "contemplated about" for a lifetime, no?)* When Aline was growing up on the farm, her parents didn't have enough money to buy her a doll. (And how much, I wonder, did I spend on Chester, without even thinking about it?) But Aline, in the resourceful way of children, found a solution to that problem. She got a length of rope and tied it to a Coke bottle, and there she had it: her Coke-bottle doll, which she would drag with her everywhere, through the dirt. That image has never left me. And I wonder, in light of the Coke-bottle doll, what she made of my ten-foot-tall toy closet, into which all manner of board games and battery-operated playthings and stuffed animals were crammed to the rafters for many, many years. (In fact, until they were replaced by toys that my parents bought for Zack.) But I never asked her *(shades of Willie Dillard?),* nor would it ever have occurred to me to do so—or even to consider the question.

I wonder, also, if Mom knew of the Coke-bottle doll. If so, she never mentioned it, which is kind of odd, because it's the sort of thing that would have left an impression on her as well—as indeed it would on anyone; but especially Mom, the Queen of Empathy. Mom and Aline were close, and shared a lot of stories together, which is why I find it hard to believe Aline wouldn't have shared that particular one with her. And their closeness in life was replicated in death, with a certain bittersweetness—more bitter than sweet, I'm afraid—that has never left me, either.

In September of 1993, Mom was diagnosed with a rare and incurable blood disease called amyloidosis. Some cases of amyloidosis have been linked to Malathion, a potent insecticide (now banned) that Mom used to spray on the orchids she raised. At first, the amyloidosis manifested as bruises on her arms and legs that didn't go away. (The bruises were what brought her to the doctor in the first place.) For a while, the amyloidosis was mistakenly treated with chemotherapy; but this only made her sicker and weaker, and brought on neuropathy in her legs. (My father called the oncologist who'd wrongly prescribed the chemotherapy "The Duchess of Death.") By Christmas of 1994, Mom was bedridden.

It was about this time that Aline stopped coming to work, with no explanation. Mom was bitter about that, especially considering how close they'd been for thirty years; though I figure on Aline's part it was a combination of a well-earned retirement (unpaid, I'm pretty sure. *Nice going, Giddings!*) and not knowing how to deal with Mom's terminal illness. *Maybe it was just that she was finally sick unto death of being your family's Black maid for thirty years?* Ouch. Yes. Well, um, yeah. What else can I say? *Nothing. Absolutely nothing. Here I am reminded of that scene in the movie* Malcolm X, *where the well-meaning white college student goes up to Malcolm after a speech he's just given and asks him what she can do to help, and he replies, "Nothing."* Shit, Joßche. Another good question. *It wasn't a question.* Well, in any case, I don't have a good answer. But maybe I will, later. *I'm not holding my breath.* And please stop interrupting. If you don't, I will have to ban you. Don't think I won't. *Ooh, I'm so scared.* God, what an asshole. Reader, I sincerely apologize for him.

By that time, you see, Aline—who'd been suffering from diabetes for years—was not at all well herself. Had she had a heart attack? Was she having kidney problems? Did she have a stroke? And did I even call her to find out how she was doing?

Res ipsa loquitur—as your son the lawyer would say.

Mom's mental state had declined since she'd become bedridden. She spoke little now and seemed to have retreated into herself, which was uncharacteristic for someone who'd always been an empath and worn her heart on her sleeve. In the aftermath of Mom's death, Diane thought there might have been some Alzheimer's involved as well, since amyloid proteins in the brain are heavily implicated in Alzheimer's; and in amyloidosis, what eventually kills you is the buildup of amyloid in all the major organs. But there was no autopsy, and so we never found out whether or not she had Alzheimer's at the end. My point though is that for the last six months of her life, Mom became very withdrawn and uncommunicative, and almost a different person. She barely mentioned Aline, and didn't seem to know what had become of her.

Well, we found out the answer to that question the second week of June, 1995, when we got a call from a friend of Aline's to say that she had just died. By that time, Mom was also dying, and Diane, Zack, and I had flown back from Massachusetts, where I was then teaching, to be with her. Aline's friend—whose name I have forgotten, so I'll call her Katie (no, that was actually Aline's mother's name; so her friend will have to remain nameless. *Figures.)*—asked me to come help pick out a coffin, and Diane came with me. A few days later, the three of us—Diane, my father, and I—went to Aline's funeral, where I gave a short eulogy at the gravesite. Zack stayed home with my parents' close friend Beth, who—along with two caregivers, Violeta and Ada—was watching Mom while we were gone. After the funeral, we were having something to eat at Aline's friend's house when Diane suddenly had a bad feeling and phoned home. She got Ada, who said that Mom was having trouble breathing. We rushed home immediately—but it was too late. Mom's eyes were slightly open, but she was gone. I'll never forget the frozen look on her face when we came into the bedroom, and I saw her still propped up on the pillows in bed, her eyes dull and lifeless.

I still berate myself for not being with her when she died. Diane felt she "chose" that time, when we were all gone from the house (except for Zack, who was in the bedroom with her and Beth, reading *The Very Hungry Caterpillar*, where the caterpillar turns into a butterfly at the end); and Julie, to whom I've told the story, thinks so too. I've always wondered whether Mom, in her empathic way, somehow intuited that Aline was dead, and so figured she could go now, too. I say "intuited" because we had decided, after we heard from her friend that Aline had died, not to tell Mom, out of fear that it would hasten her own death to know this—or at least cast her into an end-of-life dejection that would have brought her additional pain. But now I think it was a mistake not to tell her. She deserved to know the truth; and Aline deserved to have her know it, too. But maybe, despite our best efforts to conceal it, she figured it out on her own, and then took action.

Over the years since she died, the memory of Aline has become a kind of touchstone for me: the painful memory touchstone of a funky-music-playing white boy's guilty conscience. But actually, now that I think of it, Aline's touchstone power predated her death, by around ten years. Starting in 1986, when I began graduate school at USC, I also began swimming in their outdoor pool, next to the new gym. And when I swam, I would find myself thinking for some reason of Aline, and the intersection (and contrast) of our lives. Partly I think it may have been because University Park, where USC is located, is not all that far from Compton. A redoubt of still-mostly-white privilege, surrounded on all sides by poorer, darker neighborhoods. As I swam my leisurely laps outside in the sunny afternoons after classes, or to break up long stints in the library, my mind would drift to Aline and all the differences in our histories and circumstances. I don't think Aline ever learned how to swim. As I mentioned, she was morbidly obese—with diabetes—and so any kind of exercise was hard and probably even dangerous for her. What came easily to me probably wouldn't have even been on her radar. And there was something a little uneasy that happened in my stomach when I thought of this: a guilty sense of my energizing, healthful back-and-forth in the outdoor, sun-filled pool, in contrast to the diabetic life she lived in the cramped, dark little house in Compton, not too far away.

I had been to that house only twice in thirty years: once after the funeral of her mother, Katie (the "real" Katie), and once with my friend Nick from New York, on our way either to or from Watts Towers. Two privileged white boys on a sightseeing tour of the ghetto would be an uncharitable but not inaccurate way to put it. And I can't even say that what I felt when I thought about Aline as I was swimming was com-posed entirely of guilt and shame at the sense of unfairness and social injustice in our respective lots. I think there was something less benign going on as well. It was, if I am to be completely honest with myself, a feeling also of gratitude—gratitude for all that I had that she didn't. A "There-but-for-the-grace-of-God-go-I" feeling, except without the God. Gratitude for the luck of the draw. The white boy with the jam-packed toy closet, as opposed to the Black girl with the rope-and-Coke-bottle doll.

These are hateful things now to think about. And I knew at the time they did me no credit, either—nor Aline any good. It was as if my swims were at once an occasion for and attempt at cleansing myself of these thoughts. An eruption of the same thing—smug self-satisfaction—that was to be purged. Except it never got purged, because it couldn't be. It could only be repeated. Over, and over, and over again, lap after lap, almost every time I swam....

Also, mein Freund. *I think some deeper reflection is now called for. And I ask: What is all this really about? What exactly are you confessing here? Do you really think you're a racist? Why is it necessary to share all these stories—Aline, Willie, the HMI? Will rehearsing accounts of your sup-posed racism, and your guilt about it, make up for the actions themselves, or really accomplish anything at all? I think not. What, then, is the pur-pose of writing about these things? Just to ease your own conscience, and perhaps garner praise for your honesty and forthrightness and "courage" vis-a-vis your unsparing self-criticisms? Isn't what you're doing here just another form of the virtue-signaling you abhor? "Hey reader, I'm really not a racist because I'm confessing that I am, or might be, a racist." Is that what's going on here? Is that finally what this is about—your own racial sins? Because, as you rightly say, none of this*

does Willie, or Aline, or the father and his family at Herb McCarthy's any good. What good can or will come of any of this?

He's right, you know. I have to admit I've been asking myself the same questions. As a student of the English Romantics—Wordsworth especially, but also his pal Coleridge, as well as Byron's long poems *Childe Harold* and *Don Juan*—I'm big on process. You don't really have to know what you're writing about, what your end goal is, while you're writing. Coleridgean "Organic Form," right? Your content, what you have to say, will determine the form. And you don't really know what you have to say until you try saying it. Meaning is something that is only gradually discovered and revealed—constructed, really. We create the meaning we seek. It is not something that can be known or outlined beforehand. *And the rest of us are just expected to come along for the ride, is that it?* No, Joßche, nobody but you. *You* are expected to come along for the ride, because you really have no choice. If I'm writing, you are along for the ride, too. Because remember: you are me. *No I'm not.* Here we go again. The infinite loop. But whoever you are, you're also a literary biographer, and so you should know about such things as creative process, exploration, evolution. That's a foundational part of the Romantic project—the part that self-consciously reflects on its own imaginative process. And in such an endeavor, you cannot really know where you are going beforehand. All knowledge is retrospective, as Emerson said. And that is certainly true of the kind of knowledge on offer in autobiographical writing. I can only know where I've been, not where I'm going. And if you think that's a poor excuse for this narrative, so be it. What I do know—and this as a consequence of that other knowledge—is that I have a special fondness for the past, and especially my Major and Minor Periods: my life with and then without Diane. It's odd that I should be almost as attached to my period of bereavement—the eleven years after Diane's death, before I met Julie—as to the twenty-three and a half years I spent with Diane. But so it is. And why it is is perhaps worth exploring. *And perhaps not?* Perhaps not; but there's only one way to find out.

When I met Diane, in late January of 1981, I was already beginning to emerge from a serious depression, brought on by my relationship and subsequent breakup with a woman I'll call "Cindy." Cindy and I first got together in the early spring of 1980 in New York City, where I was living at the time. Our relationship was rocky from the start. She had a serious problem with intimacy, and I suppose I must have struck her as needy—or needier, at least, than she was willing to accommodate. We broke up for the first time later that spring, whereupon—since there was nothing else keeping me in New York after I had quit my restaurant job—I decided to return home to LA. Just before I left, however, Cindy and I had a rapprochement, and she decided to come out to LA for a couple of weeks in August. But things really didn't get any better between us during her visit, and when she left later in August, I fell into the depression that had been looming since our first breakup in New York.

That fall in LA was rough. I had no job. Although my novel had been published at the end of the summer, it was basically DOA: no blurbs, no good reviews (a mild pan in the *New York Times Book Review* and a more severe one in *People*), and no second novel in the works. Although I had drafted a second novel manuscript—really, a novella—called *The Man Who Spent the Night in Disneyland* (which had long been a fantasy of mine; that, and spending the night in a department store), it was deemed unpublishable by my editor, and I could hardly disagree. It basically had no story beyond the quirky premise named by the title. I had spent an unsatisfactory two weeks with Cindy in LA (though the *coup de grâce* did not come until I returned to New York in December, for a brief visit), and I was now without romantic or literary prospects—or any employment. At the age of twenty-six I was living once more with my parents, in the house I'd grown up in. I awoke every morning with a gnawing sense of dread in the pit of my stomach; and while this feeling became somewhat milder as the day wore on, it never entirely left, and the next morning it was back again, in full force. This feeling was all too familiar to me from the fall of seventh grade, when I had begun attending a new school, Buckley, in the Valley. (No relation to the high-profile private school in Manhattan.) So I was not only back at home now but also, in a sense, back in seventh grade, with all of its attendant anxieties. I had become a published novelist—a status I had long thought I wanted to achieve more than anything else in the world—only to find that I felt worse than ever, or at least than at any time since seventh grade. I did not feel right in my own skin; everything was spooky and alien—"fear in a handful of dust," as the poet said—and each day was something to be suffered through and endured. I knew not what would become of me, nor how I was to live. I wasn't exactly suicidal—the depression wasn't quite that bad, nor has it ever been since; but the world was a strange and unfriendly place. And yet, looking back on those gray fall days of the pre-Early Major Period, I feel a certain attachment to them—as indeed I feel a curious attachment to the memory of the anxiety-filled beginning of seventh grade. (Cf. the Virgilian attachment to our sadness when it is looked back on from a better time, at a distance of years. " ... *Forsan et haec olim meminisse iuvabit*," Aeneas rallies his comrades during the storm in Book I of *The Aeneid*: "Someday it will be a help to look back even on these things.") *Is this pedantry really necessary?* Probably not; but just as with your interruptions, I couldn't resist.

I think that part of the pleasure in the sad memories here is a proleptic one. This was the time period—the pre-Major Period—just before I was to meet Diane; and knowing this now confers a retrospective happiness on the sadness I was feeling back then. Little did I know I was about to meet the first love of my life—the woman, and the relationship, that would change everything for me, that would bring me into adulthood and the Major Period. So how could the memory of the pre-Major Period, even with its depression, not be dear to me?

As a means of combatting the depression, I took to jogging on the beach. I remember the weather on those runs as overcast, which I liked (and which I have always preferred, since overcast weather is the exception rather than the rule in Southern California, and so seems special—and also comforting, as a respite from the unremitting sunshine). I would sometimes finish my jogs by plunging into the chilly ocean of October and November. Those jogs and swims were briefly invigorating, and occasion for the rare feeling that fall of being rather proud of myself. In September I had gotten a piecework job synopsizing screenplays and novels for my father's literary agents—a gig that turned into a full-time studio job the following February, after I'd met Diane; so having something to do during the days helped my depression a little. But it never really lifted until I met Diane at a pub in Santa Monica—The King's Head—at the end of January '81. We slept together on our second date, and after that I spent most nights at her apartment in West Hollywood. I signed my first valentine to her "your permanent date"—a move whose boldness impressed her, though to me it seemed merely obvious. We both knew this was it.

Around this time—actually, a little bit earlier, that previous fall—I had begun talk therapy for the depression. The first therapist I got didn't take with me—nor I with her—so she recommended a colleague of hers, Dee Barlow, who had an office on Santa Monica Blvd. in West LA. I began seeing Dee about the same time, or maybe a little after, I met Diane, which was also when I got the full-time reading job (the official title was "Story Analyst") at Warner Bros. Pictures in Burbank. So by early 1981, things were definitely looking up, and the depression had mostly abated. It came back in the summer of '81, when I got temporarily laid off, but then went away (for many years) after I was rehired at Warner's in the early fall of '81. I remember that time as a particularly happy one. I was in love with the woman I would marry, I was living with her and making good money—with benefits—working full-time at the studio, and the Dodgers won the World Series.

That fall I read a book that changed my life: *Images of Hope: Imagination as Healer of the Hopeless,* by William F. Lynch, SJ. Dee Barlow had recommended it, and I fell into it and lapped it up—every page. It was just what I needed at the time, and it marked the end of my depression. In memory this book cannot be separated from my starting to live with Diane (I "officially" moved into her apartment and started paying rent right after Thanksgiving), and the contrast of that fall with the previous one, when I had been so low, could not have been greater. Diane once described the feeling of our getting together as "coming home". That puts it exactly right, and the Lynch book accompanied me into this new era of my life. It opened up—or was a participating witness to the opening up of—a new landscape of feeling and thought, inseparable from both my love for Diane and the insights and support I was getting from Dee Barlow. "Perhaps it is impossible to really despair with someone," Lynch wrote, and that one sentence really says it all: my despair finally ended when I met Diane. (And interestingly, it did not return when I lost her, twenty-three and a half years later. Though there was much sadness during the Minor Period, as well as a few short-term depressions—and one notable longer one, in the summer of 2009—there was never any more despair.)

In accordance with its title, the Lynch book witnessed and helped to spark a new kind of hope in my life. That hope felt substantially different from any I'd felt before. It was the hope brought on by the recognition that I'd found someone I could share a life with. In that way it was perhaps my first "adult" hope—the hope of the Major Period that was just now beginning. This feeling of new hope would probably have come regardless of the book, but the book "ratified," "certified," and "validated" the feelings, as books that are important in our lives tend to do. (I will have more to say later about the desire for validation, and how books serve to gratify—but can never finally satisfy—that desire. *I'm sure you will. Ignore him.*) Proust, for me, is the Great Validator; he has "definitively" and "magisterially" validated most of the principal thoughts and feelings of my own life. (I admit that the descriptors "definitive" and "magisterial" are like catnip to me. How I long to be the author—and better yet, the

subject!—of a "definitive," "magisterial" study. *Just you wait, Schatzi.*
What are you talking about? *You'll see.*)

Another book of the Early Major Period that had a formative effect on
me, about a year later, was Jacob Needleman's *The Heart of Philosophy.*
The circumstances surrounding the discovery of this book are worth
mentioning. *(We can only hope.)*

In the fall of '82, Diane and I moved from West to East Hollywood,
from a characterless apartment in a characterless building to the top floor
of a house in what is now—and was then in the process of becoming—Little
Armenia. The house was on Winona Blvd., a block west of Normandie,
between Hollywood and Sunset. We lived for twelve years in that house.
We were living there when Zack was born in 1987, and for seven years
after that. We left in 1994, at the beginning of what I call the Heart of
the Major Period, when I got my first faculty job back east at Holy Cross,
in Worcester, MA. That house on Winona is not infrequently the scene
of dreams of the Major Period, when Diane was still alive and before she
even got sick. (She was first diagnosed with breast cancer in October of
1999.) As a locus of my dream life, it is not quite as important—and not
nearly as frequent—as Vance Street, in the Palisades, but it is important
nonetheless, and full of memorial "juice."

This was a term that Diane and I used to denote the molecular traces
of a person left in a place or on a thing. For example, there must be traces
of skin cells or DNA left in a place where that person had lived, or visited,
or touched things, or just shed skin cells in passing through. The trace of
Diane's blood on the wall in our apartment on Long Island, where she
fell a few days before she died, and which I never washed off, is an example of her "juice." (I'll have more to say about this later. *What a surprise.*)
And although Diane never lived in the house on Long Island where I lived
during all of the Minor Period—which was bought two years after she

died—there were many things in this house that she had lived with, many things that she had touched: linens and pillows and blankets and cooking utensils and stuffed animals (her toy frog Debbie especially) and books, and her journals and artwork. So her "juice" was undoubtedly there as well, even in a place where she never lived. And the thought of it being there made me feel better during the eleven years that I lived there without her. For where her "juice" was, I told myself, so was her wisdom, and understanding, and laughter, and words, and sympathy—many of the things that helped sustain me during the Minor Period.

Our East Hollywood neighborhood was a sketchy one—drug-dealers across the street, prostitutes on the corner of Sunset, gang-bangers up and down Winona—but the house itself was a gem. Diane fell in love with it on first sight. It was a two-story, 1920s California Bungalow: square wooden pillars at the entrances to the first and second floors, and gray-shingle siding, with an enclosed front sun porch and a side deck on the second floor, where we lived. Inside it was all dark wood paneling, cream-colored walls, and chocolate-brown carpeting, wall-to-wall. There were old varnished, built-in bookcases, and china cabinets with beveled-glass doors; a double pull-out oak partition between the living room and dining room; old sconce lights in the dining room; old-fashioned, push-button light switches in all the rooms; the remains of an old voice-tube connecting the upstairs hallway with the stoop downstairs; and a secret compartment to stash valuables under the bottom shelf of the built-in bookcase in what was first my study, and then became Zack's room. Connected to that room there was also a tiny half-bathroom, containing just a sink, a mirrored medicine cabinet, a towel rack, and an old light fixture that you turned on at the stem. There was a window on the left that looked out over the apartments next door, all the way to the Equitable Building downtown on Wilshire, several miles away. Before Zack was born, I used to brush my teeth every night in this room. Seeing the red lights flashing on top of the Equitable building in the distance always made me feel good, for some reason—just as seeing a small plane flying at night always makes me feel good: cozy and secure.

I come back to that bedroom often in my dreams, sometimes with Zack in it, sometimes without. But even without Zack, it is still his room, waiting for him to arrive—to be born, come home from school, or go to bed, when one or both of us will read to him before he falls asleep. And when he is ready and rubbing his eyes—or after his eyes are already closed—I tuck him in, kiss him good night, get up gently and push out the light, and then turn back for a moment to look out the window and see the red lights of the Equitable Building, blinking faithfully in the night.

This last paragraph is rather touching, I have to admit; but what, pray tell, does it have to do with the Needleman book? And why is that particular book so important to you? All in good time, Fritz. *You keep saying that, and then you keep going off again. How can you expect any reader—even a sympathetic one—to stay with this?* OK, fair enough. I take your point and will try to rein in the digressions. But please stop interrupting, or I will have to ban you. *I'd like to see you try.* Is that a challenge? *Consider it whatever you like. I'm just trying to help the narrative along—what there is of it.*

In the fall of '82, shortly after we had moved to East Hollywood, I was walking down Western Ave. on my way to get a haircut at the barbershop of Mits Akino. In the window of a Crown Bookstore a hardcover book with a red cover and white lettering caught my attention: *The Heart of Philosophy,* by Jacob Needleman. The title spoke to me immediately. Without a conscious thought, I found myself entering the store and buying the book, which I began reading in the barbershop. It was as though I had been craving exactly such a book without knowing it. As with Lynch, the book took at once, and I was hooked on Needleman (I followed *The Heart of Philosophy* with *Lost Christianity,* a book on Gnosticism), and also on existentialism. The following spring, I signed up for the first of what would end up being five evening courses in philosophy, taught through UCLA Extension. This was the germination of my academic career. For a while I considered going to graduate school in philosophy, but the thought of all the gruesome reading I would have to do put me off (especially after I learned that the focus of study would be on analytic philosophy, not existentialism, which as a field of academic study was a nonstarter), and steered me instead to what I figured would be either English or comp lit (the latter because of Proust). I ended up doing English.

Walking back to the barber's a couple of months after buying *The Heart of Philosophy*, I found the shop closed and a horrifying notice stuck on the door: anyone with any information connected to the robbery and murder of Mits Akino was to contact the LAPD.

I'm sorry, but I really must intervene again. Why, may I ask, include this detail about your hapless barber? What is its purpose? What relevance does it have to the story you are telling? And, for that matter—once again—what exactly is the story you are telling? Are you trying to destroy me, Joßche? What are you after? Why do you keep interrupting me? I ask in turn, What is your *purpose? Are you trying to kill the narrative here? Funny, I was just going to ask you the same question. But now that we're at it, what narrative are you speaking of? Or rather, which one? The narrative of the Old White Man you started with? Whatever happened to him—that dried-out old dust bunny in the corner? The unseemly detritus swept under the rug? The straight, cis-gendered (to use the woke parlance of the present moment), superannuated, superseded, irrelevant writer, whose story (that nobody wants to hear) you appeared at the outset so keen on telling? Or is it the story of the WAGS and the unfortunate Suzette? Remember her? Wasn't it that experience that originally sparked this whole flood of memory—including your desultory meditations on Willie, Aline, and the Black father you were staring down at Herb McCarthy's? Where have they gone? And where are we now? It appears, from what you say, we are currently near the beginning of the "Major Period." And how many more of these "periods" must we go through? And to what end? Where is all this headed? I have asked this before, and I am asking it again.* Quo usque tandem abutere, Catalina, patientia nostra? *Remember*

*that one from your Exeter Latin, junior year? The opening sentence of
Cicero's First Catalinarian? "How much longer, finally, will you try our
patience, Cataline?" Or, if you prefer a slightly different question from
another part of your heritage—your genetic heritage, rather than your
elective one: "How long, O Israel, how long?"*

*Is this really just a novel after all? The novel you claim to be inca-
pable of writing? Or is it perhaps—and this is a rather teasing question,
as you shall see, by and by—that very "biographization" you have
hypothesized (at considerable length, I might add)? An enactment, an
inscription—or rather "inscripture," if you will (since you seem so fond
of neologisms)—of your so-called theory of "biographization"? Are you
not the nobody, the "biographically invalid" person of whom you write,
who deserves a biography, too? Are you not that person? But maybe,
come to think of it, you should be writing a biographization of this Mits
Akino person, the murdered barber, instead of yourself. Because after
all, Schatzi, you are really not a nobody. You are a published author with
two books to your credit—or discredit, as the case may be, and as you
would (rather disingenuously, haha) have it. Hardly a nobody. It doesn't
even matter if your books are shit—*Now wait just a minute, buster. Who
are you to say that? Who are you to judge? *I am a literary biographer.
Who better to judge such matters? Besides, am I not only reflecting your
own self-assessment in this? And have you not invented me (according
to you) to do precisely that? Am I not, at least following your account,
a mere projection of your own miserable self-hatred?*

Listen, I don't give a fuck *who* or even *what* you are—I'm not going
to allow you to destroy this narrative. Get thee behind me, Satan! *Teufel!*

*But I'm not destroying the narrative, Schatzi. I am only commenting
on it.*

Moot point, the way you are doing it. You are making it impossible
to continue, and impossible to read, too.

Ah, so now you have readers? I always had readers. Well, at least one.
I address this reader repeatedly—hadn't you noticed?

In your mind, yes. As your beloved Clint Eastwood would say (his production office was across the alleyway from you at Warner Bros., remember?), you have readers in your mind.

Speaking of the narrative, though—such as it is—I'd like to see a little more of Diane here. Less of your abstract philosophizing, and more of Diane. A little more "human interest," let's say. Not to mention that she was, as you aver—and I don't disbelieve it—the first real love of your life. And they say our first love makes the deepest impression, and never leaves us. But—and not to sound like a hack writing teacher or anything—you need to show *us, not just* tell *us, that this is true for you, too.*

Fair enough. You have a point. Diane may now be with the angels, but perhaps she has not been enough with us in this account. And that is a shortcoming, since she was at the center of both the Major and Minor Periods; nor is she absent from the Julistic Period, either. Julie and I reference her often. She is one of my life's touchstones, and as such, Julie has come to know her too—and even perhaps, in a way, to rely on her, at least as a kind of presiding spirit in our life together. I have often thought, and said to Julie, that if they had known each other, they would have been friends. And the realization of the impossibility of such a paradox does not dispel the fantasy.

PART II

Earlier I mentioned the moment in Westwood Books in the fall of 1978 when I first encountered the idea of someone (in that instance, Henry James) having a "Major Phase" or "Period", and then conceived the grandiose idea of applying such a classification to myself. In the event, though, my Major Period did not come in the form of a book, much less a collection of books. It came in the form of a woman: Diane. It came, it lasted twenty-three and a half years, she died, and it was over. And at the time—the whole time—I did not even recognize it as my Major Period. You never do, though; for it is one of the features of periodization not to recognize one's periods for what they are at the time. It requires the retrospective vision of the biographizer to discern these things and periodize them accordingly.

Another reason I never realized I was in my Major Period when I was was because I was too busy taking it, and Diane, for granted. But that didn't last forever. In October of 1999, she was diagnosed with third-stage breast cancer. She was treated with aggressive chemotherapy, then radiation, and in the summer of 2000 she went into remission for almost three years. But in the spring of 2003, the cancer came back, having metastasized into her ovary and abdomen. The ovary was removed, but the cancer scattered throughout the abdomen was inoperable, and a year later she was dead.

I remember the last "true" summer of the Major Period (2002)—the last summer before the recurrence—as being a particularly happy time. Diane was still in remission and, for all we knew, would continue so. I was hard at work on an autobiographical childhood novel ("The Bohemian Period"), set in and around the neighborhood in Pacific Palisades where I grew up. I was caught up in the world of this novel and loved writing it. Though it would not be published (and I suspected this even at the time), that didn't really matter: I was writing every day, and was filled with the sense of purposefulness and accomplishment that went along with that.

This was also the summer of my Biblical obsession. Every night I would read Donald Harman Akenson's *Surpassing Wonder: The Invention of the Bible and the Talmuds*, in preparation for a course in the Bible as literature I would be teaching in the fall. For my birthday in June, Diane had given me, in addition to the Akenson book, both the *Harper-Collins Bible Dictionary* and *Commentary*. On the dictionary she had stuck an embossed name tag that read "i love jojay" (my nickname). The combination of fiction writing in the daytime and scholarly reading at night was particularly gratifying: the best of both worlds.

The summer of '02 had also about it the sense of having survived, of having come through the valley of the shadow of death and out the other side, into the sunshine. This was not only because of Diane's remission, but because of two other things as well: the catastrophe of 2001, and the sudden death of an old friend in June.

It may seem callous and frivolous to juxtapose the enormity of 9/11 and the death of a friend. I am in no way comparing them. I am just trying to recapture the particular feeling surrounding our small family circle during the summer of 2002. It is not a feeling I am proud of having had, nor does it speak well of me, or of my type of self-concern. But it is a feeling I need to acknowledge all the same, because it was mine ("a small thing, but mine own"), and because I have thought a lot about it since Diane's death. It was a feeling of having been spared the unimaginable terror, agony, and death in the infernal planes and buildings on that day almost a year before. And not just my death, but—even worse, when I tried to imagine it with myself as a survivor—the death of my wife, and/or my son, and/or my father. (My mother, you may recall, had died of a rare blood disease in June of '95.) We had been spared, and this recognition hung over the summer of 2002 like a sort of unearned and therefore slightly shaming gift—arbitrary and capricious, yet not to be refused.

I was also aware, that summer, of having been spared another death, on another scale altogether: the death of my old friend, Jeff Naideau. Jeff was a pianist and singer, and in eighth and ninth grade was the coolest person I'd ever known. He got me stoned for the first time. It happened over Christmas vacation of ninth grade, after we'd gone to see the musical *Hair*. (The triteness of the whole situation now embarrasses me to remember, but it seemed like a good idea at the time. We were fourteen.) We stayed up all night talking, playing records and guitar, smoking cigarettes, and playing canasta. Just before dawn, we went outside and smoked the dope in my old childhood fort, then walked down to the beach to watch the sun come up. For years afterward, the smell of dope would bring back that long winter night at the end of 1968 and its mysteries of initiation, with Jeff as the *magister ludi* (a book I didn't read, oddly enough, until I read Diane's hardbound copy the spring she died). We continued to be friends throughout high school, but lost touch after that.

Near the beginning of June 2002, around the time of my birthday, I got to thinking of Jeff again. Zack, who'd just seen *Apocalypse Now*, had expressed interest in the Doors' song "The End," which is featured in the movie, and which Jeff and I listened to a lot when I was around Zack's age. I bought Zack a CD of the Doors' greatest hits, but he soon lost interest, and I ended up listening to the whole CD myself, chasing the nostalgia with a beer or three. Memories of Jeff came flooding back. I decided to google him—and what do you know, there he was, now playing jazz piano in New Orleans! I sent an email to his website, giving him my phone number, and the next day he called. We had an emotional phone reunion. He cried. We made plans to see each other that coming August in New Orleans, and we talked a few more times after that. Then, when I called again around the middle of June, I got the shocking news of his sudden death by coronary, only a few days after I'd last spoken with him. The next morning I was on a plane to New Orleans for his funeral—a jazz funeral, with a brass band leading a white, horse-drawn hearse through the streets of the French

Quarter. Construction workers on buildings along the route took off
their hard hats as the cortège passed by.

The following day I flew back to Long Island. It was Midsummer's
Day. I changed planes in Atlanta, and we took the coastal route north.
Out the window, under the afternoon sun of the longest day of the year,
I saw the boats of summer coming and going through the inlets of the
Eastern Seaboard. The summer was still young—officially only just beginning. I had many full days and weeks of writing yet ahead. I was already
well embarked, and if I was lucky (and I was feeling lucky that day), I
could finish a first draft by summer's end. I was headed home to my wife
and son, who were waiting for me. Diane was in remission. There was
much to be thankful for. I felt not only spared from Jeff's sad fate, but
blessed. Blessed, and flying home in the sun.

Another nice paragraph. But aren't you leaving something out? What
is it now, Joßche? *I speak of the affair. The affair with the woman—the
old girlfriend, as a matter of fact—you call "Cindy."* I already wrote
about that at some length in *Failure. Yes, you did. But isn't it a bit disingenuous (pardon the expression) not to at least mention it here?* But I
stopped communicating with Cindy in the summer of '02. *Yes, and doubtless that's another reason that time seems so happy in retrospect. You
were relieved, at least temporarily, of the guilt brought on by the affair.
Though you started it up again in 2003, and did not stop it conclusively
until after Diane had died.* Yes, that's true; but why dredge all that up
again here? *Because this is—whatever else it is—a true confession, no?
In a true confession, you must give not only the truth and nothing but
the truth, but also the* whole *truth. A truth omitted is not the whole truth.*
This is not a court of law, Fritz. *No—but no less requiring of the whole
truth for all that.*

Very well. By the summer of '02, then, I had stopped communicating
with Cindy on AOL Instant Messenger—which, by the way, is all we ever
did together, besides meeting twice for lunch in Manhattan—*which you
didn't tell Diane about*—Yes I did—*but not until after she confronted*

you, a month or two into the affair. Well, yes, that's also true. And I'm ashamed of all of that, and will feel guilty about it for the rest of my life. *I know you will. But that's not the point, Schatzi.* So remind me what the point is? *The point is not to withhold inconvenient truths in order to make yourself look better than you are.* I can't believe you said that. Do you honestly think that's what I'm doing here—trying to make myself look better than I am? Have I ever withheld any inconvenient truth? *Yes. This one.* But I told you I already wrote about it in *Failure.* Why rehearse it again here? *Because it's part of this story, too. But again, I think you're missing the point. I'm not saying you need to recapitulate everything that happened—and didn't happen—with Cindy. You just need to come clean about the other reason you were so happy during the summer of '02. That reason being that you had stopped—for the time being, at least—your AIM communications with Cindy, and had no (conscious) plans to resume them. That took a huge load of guilt off you, since you had explicitly promised Diane—several times—that you would no longer communicate with Cindy.* Yes, that's true. All of that is true. *And what else is true?* What do you mean? *I mean, did you keep that promise?* No. No, I didn't. I resumed communications in the summer of '03, after Diane had the recurrence of the cancer and was diagnosed as terminal. And after that, the messaging was on and off until she died. *And did you tell Diane this?* No, I didn't. *OK, that's all, Your Honor. I have no further questions. Just keepin' it real, as you Americans say. (And also trying to check the ongoing unreliable narrator problem.)* Thanks. Thanks a lot for your efforts. Though I suppose the correction was necessary. I mean, I really don't want to get away with anything here—or even seem to be getting away with anything. Unreliable narrator or not. Which, incidentally, I don't think I am. *Of course not. They never do.* Can you believe this guy?

So anyway, yeah, the summer of '02 was a happy interlude—a happy, brief interlude, for all the reasons given above. But looking back on that summer now, twenty-two years later—and twenty years after the deaths of my wife and father within a month of each other—I think that maybe even then I had a premonition of worse days to come. My father's health was in decline. He had the beginnings of congestive heart failure and water on the brain (a not-uncommon ailment in the elderly), and we knew that Diane's remission might only be temporary (as indeed it proved to be). She was a cancer survivor, and no matter how long she survived, she could never be fully clear of the danger of a recurrence. But on the strength of her remission, she—we—had resolved to live every day to the fullest. Nothing was to be taken for granted anymore. Nor was this resolution made under a sword of Damocles: we were seizing the day—not out of desperation, but in the conviction that the only way for us to live was in hope and great expectations.

Yet in the midst of our good faith there was also a sense—on my part at least—that, like the industrious ant of Aesop's fable, I was storing up happiness against a time of dearth, thinking that a life not lived to its fullest now might be a cause for reproach in harder times to come. The Lambert Strether approach to experience, if you will, when he exhorts Little Bilham, at the Parisian garden-party in *The Ambassadors*, to "live all you can; it's a mistake not to. It doesn't so much matter what you do in particular, so long as you have your life. If you haven't had that, what *have* you had?" And to the hortatory philosophy of Strether was added a more superstitious belief of my own: if I did not make the most of this summer, I would somehow be punished for it later on; whereas if I did, the memory of it would provide some sort of solace in the future. (The latter is a Wordsworthian idea, put forth in "Tintern Abbey": "That in this moment there is life and food / For future years.") *(Of course. Good old Wordsworth.)*

We may have refused, Diane and I, to live under the sword of Damocles, but I was secretly waiting for his other sandal to drop. Soon enough, it did. In the spring of 2003 my father collapsed after a walk, and his heart briefly stopped beating. He was brought back to life, miraculously, by his second wife, Chun Ling—a doctor of Chinese medicine, and also his nurse, herbologist, and acupuncturist, whom he'd married in 1998—who stuck a needle in the little channel under his nose, twirled it, and made his heart start up again. (When I told him we couldn't make it out for Passover that year but would be there for Easter, he replied, without missing a beat, "Good—we can celebrate my resurrection.") But his brief trip to the hereafter and back had further weakened him, and by the fall he was bedridden.

That spring was also the beginning of the end for Diane. After returning from my father's resurrection party, she began to have severe abdominal pain. This led to the removal of one of her ovaries, as previously mentioned; but the cancer had already spread throughout her abdomen, and was inoperable. Even if it were to respond to more chemo and/or hormone therapy, we were told, it would always come back. She would never be cancer-free.

Life now became very concentrated for us. It centered in the living- and dining-room area of our small apartment in Huntington, and in the bedroom—now more than ever an intimate shelter. Daily tea was a ritual not to be missed. (After chemotherapy, Diane's taste buds had changed, and she no longer liked the taste of coffee, so she switched to tea, which had always been my drink. Now we drank it together.) Little pleasures became big ones. The big worries—money, the future, even Zack's troubles at school, brought on by his mother's illness—became trivial. All that mattered was the three of us being together. ("WE 3," I once saw, with a pang, on someone's license plate, a few years after Diane died.) She quit the job at the community mental health center that she'd loved so much, but continued to visit there regularly, and joined a local cancer support group. Our life—now lived in the presence of death—became heightened, more intense, more full, just as fruit sprinkled with salt becomes sweeter.

In the winter of that final half-year (Jan.–June 2004), she almost didn't make it. It seems perverse now to think of it: six months before she died, she almost died—and then she died. But that wasn't how I saw it at the time. Since every day was precious now, and every moment mattered, any more time squeezed out was something to be grateful for. As would happen again in May, her sickness that winter followed close upon another visit out to LA in late December to see my father, who was now bedridden with congestive heart failure. We had planned to stay for New Year's—it would have been the last New Year's we spent with him, and we suspected as much at the time—but we had to return before that because Diane was in such pain. I remember the trudge through the slushy long-term parking lot at JFK to get the car, while she and Zack waited with the suitcases inside the AirTrain terminal. I think it was only then that the full realization of how sick she was really hit me.

She went into the hospital on Jan. 2. The pain was getting worse, and she couldn't stop vomiting. They put her in the ICU, and inserted a tube through her nose down into her stomach to pump out the accumulating fluid. This newest turn of events was especially hard for her, because ever since childhood she'd hated vomiting more than anything: the anticipatory salivation and nausea, the uncontrollable violence of the vomiting itself, the dread of the next wave. The painkiller and anti-nausea medication they gave her helped a little, but not that much. The first ten days in the hospital were touch-and-go. When they were finally satisfied she had turned a corner, they moved her out of the ICU and down to the cancer ward, where she shared a room with several others. The nose tube stayed in, though. This was becoming her bane, but it helped reduce the vomiting caused by all the fluid in her stomach. The fluid, in turn, was caused by the tumor mass in her abdomen. Because of the vomiting and the tube, she wasn't allowed to take any liquids by mouth; they had her on intravenous saline. But she craved Coke, so we would sneak her some when the nurse wasn't looking. It was more for the taste—and just to wet her mouth—than anything else, because as soon as she drank it, the pump would suck it back up again, and you'd see it bubbling through the clear plastic nose tube. Her brother Robbie, an advertising copy writer with a black sense of humor, thought it would make a good ad for Coke (which, as they used to say, things go better with).

She was released from the hospital near the end of January, just in time to attend the Robert Burns party that friends of ours on the Upper West Side threw every year. It was always a great party, with bagpipes, recitations of Burns's poetry, and much good food and drink (and some vile stuff as well: the horrible haggis, customarily served as the *pièce de résistance*). Diane had never been an avid party-goer, but she always made an exception for Burns Night, and this year it was especially important that we make it to the party. It was one of the reasons she was determined to get out of the hospital before the end of January. *(Just a quick note here. Cindy was at this party, too, wasn't she?* She usually was. She was a close friend of Adam and Liz, who gave the party, and she worked for Adam's business, too. But I honestly don't remember if she was at the party that year or not. If she was, maybe I've blocked it out. *Well, I wouldn't blame you if you have. Talk about awkward.)*

That weekend we left Zack with Robbie at his place in Brooklyn and stayed at a small, new, modest hotel on the Upper West Side, eating our meals in the neighborhood and going for short walks up and down Broadway. We bought shoes at Harry's, where they were having a sale. There was a pair of elegant boots that Diane coveted but didn't want to buy for herself, so I bought them for her; she bought me a pair of heavy winter boots. We had brunch at a coffee shop, and found ourselves sitting at a table next to Paul Simon and his young daughter. And, of course, we went to the party on Saturday night.

At the time, I think we both deliberately downplayed its significance, while secretly knowing better. It was unnecessary to state the obvious: that Diane had come close to dying just a few weeks ago, that she'd been given a reprieve, and that her cancer was now Stage Four. Our hosts knew this, and so did a few other friends at the party, where Diane was the calm, quiet center of a tight nucleus. *(Not including Cindy, I take it?* I told you, I honestly don't remember. Will you please get off my case?) I think we all felt protective of Diane that night—I know I did.

She was quite thin from her recent ordeal, which had aged her considerably. The hormone therapy she'd received over the past six months had caused most of her hair to fall out again, and she kept it cropped short; she'd stopped coloring it, too. As I write this, I am looking at a photo from this period that I keep on the windowsill of my study. She is looking into the camera with her trademark level but slightly humorous glance: the hint of a smile playing about the lips, and the eyes slightly playful, too—yet quietly serious as well, as if to say, "Yes, this is what I've been reduced to—I, who was once the Queen of the Strawberry Festival in kindergarten, and had a toy field mouse named Sillary. 'Ain't this a revoltin' development?'" (A quote she liked to attribute to Jackie Gleason in *The Honeymooners*, though it is actually from Jimmy Durante.) All of this is in that look, plus a hint of connivance with the taker of the photo. Was it me? I am such a terrible photographer that I hesitate to take credit for this one, since it is not only in focus but captures her as she was then: ironically disbelieving, knowing, witty, and wise. Yet I cannot think who else might have taken it, and the look was such as she might have given me, and sometimes did, with the Mona Lisa smile and the playful eyes.

But the eyes didn't stay like that.

Right after we got home from my father's memorial service in May (he died on May 2), she began to be very sick again. Her oncologist said the plane trip might have brought on this latest bout of inflammation. She went back into the hospital for a few days—no corner room this time—and when they'd gotten the pain under control they released her, giving her lots of pain patches that she stuck on her shoulder blades. I don't recall any nausea this time; maybe that was why they released her so soon. Or maybe it was because they knew there was nothing more they could do.

The beginning of the end came just before the start of Memorial Day weekend—the same time her father had died, eighteen years earlier, from complications following open-heart surgery. She was admitted to the hospital again with pain and nausea—this time worse than ever. The "tumor" (this was the oncologist's collective-noun word for the conglomeration of tiny, grain-sized tumors lumped together in her peritoneal cavity) was larger now—virtually a solid mass all over the abdomen. The doctors made it clear that all they could offer at this point was palliative care, and that the hospital wasn't the place for that. They recommended she go to a hospice care center. They told me this in a morning meeting—the oncologist, the head cancer nurse and I—the Tuesday after a hellish, unforgettable Memorial Day weekend.

Since she'd been admitted, I had been staying overnight in her room (a private room this time, for terminal patients), sleeping on a reclining easy-chair next to the bed, holding her hand all night. There was a storm over the weekend. I remember looking out the window at various times during the night, watching the rain whip past the floodlight outside. By this point she was in such pain she was on a Dilaudid drip, which they gradually kept upping to "keep her comfortable." The pain specialist was a young twit in a bow tie. I disliked him immediately, and soon came to hate him because of what happened later. In the middle of the night—I'm not sure whether it was Friday or Saturday night of Memorial Day weekend—I had a run-in with one of the nurses. Diane was in pain, so I went to the nurses' station to ask for more medication, wearing only my boxer shorts and a t-shirt. The nurse at the station scolded me for going out into the hallway dressed "inappropriately." I've always hated that prissy, euphemistic word—and I didn't like her tone, either. It pushed my righteous-indignation button, and I let her have it.

"My wife is dying, and you're talking about 'inappropriate'? You should be ashamed of yourself." I said I was going to report her to Dr. Bucholz, Diane's oncologist, who ran the cancer center, and also to the head cancer nurse.

The following night, a nicer nurse was on duty—one I knew and liked. Around midnight, she told me I should go home and try to get some sleep; there was nothing more I could do for Diane at the moment, I needed to take care of myself, etc. This time I was compliant. I guess after my outburst—news of which must have made the rounds; maybe that was even why they suggested I go home—I wanted to show that I could be reasonable and well behaved. The "nice" nurse told me they'd call me if there was any change.

Which they did, not long after I got home. They said I'd better come right away—there had indeed been a change. What sort of change? Was she dying? No, not that; I just better come. I rushed back to find Diane sitting in a chair in the hallway. Even from a distance I could see there was something terribly wrong. It looked as if her soul had been sucked out through her eyes. I think it was the most horrible thing I'd ever seen. Her pupils were as small as pinheads; her head was lolling from side to side, like an animal that had been stunned. She clearly didn't recognize me or understand anything I was saying to her.

"What have you done to her!" I cried. "That's not Diane! What's wrong with her! Where is my wife!"

"Relax, sir, and keep your voice down, please."

"What do you mean 'relax'! This isn't my wife! What did you give her! She's obviously OD-ing! Do something!"

"Sir, calm down."

"But look at her! She's a zombie! Do something! Call a doctor! I want my wife back! Diane, Sweetie, can you hear me?"

Her head continued to loll, the pinhead eyes unseeing. It was chilling, hair-raising—ungodly. Her soul has been sucked out through her eyes, I kept thinking. I wanted them to put her soul back; I wanted my Diane back.

"Call a doctor! I want to see a doctor!"

They got a doctor from the emergency room, who briefly examined her and diagnosed acute narcotics poisoning. (Except of course he didn't say "poisoning"; he said something like "reaction.") There were two things he could do, he said. He could give her an antidote that would bring her out of the stupor but also bring back the pain (immediately), or he could begin an IV saline solution that would gradually dilute the pain medication (and more slowly bring back the pain). "But she'll basically have pain either way. Her pain has reached the level where it's not responding to lower doses of medication."

"That's OK," I said. "I just want my wife back. We'll deal with the pain."

"That's easy for you to say."

"No it isn't, Doctor. It's not easy at all. But this isn't my wife. I want my wife back. I know she wouldn't want to be a zombie."

So they put in the saline IV, and I spent the rest of the night in her room. (This time I wore a hospital robe over my boxer shorts.) By the next morning, Diane was back, and the horrible zombie creature of the night before had been banished back to the nether-world of Dilaudid. Then I let the bow-tied twit of a pain doctor ("dolorologists," I think they're called) have it.

"Doctor, you gave her too much pain medication last night. She was a zombie. I don't want her ever to be like that again."

His bow tie seemed to swell in indignation, like a cobra's hood. "Listen, I've seen what pain can do," he replied. "I saw what it did to my grandmother when she had cancer. No one should have to go through that. That's what these medications are for—to spare our patients unnecessary suffering."

"Not if it turns her into a zombie."

"I understand your concern, sir—but with all due respect, you haven't seen what I have."

"And you didn't see what I saw last night. My wife was a zombie. You gave her too much. She was like a—like someone I didn't know. She wasn't even a person. Her eyes were dead."

Maybe he smelled a lawsuit in the making, because he softened a bit and tried another tack. "What you saw may also have been the metabolic changes that patients at this stage of the illness go through. I understand how difficult it is to see someone you love going through something like this. As I said, my grandmother—"

"The emergency-room doctor who examined her said it was the pain medication," I interrupted. I wasn't going to make it easy for him. Why should I? This was as much a part of his training as his grandmother. "He took her off it immediately, and today she's much better."

He stiffened again. "Yes, I heard about that. But he isn't her doctor."

"Maybe not—but I'm sure glad he was here. He knew right away what was wrong." I let that sink in; then it was my turn to soften. "Look, I know you are just doing your job, Doctor, but you overdid it yesterday. I never want her to get that way again."

"So we'll put her back on a lower dose of the Dilaudid. But I'm warning you right now, she'll have breakthrough pain."

"I understand that. But I know my wife, and I know she would rather have pain and be aware than be a zombie."

"Very well, then," he said, and turned on his heel.

It's interesting to note that there was no discussion of what Diane herself might have wanted. You seem to have had no qualms about speaking for her. Well, what should I have done? What would you have had me do? Ask her what she wanted? But she was insensible! She was barely conscious! *True enough, but you still made the decision for her—that she would prefer to have sensible pain, so to speak, than insensible comfort.* That's a strange way to put it. But I suppose you are basically right—I did make the decision for her. But somebody had to; she was in no condition to make it herself. But I still don't see your point, really—other than that I made a decision contrary to what the twit of a dolorologist thought I should do. *OK. Let's drop it for now.*

Later that morning, I had the aforementioned grim conference with Dr. Bucholz, the oncologist, and the head cancer nurse, Gail Probst. They corroborated what the pain doctor had said about the "metabolic changes," and there were tears in their eyes as they told me that Diane was now under palliative care only—there was nothing more they could do for her medically. They said I should put her in the hospice care center they had in mind, which they described as "intimate" and "personal." (I believe they even used the term "cottage-like atmosphere.") They gave me a brochure, and a social worker arranged for the transfer. Diane's friend Irene and I packed up her belongings, and a few hours later, leaving my car in the hospital parking lot, I rode with her in the ambulance to the hospice care center.

Its description as "cottage-like" couldn't have been farther from the truth. At one end of a new development of sterile, cookie-cutter condos with vinyl siding and fakely partitioned windows (the kind that are cross-hatched with white plastic strips), the hospice care center was more like a palace than a cottage—the "Palace of Death," I called it, remembering the title my father gave to my mother's oncologist: "The Duchess of Death."

I will never forget the smell of that place. It hit you as soon as you walked through the automatic sliding-glass doors: an overwhelming smell of new plastic, or linoleum, coupled with a floral-scented industrial cleaner and something else, carried through the air-conditioning ducts. It was the chemical smell of death—or whatever chemical they used to cover up the smell of death. Then again, what was I expecting—Mother Theresa's Calcutta hospice? High-tech is one of the things Americans do best. Is it any wonder that if we use it to raise the standard of living (at least for those who can afford it), we should also use it to raise the standard of dying? I can't say I was surprised at the sterile efficiency of the hospice care center—in spite of the "cottage-like atmosphere" Dr. Bucholz and Gail had claimed for it. The nurses' station upstairs looked like a larger and only slightly simpler version of an airplane pilots' cabin, with tilted, ergonomic consoles of lights, buttons, switches, and monitors. But this was a trip no one was looking forward to. (Or coming back from, either.)

The room they put us in was spacious, clean, private, carpeted—"comfortable," I suppose would be one way to describe it. A double bed, cloth-upholstered sofa and easy chairs, several of the fakely partitioned windows (overlooking the parking lot of the new housing development), and soft, incandescent lighting. So this was to be her last room on earth. Out of all the rooms we had lived in together over twenty-three and a half years—apartments, houses, hotels, and motels in LA, New York, Baja California, Santa Barbara, San Francisco, San Diego, Carmel, Venice, Paris, Prague, Toronto, New Mexico, Maine, Morro Bay, Washington, D.C., Baltimore, Massachusetts, and Long Island—in all of those places, this sterile, soulless room, hard by the Long Island Expressway, was to be her last.

"Are you going to leave me here?" she asked—meaning not only, "Are you going to abandon me?" but also, "Are you going to leave me here, of all places?"

"No, Sweetie—never. I'm never going to leave you here. I'll be with you the whole time. I'm just going to leave for an hour to pick up Zack and bring him here. I'm coming right back." But I knew, from the way she looked at me—as though her final hope was gone—that she didn't believe me.

Another thing I'll never forget was the cab ride back to the hospital to pick up the car. We got caught in a summer thundershower, and the windshield fogged up. At first the driver didn't know how to work the defogger, and we had to pull over to the side of the road while he tried to figure it out. It was during this little crisis that it suddenly and finally hit me: Diane was going to die. Very soon she would be gone. From my life, from Zack's life, from the world. And the world would continue without her. How was this possible? It could not be, yet it was going to happen. And it would happen soon. All of this as we fiddled with the window defogger. On the one hand, we had to figure out how to get it to work; on the other, Diane was in that horrible room, and she was going to die. I had to get back to her—that was as far ahead as I could think; what lay beyond that was only dimly imagined. But we weren't going anywhere until the windshield cleared. After a few minutes, the driver pushed the right button, the glass defogged, and we were on our way again. But the world was now a different place. The streets and buildings, the very air, felt desolate and unfamiliar. This was the world without Diane; this was what things would be like. I had to get out of this world and back to her as soon as possible. That was the only thing that mattered.

I got the car at the hospital, picked Zack up at home, and returned with him to the hospice care center; but he couldn't take it for very long (the smell got to him, too), so we left. (Was it then that Diane asked me if I was going to leave her there? Or maybe she asked me twice.) We ate the grimmest meal of our lives at a diner I'd never been to before (though any place we'd gone to with Diane would have been unbearable, too), and then we drove home. I didn't feel great about leaving Zack, then sixteen, alone overnight, especially under the circumstances, but leaving Diane alone in that place, as she had feared, wasn't an option. So I took my toothbrush and cell phone and told Zack to call for any reason—or no reason at all—and returned to the Palace of Death.

When I arrived in her room there was a young nurse watching TV with her; or rather, the nurse was watching TV while Diane lay in bed. She was hooked up to the nasogastric tube again. (Not even in hospice could she be free of the thing.) I told the nurse I wanted to be alone with my wife, and as soon as she left, I turned off the TV and climbed into bed with Diane. I was damned if we were going to spend our time now watching TV. But apparently they didn't like the idea of me being in bed with her, and soon brought in a cot and placed it next to the bed.

Later that night, after we'd turned the lights off, she pulled out the tube, took off her robe and underwear, and climbed into the cot with me. By now she was incoherent, speaking nonsense—or what others would have called nonsense. But I didn't mind. It seemed to make a kind of sense to me, and I wanted to hear the sound of her voice, so I replied in kind. I took off all my clothes and lay in the cot with her, holding her close, as though we had just made love or were about to. Except we were both conversing in gibberish. The *lingua franca* of our last room on earth. Outside, it stormed off and on all night, and the lightning came in flashes through the fakely partitioned windows.

Sometime during the night she must have gotten up from the cot and moved back to bed (or maybe the nurse moved her, I don't recall), because when I woke up the next morning—a beautiful, bright, sunny day, post-storm—there was Gordon, her old childhood friend, sitting quietly across the room, watching her sleeping in bed. (It was Gordon who'd told me the story of Diane being crowned Queen of the Strawberry Festival in kindergarten.)

"Good morning," he whispered.

"Good morning, Gordon," I said. "How good of you to come. How did you know where we were?"

"They told me at the hospital. Hey you," he said to Diane. "Good morning."

It was indeed. The sun was shining, the storm had passed, Gordon was here, and I'd had a sudden revelation: I would bring her home. Today. This wasn't the place for us. The place for us was at home. I said as much to Gordon, then to the head nurse, then to the medical director. At first, everyone was very nice about it—they seemed to share my enthusiasm about getting her home. After all, that was one of the basic ideas of hospice care, wasn't it? That the dying should be cared for at home, if that was what they wanted.

But as I soon found out, it wasn't quite so easy. The medical director said that in order for her to be discharged, I would have to have a home-health-care plan already in place. That meant, basically, hiring a licensed practical nurse who would be on hand as soon as Diane got home. Hospice nurses would be on call 24/7, and would give me full instructions for the administration of oral pain medication before we left the care center. The director thought she could be ready to go home in a day or two.

"No, Doctor," I replied. "She has to come home today. She can't spend another night here."

"Why, if I may ask?"

"Because I have had a kind of revelation," I declared, hearing a strange new kind of excitement in my voice. "Nothing religious, but a revelation all the same. I have to get her home today." I didn't tell him about the Palace of Death and the House of Life; he probably thought I was weird enough already.

"And what does she want?" he said. "Have you asked her what she wants to do?"

(Good question, Doc. And same problem here. Again, there is a kind of over-riding of her possible wishes that I find troublesome. You seem to take it for granted that her wishes are always the same as yours. I think you need to back off here, Joßche. You are out of line. I was married to Diane for twenty-one years, and lived with her longer than that. I should well have known what she wanted. Objection overruled. So now this is a court of law, apparently. And besides, according to your "alter-ego" theory, I was with Diane too for all that time, and knew and loved her as well as you did. How dare you pull rank on me! This isn't a game, Joßche. This is my life, and Diane's. Please let me continue. And I'm not asking your permission, either. If you continue to interrupt, I will ban you. Don't think I won't. Wishing and willing are two different things, Schatzi. And you were the one who mentioned your "weak will" earlier. But go ahead.)

"She's not making a lot of sense right now," I answered the director. "She's mostly incoherent—talking gibberish—but I understand her. I told her we were taking her home, and she seemed fine with that. I know it's what she wants. Will you agree to discharge her today, if I can get the home health care set up?"

"We usually require at least twenty-four-hours' notice before discharging a patient. It's in their own best interest."

"It's in her own best interest to go home now, Doctor. We can't spend another night here. Nothing personal. It's just—well, actually, it is personal. Very personal. But nothing against you. You run a very professional organization, and everyone has been very nice, but it's just ... not our style." I paused. "Doctor, I believe we will both die if we have to spend another night here."

He actually smiled slightly at this—not, I think, because he thought I was crazy, but because on some level he got what I was talking about. He couldn't admit it, but he understood we wanted out of his Palace of Death, and didn't hold it against us. Maybe he wanted out, too.

"You understand that I will have to inform Dr. Bucholz of your decision?"

"I understand."

"And that he will no doubt disagree with it—as I do. You will be acting against medical advice."

Here I had to restrain the impulse to tell this decent man that I didn't give a shit—that it felt *good* to be acting against medical advice, especially when the medical advice was tainted, because it was coming from the Palace of Death. But I bit my tongue, and just nodded. All that mattered was that we were going to get out of there, and he wasn't going to stand in our way.

The social worker gave me a list of home-health-care agencies and a sunny room with a phone to make my calls in, and within an hour or so I had it all set up. The day before I had been in despair—the worst day of my life, with the fogged-up windshield and the world without Diane. Today, I felt triumphant. Out of the Palace of Death, into the House of Life.

But the medical director was right about Dr. Bucholz. He called shortly after, and he wasn't happy.

"As Diane's doctor, I have to tell you in the strongest of terms that you're making a terrible mistake."

"That's your opinion, Doctor."

"Not opinion—medical fact. You are simply not equipped at home to give Diane the kind of care she needs. She will be in terrible pain. She will die a horrible death. Certainly you don't want that?"

"Doctor, with all due respect, I disagree. *This place* is a horrible death. I know you think it's great, but it's not. It's a Palace of Death. We have to get out of here."

There was a pause as he considered my description. "Mr. Gidding, I understand your pain and anguish. But that is not a good basis on which to make a decision of this magnitude. This decision will be with you for the rest of your life. Our first consideration should be Diane's comfort."

"Doctor, there are things that are more important than comfort. *Life*, for example. *Life* is more important than comfort. This place is death." I was again aware of a strange, slightly grandiloquent ring to my voice—the same sound that had appeared when I was telling the medical director about my "revelation" that morning—that was both exciting and foreign to me. (Perhaps a little mad, too.)

But if Bucholz was thinking any of this, he didn't let on. After all, scenes like this must be nothing new to him. "Diane's life is nearing its end, Mr. Gidding. As her doctor, I would like for that end to be as comfortable as possible. And I'm sure you want the same for her. If you take her home, it won't be—I can guarantee you that."

"Doctor, there is no such thing as a 'comfortable death.' That's a euphemism, a lie." I knew I was getting carried away now—high on my own rhetoric and fine feeling—so I reined it in a bit. "Look, Doctor, I don't want her to die here. I want her to die at home."

"And what does Diane want?" These guys had their act down.

(Your interpretation. But what if it wasn't an act? That's only a manner of speaking, Fritz. This is my story. Let me tell it. And one more interruption like that and you'll be banned. I mean it. *Do you really have that power?* Try me, Fritz. Just try me.)

"She wants what I want," I answered him. "I want what she wants."

"Diane is not in a condition, at this point, to make a rational decision." *And neither are you*, was the implication.

"Maybe not, but I know what she would want. I have never been more sure of anything in my life." Again, my voice rang with a strange but unchallengeable righteousness—the feeling that had come to me with the morning light. Maybe I did sound a little nuts, but so what? No wonder the prophets of old hadn't cared what people thought of them.

Compared to the visionary radiance, the blessed aura of righteousness, what was the scorn of the naysayers? Careful, though: there was a fine line between craziness and utter conviction, and I was walking it. (Blake: "Does a firm perswasion that a thing is so, make it so?") But I was no Blake, no visionary (notwithstanding the morning light). I just wanted out for Diane and me. Maybe this wasn't the best way to go about getting it, but instinct told me otherwise.

"You realize you are making this decision against medical advice?" Bucholz asked.

"That's what the other guy said, too."

"Well, that should tell you something."

Yeah, that you guys have your rap down, I thought to myself. *That you're afraid of lawsuits. That you still want to be the boss, even in death.* But I said nothing.

Perhaps he read my silence as vacillation, because he went on: "I wish you would reconsider, Mr. Gidding. Consider what is best for Diane. I know you don't want her to suffer needlessly—which she will, I assure you, if you bring her home."

"Doctor, I appreciate your concern—I really do. But I've made my decision. We're going home."

And that was that. I drove back to the house to meet the home-health-care worker and give her my deposit, then back again to the hospice center to give them the receipt so they could officially release Diane. This all took an hour or two, and when I returned to her room, she was gone. The bed was made up, the cot had been removed, the room tidied—and she was gone.

I ran to the nurses' station. "Where's my wife?" I cried. The nurse read my panic—perhaps a not uncommon one, in this place—and smiled reassuringly.

"She's in the courtyard with some friends. It's such a nice day that we thought she would like to be outside in the fresh air. I'm sorry, we should have told you that's where she was."

The "courtyard" was an outside area enclosed by the inner walls of the hospice center. Diane was sitting in a wheelchair in the shade, with a hospital-green cotton blanket draped over her, though it was a warm day. (I have this blanket still. I keep it in the hall closet. I don't want to look at it, but I can't bring myself to throw it away.) Diane's friend Irene and two other friends from her cancer support group were with her. From a distance, Diane looked like a frail, sick old lady: sparse, close-cropped gray hair; drawn face—the cheekbones now showing; thin feet in slippers. (Her feet, and the slippers, reminded me of her mother's.) And she was sick and frail—but not old. She was fifty-four. The thing that got me most, though, was her eyes. Large and glassy, wide, focused on something in the distance that the rest of us couldn't see. The shine of death. A radiance—but in the eyes only. The rest of her face was pale and sickly. Everything was concentrated now in her ocean-blue eyes. The eyes that had looked so deeply into mine for all these years, that had seen me so well—better, much better, than I could see myself. And now they were seeing something else—something that I couldn't see, something great and intimate, that was hers alone. It must be this that gave her eyes their distant radiance. I took her hand and she smiled, and her eyes looked into mine; but they also looked beyond me, with her characteristically unflinching gaze.

Her things had already been gathered together, so we loaded them and her into the car, one cancer-support-group friend on either side and Irene in front, and drove home. Diane needed help up the path and steps to the front door, but she was smiling and clearly happy to be back home. It was the first of June.

Oddly, this will always be one of the most memorable—can I say maybe even "happy"?—days of my life. Right up there with the day we got married, the day Zack was born, the day I found out I got my first full-time teaching job back east, at Holy Cross. Though maybe it's really not so odd after all, considering the horrors we'd been through the previous few days, including the Dilaudid overdose and the Palace of Death. There was an aura of triumph on that day—what the Germans call *Feierlichkeit*: a solemn celebration. *Yes. This is nice. All of this is quite nice.* Why thank you, Joßche. (Our last exchange seems to have had an effect on him.) We were celebrating her emergence from the Palace of Death into the House of Life—the triumph of bringing her home, where she wanted to be; and I had the proud sense, that day, of having made it happen for her. We could have been stuck in the "cottage-like atmosphere" (not!) of the Palace of Death, but I got us out. I might not have been able to prevent her cancer, or its recurrence and inevitable course, but I kept her from having a "comfortable death" in that horrible place, according to the doctors' plans. In my half-mad state I did not think of her dying in excruciating pain, as the doctors had warned. (And they were wrong, as it turned out. She died peacefully.) Was that thoughtless of me? Selfish? Insensitive? Maybe. But it was also part of the visionary spirit of the day, begun that morning, and under whose aegis I felt myself to be operating.

Her first night home, and for several nights after, we slept on the futon in the living room—both naked, and talking to one another in the private language of gibberish, as we had begun to do that night in the hospice center. But this arrangement turned out to be no good, because by that time she had become incontinent, and wet the futon. Did she wear diapers after that? I'm not sure—perhaps I have repressed this memory. It seems to me that I bought adult diapers for her, but could not bring myself—or allow the home-health-care aide, either—to put them on her. So I rented a hospital bed with a plastic-covered mattress, which we put in the living room, facing the west windows. I slept on the urinous futon, next to her. I have to admit, I didn't really mind the smell—it wasn't that strong, and besides, it was hers. Early on in our relationship, before we were married, when she once got sick to her stomach and threw up, I cleaned it up. She was impressed by this.

"You cleaned up my vomit," she declared.

"What were the options?" I replied.

So sleeping on a sheet on top of her (mostly dried) urine wasn't such a big deal. It's not that I'm not squeamish; about bodily fluids I'm as squeamish as the next. Maybe it was just that I was holding onto her, and would take her in any form I could get—even with pee. (In the end, though, I did send the futon cover out to be dry-cleaned—but only after the funeral.)

Other excretory indignities were visited upon her in that last week, but these I will pass over. There was one heart-breaking incident, though, that I will mention—since it, too, is dear to me in the chronicle of her suffering. This was when she was rushed to the emergency room because of a cut on her forehead—the medical version of rearranging the deck chairs on the Titanic. It happened when we were still sleeping on the futon, and was the main reason I decided to get her a hospital bed with safety railings.

In those final days her legs were failing her, and tended to give out unexpectedly. One time she was standing before the bathroom mirror when her knees suddenly buckled; fortunately, I was right there, and able to catch her before she fell. Another time, she was not so lucky. We were lying (clothed) on the futon when she suddenly got up and made a mad dash for the bathroom; but her legs buckled again, and she fell in the hallway, hitting her head against the corner of the dividing partition and opening a bloody gash in her forehead. I called an ambulance, and rode with her back to the hospital—the emergency room this time—where they gave her stitches and then sent her home. For a moment, I felt good about this: the problem had been fixed, the doctors had made it all better, and she was on the road to recovery. Then I remembered: she would probably be dead before the wound healed. (As indeed she was: they cremated her with the stitches still in.) This incident was a more permanent form of the Urinous Futon Syndrome: I deliberately did not wash the little smudge of her blood off the corner of the partition (it was part of her "juice," and I wasn't going to expunge it), where it remained for two years, until Zack and I moved out of the apartment. For all I know, it is there still.

Two days after she came home from the hospice center, I turned fifty. We had a birthday party in the living room, with Irene, Gordon, and a few other friends. Was this the best birthday party of my life? Could be. It was certainly the most important, and the saddest—but its sadness was transcendent, and so not really sad at all. We ordered a huge sushi boat from Nisen, the best sushi restaurant on Long Island at the time (IMHO). Diane, at that point, wasn't eating anything solid (though she had conceived a passion for Yoo-hoo, which she called "chocolate." "Chocolate! Chocolate!" she would cry in a whisper), but the rest of us made up for that, and I drank more than my share of beer. I remember at one point going into the backyard and phoning Dr. Karpas, who'd been our family therapist when Zack was having trouble in school after Diane's first diagnosis, and then again after the recurrence. I filled him in on the latest developments regarding the Palace of Death and the House of Life. I'm not sure what he made of it all. He probably could tell I'd been drinking. As I unfolded the recent events for him, I was pacing back and forth in the backyard, with a strange feeling of well-being that sat very oddly with the awareness that Diane was dying. Was I merely in denial? Was I (once again) putting my feelings before hers? Probably a little of both. But I think it was also that I was just happy, and proud, to have her safe at home again, knowing it could well have gone otherwise.

When I came back inside after talking to Karpas, Irene said that while I was gone, Diane, who'd been lying down on the futon and not saying anything, suddenly sat up and exclaimed, "Josh is fifty!" I guess she wanted us to see that she was still with it—still lucid enough, despite the morphine drops we were giving her now, to know it was my birthday. And I wanted only to be with her, not to let her go. Which was the thing that was most impossible.

Bucholz had assured me that even with the morphine drops, Diane would be in horrible pain at the end; but this was not the case. She didn't complain of pain, at least—nor did she make any of the sounds indicating that she was in pain. But she was terribly thirsty, and we weren't supposed to give her anything to drink. Her system couldn't process fluids anymore, the hospice nurse told me, and if she drank anything she would become bloated. There was a risk that her lungs would fill with fluid, and she could get pneumonia or suffocate internally. All I should do, when she was thirsty—which was all the time—was swab out her mouth with little wet green sponges on sticks. They looked like lollipops—the Lollipops of Death. But she continued to call out for "chocolate," and this I could not refuse her. I gave it to her with a straw, of course, but she still wanted to drink the whole bottle of Yoo-hoo in one gulp. "No, Sweetie, easy does it, just a little at a time," I would coax, gently drawing the straw out of her mouth and replacing it with a wet swab. She did not object. Even in death she was considerate and well-mannered. She didn't want her dying to be an inconvenience to anyone.

Which didn't mean she had lost her spirit. Her eyes told me that. Her eyes—and her nose. At some point in the last couple of years, she'd had a tiny diamond stud put in at the side of one nostril. Was this before or after the cancer came back? I want to say it was after—an assertion of her femininity, and even a slight raciness, in Stage Four—but I'm not sure. Even if it was before, while she was in remission, it still broke my heart. I didn't tell her that, of course. I told her I loved it, and while that was maybe an overstatement, it wasn't a lie. I liked the idea of the nose stud, and I liked that she'd had the spirit of youthfulness and slight rebelliousness to get one. (This was back in 2004, when nose studs were not as common as they are now.) A middle-aged cancer survivor with a nose stud—why the hell not? But secretly, it broke my heart. I said to myself, with a pang, "Just trying to jazz herself up a little … " To reaffirm her attractiveness, her sexiness, even a slight feistiness, against the memory of her chemotherapy and baldness, and the cruel fact of her one-breastedness. To declare herself *not* a cancer patient, not even a cancer survivor, but something other: middle-aged-but-not-quite, and recalling perhaps her interest, as a young woman, in classical Indian dance. She'd also always found Indian women particularly beautiful. But whatever it was that prompted the nose stud, it broke my heart. And this response, unlike almost all of my other responses to things we'd experienced together, wasn't something I could ever share with her.

But maybe I didn't need to. Maybe she could intuit it anyway—just as she could intuit practically everything I was feeling. A painful example comes to mind from that last year. We were embracing in the kitchen, and she turned her face up to me, wanting to kiss me—passionately, I knew. But instead, I gave her a chaste little peck on the lips, then moved my face away, back over her shoulder. In that split second when our eyes met, I saw the hurt in her face, the pain of the rebuff, as clear as any declaration: "I see. You don't want me anymore." I hugged her extra tight, but that was just a lame consolation and, in fact, confirmation of the truth I had seen in her eyes: "I even put in a nose stud, but you still don't want me."

Despite Bucholz's warnings, the end came quietly—though not without a gruesome final flourish. After the recurrence of the cancer, Diane had been getting Reiki treatments. She stopped going for these when she was hospitalized for the last time, but when she came home from the hospice center, Gordon arranged for a woman from his church—Ruth, a Reiki practitioner—to come to Diane and give her what comfort she could. Ruth would pass her hands gently over Diane's midsection as she lay in the living room. She seemed to recognize what Ruth was doing, and it appeared to have a calming effect, over and above the morphine.

On Tuesday afternoon, a week after Diane had come home, Ruth told me she could feel her pulse weakening and her energy dwindling. She had stopped calling out for "chocolate", and was sleeping most of the time. When she awoke, I would swab her mouth out. That evening, after work, Gordon came over to sit with her and hold her hand. The idea of a death watch wasn't really my style, and I knew it wasn't Diane's either; so although neither Gordon nor I was hungry, I decided to make a pot of pasta for dinner, as I had one night six months ago, when Gordon and I had celebrated Diane's taking a turn for the better in the hospital. Maybe

I was indulging in a little magical thinking, too—though I knew that even at her sickest last winter, she had never been like this. Her eyes were closed, and her breathing was shallow. Gordon sat by the bed, holding her hand, while I futzed in the kitchen. I had been with her all day, except for a little while earlier that afternoon, when I'd gone out for a walk and left her with the home health aide. I'd felt guilty about this, of course, but told her I'd be back very soon. I had to get out of the house, had to walk and feel my blood circulating and "contemplate about" things, but found—unsurprisingly—that all I could think about was her, and how she could die while I was out for a walk, contemplating about things; so after a block or two I came home. Perhaps I was thinking also of the day my father died, only a month earlier, when I'd left his bedside at Santa Monica Hospital to go out to lunch, and stopped afterward at a used bookshop on Wilshire, where I'd bought a biography of Heidegger and a book on "metahistory"—whatever that was—so I'd have something to read back in the hospital room. That was in the afternoon; he died later that night. It shocks and shames me that I could have been thinking of books, and actually buying them, while my father lay dying in the hospital. I may have told myself, while I browsed in the bookstore, that I was just distracting myself, that this was natural and something he might have done too, bibliophile that he was. Maybe I even believed I was doing it in honor of him. Besides, he'd been rallying that day—it was a Sunday—and his gerontologist, who knew we wanted him to be at home when he died, said there was a good chance he'd be able to leave the hospital in a day or two, if he remained stable. So I guess I told myself he was coming out of the woods—another rationalization for my leaving his bedside. But the truth is, I really don't know what I was thinking that day—except of myself and not of him. And it was the same with the walk I started on the day Diane died. The fact that I cut it short, remembering the day of my father's death, didn't erase the fact that I'd had the absence of mind to start on it in the first place.

And so there I was, later that night in the kitchen, cooking spaghetti sauce, when Gordon called me from the living room.

"I think you'd better come here."

I turned off the range and came to the bedside.

"She seems to be having trouble breathing," Gordon said.

I took her hand in mine and inclined the head of the bed so she was in more of a sitting-up position. "It's OK, Sweetie, it's OK. I'm right here with you," I said. Then she vomited up a stinking, dark-brown fluid—black death, it was—which I wiped up with a towel. And then, in my arms, she died. It was a little after eleven.

We waited until Zack got home to call hospice and tell them she was dead. Irene had taken Zack and her son Max, Zack's best friend, out to a movie. (It was "Harry Potter and the Prisoner of Azkaban." It seems important to remember this.) I wonder now if I should have insisted that Zack stay home that day. Was this another version of my going out for a walk? But he'd hated going to the hospital; he'd hated the hospice center; he'd hated seeing the hospital bed in the living room. A few years earlier, when Diane became bald from the chemotherapy, Zack had made up what he called a "Head Spa," complete with flyer and coupons. He would spread Noxzema on her bald head and give her a head massage. He also got an idea for a website, "mommysbald.com." He was thirteen at the time.

But now he was going on seventeen, and much had changed. He'd learned the word "inoperable", and what it meant. When the news came in after the second surgery that the cancer had spread throughout her abdomen, Robbie told me Zack had asked him, when I was out of the room, "You mean she could die?" The innocence of the question broke my heart, too. But that was last summer. Now he'd closed himself off to such questions, and had adopted a defensive stance of not being able to "deal with" what was staring us all in the face: "I can't deal with the hospital"; "I can't deal with this place" (the hospice center—and he wasn't the only one); "I can't deal with that thing in here" (the hospital bed in

the living room). I figured it wasn't anybody's job to make him deal with
these things. After all, I hadn't shown such great coping skills either.

It was no surprise, then, that when he came home with Max and
Irene, Zack couldn't deal with seeing his mother's body lying in the living
room. After looking at her briefly and touching her lifeless hand, he went
into his room, followed by Max. Irene stayed in the living room for a little
while, softly reciting some Buddhist prayers for the dead. (She was a
practicing Buddhist, and Diane wanted her to lead a simple Buddhist
funeral service at the beach, which she did.) By this time, Gordon had
left, and Robbie had arrived with his wife—whose name was also Diane.
(Her married name was the same as Diane's maiden name—a fact which
was now, and ever after, to unnerve me. Whenever I heard her full name,
Diane Austin, spoken on her voicemail, it gave me a cruel little jolt, a
momentary confusion in which the tiniest spark of something—Hope?
Wishful thinking? Magical thinking? Hallucination?—would be both
ignited and, at the same time, snuffed out.)

Through the hospice center I had arranged for the Hemlock Society to handle the cremation, and after midnight a large man in a
Hawaiian shirt arrived to take the body. I remember Robbie engaging
him in conversation as he filled out the paperwork and had me sign it.
Robbie asked him how he'd gotten into this line of work, what he'd
done before that, etc. I wasn't inclined to follow their chat. I understood that Robbie was only trying to distract himself, and maybe also
do the decent thing by acknowledging the man's presence. But there
was also something that really bugged me about his show of interest,
under the circumstances, in the undertaker's job history. How could
he honestly want to hear this stuff right now? Or was he not really
serious, and just playing one of his head games? There was an element
of sangfroid in his talk with the man that rubbed me the wrong way.
Diane ("my" Diane) and Robbie had had a long and sometimes troubled history together. Suffice it to say that she had more than once
been the guinea-pig for his mind games. She had forgiven him; but she

was always more forgiving than I. Or maybe, as an only child, I just didn't know what it was like to have (or to be) an older brother. It wasn't his fault that he wasn't his younger sister; but at the time, in the temporary insanity of grief, I was finding it hard to forgive him for that. And for not being able to do what I suddenly wanted him to do, which was to switch places with her.

The undertaker asked me to remove her jewelry. The rings slipped off easily from her thin fingers, but I had some trouble with the fixing of the nose stud, and had to poke my pinkie into her nostril to retrieve it. And as I did so, I caught a whiff once again, faint but unmistakable, of the stink of black death. I put the nose stud and its fixing into an envelope, along with her wedding band, and placed the envelope in the top drawer of my dresser. The other rings I gave away.

And so began the Minor Period, which I'd had a taste of even before she died, in the form of the Widower's Bed, and the Library in Winter. The account of these things will require a bit of backtracking, for which I again ask the reader's indulgence. *(Sigh.* Oh shut up.)

It was early January, 2004. Diane had gone into the hospital just after New Year's, suffering from nausea and intense abdominal pain. The previous summer, three and a half years after her mastectomy, they had operated to remove a cancerous ovary and found tiny metastasized tumors scattered "like grains of millet" throughout her abdomen. Speaking with the surgeon as he came out of the operating room, Robbie, Zack, and I had asked him if there was any hope. "Well, there is always *hope* … ," he conceded grudgingly, as if this were now beside the point. Which I guess it was, to him. I had already concluded he was an asshole after he'd pushed back the operating date to accommodate his schedule, though he knew Diane was in severe pain. When I expressed dissatisfaction with the delay, he told me I was free to look for another surgeon. I wondered after the surgery if I'd made a mistake in not doing just that; but by then we knew the cancer was inoperable. It was producing a buildup of fluid—edema—that had to be drained regularly through a long needle.

That fall, after Bucholz had decided against further chemotherapy in favor of hormone treatments, we went to Sloan Kettering for a second opinion. The specialist there proposed a different chemo regimen, which we tried for three months. But this proved worse than useless. By early January, in addition to the edema, there was the palpable mass of "tumor"—along with more severe pain—and she went into intensive care. For ten days she was in critical condition. I was spending all day at the hospital (my college was on instructional intersession in January, but I wasn't teaching during this time), but they wouldn't let visitors stay overnight in the ICU; and it was then, and in the nights that followed, when she was released from intensive care and sent down to the cancer wing on the second floor, that I first became acquainted with the Widower's Bed.

I didn't call it that at the time. But in those bitter cold nights of January, with the wind whistling around the corner windows of the bedroom—when even the down comforter wasn't enough to warm the bed in the absence of Diane, and I had to put a sleeping bag on top of it—I had my first real taste of the reality that lay ahead. "The empty bunk," I said to myself—a phrase my father and his buddies used in World War II. The wry self-consciousness (not lacking in self-pity, either) with which it was uttered now seemed to mitigate the coldness of the thought itself—as if it were a coldness I was only allowing myself under duress.

They gave her the bed by the window in a corner room on the cancer wing—Two North. She was there for most of January. The first few days out of intensive care were rough. She spoke very little. (It's not easy to talk with a tube in your nose and down your throat.) Her color was sallow, her face drawn and pinched, and she was still throwing up a lot. I'd brought her stuffed toy frog to the hospital to comfort her, but she didn't want to have Debbie in bed with her for fear she'd throw up on her. We kept a shallow, kidney-shaped metal basin within arm's reach. Sitting in a chair at the foot of the bed, alert to the feeble groans that presaged an attack of nausea, I would periodically jump up from the chair, grab the basin, hold it under her chin, and cup the back of her head while she vomited.

The anti-nausea medication she was on made her sleepy, so I brought a book for the intervals of rest. It was Mann's *Doctor Faustus*: the fictional biography of a modernist German composer, Adrian Leverkühn, who sells his soul to the devil for twenty-four years of musical genius. *(Which he wrote, as you know of course, in your schlappschwanzische hometown of Pacific Palisades.* Yes, I know. And thanks so much for reminding me of its wimpiness.) The story is narrated by his childhood friend Serenus Zeitblom, writing from "Fortress Germany" during the final two years of the Third Reich. A strange choice of book, it might seem, to bring with me to the cancer wing; but I found it engrossing and oddly comforting—as though Mann's heavy, dense German world, larded with history (medieval, Wilhelmine, Weimar, Nazi), could act as a counterweight to the load we were already carrying on Two North.

I have sometimes wished I had a taste for books of popular escapist literature: detective novels, cozy mysteries, espionage thrillers. I envy those who can immerse themselves in these kinds of stories; but on the few occasions I have tried to read them, I have never gotten very far. I can't help feeling I am wasting my time "slumming," when I could be feeding my mind with edifying works. It's as though I were a prisoner of my desire for high-mindedness. It seems to me there is a kind of imaginative limitation in this preference for the high-brow—something almost materialistic (and actually rather middle-brow, ironically) about it: as if the ideals of wisdom, beauty, and virtue were quasi-tangible things to be deliberately pursued and consumed; as if there were something salvific and ennobling about high culture; as if reading Thomas Mann could have somehow strengthened and prepared me for Diane's suffering and what lay at the end of it—an eventuality I knew to be inevitable now, since she was in Stage Four, but which I vaguely imagined could continue to be pushed forward into the indefinite future. *Doctor Faustus* promised to be helpful in this avoidance. It provided distraction because it required concentration and immersion in the details of its demanding and punishing German world, while in the bed in front of me lay my wife, slowly dying of cancer.

What a selfish bastard, to be withholding myself from her even a little in her final months, and for the sake of that dreary, great novel. But hadn't I always found a way to withhold part of myself from her? And could I not now bear the thought of the final intimacy? Did I not see that this was a precious time, when she was still precariously in the world? The thought of the future was both to be avoided and, at the same time, irrelevant. All that was important, I told myself, was that she get through this "rough spot." The drastic understatement seemed necessary not only to de-dramatize the direness of the reality, but also to reassure myself by suggesting that it was possible to look at the horrible present as if from a "safer" vantage point of future retrospection.

And, in a way, it worked. The memory of those winter days in the hospital is dear to me now, not just because they tell of a time when Diane was still in the world, but also because they hold the special value that times of trouble assume for us once they are past—once they have become personal history. Or maybe I love those memories for a much simpler reason: hope. The childish hope—so easily dismissed by the surgeon that previous summer—that the cancer would somehow go away, that the collective-noun "tumor" would de-massify, break up, and eventually disappear. This hope was as persistent as it was irrational; and *Doctor Faustus*—dark, grim, demanding, but not entirely hopeless itself— somehow became part of that hope, a companion in adversity.

But it went farther than just having the book with me in the hospital. I bought a spiral-bound Michelin map of Germany (including Austria, Switzerland, the Czech Republic, and "Benelux") so that I could locate the places mentioned in the novel. At night, after I got home from Two North for the third and last time (the first was to pick Zack up at home after school and take him to the hospital; the second to drive him home and get dinner), I would take the novel and map into bed with me and hunker down under the sleeping bag and comforter for some quality time in "Fortress Germany." Every now and then, as I looked up the location of some place mentioned in the book, my mind would go on a prolonged detour over the multicolored Michelin map, following the red, yellow, blue, and green lines as they meandered through Mitteleuropa. How comforting it was to ponder the details of this map! "Contemplational Geography," I called it. (Part of what I term the "Contemplational Sciences." Other disciplines in this dreamy field include "Contemplational Meteorology," "Contemplational Bibliography," "Contemplational Geology," and "Contemplational Cosmology.") Here, then, was my escapist literature after all—maps of Germany and *Doctor Faustus*. These were footholds for my imagination during that bitter-cold January. Better the map and the book than the thought of what lay ahead in the near future.

The Widower's Bed returned to stay on the night of June 8, 2004, when she died, and they took her away after midnight in a black plastic body bag. For the first time since she'd gone back into the hospital for the last time (just before that long Memorial Day weekend), I slept in our bed—which now, after twenty-one years of married life, was once again "my bed." As they were also now "my bedroom," "my bank account," "my taxes." According to the transformational vicissitudes of "Contemplational Grammar," the first-person possessive pronoun was singular again, and it took some getting used to. At first it sounded harsh coming out of my mouth; shouldn't I be allowed to continue to use the first-person plural a little longer? During the final two weeks of Diane's life, I stayed with her every night: a week in her hospital room; then a night—one night only—in the hospice center she'd gone into after the hospital; and then, during her last week back at home, I slept beside her on the futon in the living room. The night she died, I moved back into our bedroom. My bedroom, now.

The first few nights of the Widower's Bed, I conscientiously still slept on "my" side. Gradually, though, I migrated over to the middle of the bed; it seemed merely superstitious not to do this. Then I started sleeping on "her" side, just to prove to myself … what, exactly? That I was adapting? That I was, at least in the matter of sleeping sides, moving on? Not being morbid or pathological? That my mourning of her did not require my being superstitious? (Funny, because when she was alive, I sometimes used to enjoy making deliberate shows of superstition in front of her: throwing spilt salt over my left shoulder; never walking under a ladder—at least not when I was with her; quickly grabbing a hat or cap if it happened to land on the bed. More than anything else, these gestures were inside references to my father, who really was superstitious.) Maybe there was even something comforting about sleeping on her side of the bed now. I remembered when we'd occasionally switch sides, and how pathetically exciting that was. I remembered, too, our placement in all the different beds we'd slept in together. As with the name of the movie Zack saw on the night his mother died, it seemed important to get this right.

To vary a little the maxim of La Rochefoucauld about the misfortunes of our friends, there was something about the Widower's Bed "that did not displease me." Was this really true? I think it was. But how was this possible? What could I possibly have liked about this arrangement? What could it have been about loneliness and solitude and bereavement and enforced celibacy that I found even slightly appealing? Was it just that I like to suffer, and then feel sorry for myself suffering, and the Widower's Bed was as good a way as any—better, actually; maybe the best way—to do this? It may be that simple: just the love of suffering, and of feeling sorry for yourself suffering (which really, of course, are not that simple at all). Or it may be something else, which I don't particularly want to think about, much less write about. *But of course you will.* Yes, Fritz, I will. Suck it up.

It may go back to something I called the "Imagination of Disaster," first experienced in childhood, which I became aware of again one evening in winter, before Diane died (at least I think it was before she died,

but see below). I was at one of the local Long Island libraries I haunted—I
believe it was the Dix Hills Library, near Huntington—in the medieval
Christianity section, leafing through a book on English monasteries. It
was Michael David Knowles's *The Monastic Order in England*, which I
had read about in another book, Norman Cantor's scholarly but
accessible—in fact riveting, for me—survey *Inventing the Middle Ages*.
Cantor's book, a series of profiles of late-nineteenth- and twentieth-century
medieval scholars and their work, I had discovered by chance some years
before, while browsing in the bookshop at The Cloisters museum in upper
Manhattan. On a hunch—it looked not too academic, but just academic
enough—I bought it, and ended up reading it twice. The second time was
the summer of Diane's ovarian surgery, when her cancer was found to
have metastasized. I brought Cantor's book to the hospital to read while
she was in surgery. I guess it functioned somewhat the same way *Doctor
Faustus* was to function the following January, when she was so gravely
ill: comfort, distraction, a companion for the mind—something to hang
your attention on when the worst is coming to pass.

Knowles's work had figured prominently in one of the chapters of
Cantor's book—"The Rebellious Monk"—which was why I tracked it
down in the medieval Christianity section of the library. I remember
feeling that just having this book in my hands helped a little. Helped
what? I'm not quite sure. And I'm not sure I even want to find out,
because if I did, the spell of that moment in the library would be broken.
Now was this after Diane died? Or was it before, and was I only imagining, or trying to imagine, or being unable to imagine, what life without her would be like? Imagining how much I would be in need of
sheltering when that time came. Imagining what kind of shelter the
library would become to me then. The fascination, the curious attraction of the unthinkable. But wherever on the timeline that moment in
the library fell, it was then that I began to formulate the adult version
of the Imagination of Disaster—the thought of what life without her
would be like. I felt (and still feel) guilty even admitting the thought.

Yet this kind of thinking was nothing new to me. Ever since childhood I had flirted with the question of what it would be like if the unthinkable occurred; say, if one of my parents—or, even more unthinkable, both of my parents—should die. This was a thought that would be banished the instant it occurred. Yet it did occur. I would allow it to occur, and then banish it the moment after. It was a kind of game I played with myself—a strange, sick game. *(Perhaps a morbid version of the Friday Night Syndrome?* Perhaps.)

Back in the day, the Imagination of Disaster was not limited to the death of my parents. Other disasters fit the bill, too: suddenly becoming blind, or deaf, or losing a limb (or two), or becoming paralyzed. Or all of the above. *(Oh come now, you can't be serious.* I wish I weren't, Fritz. But we have already established that I was a weird kid.) These disasters were different from the orphaning version, though, primarily because they didn't entail guilt, which made the orphaning version something especially not to be imagined—and therefore something especially hard not to imagine.

All of this was quite compulsive, of course; and since I probably shared it with my mom—as I did everything that happened to me in childhood, at her encouragement—she would have told me so, and then would have gone on to explain the compulsion (fear, anxiety, repressed hostility, etc.), and thus help to defuse it. I don't remember spending too much time in the grip of the Imagination of Disaster, and it never got so bad that I had to go to a shrink (not as a child, anyway). It was just something bizarre that happened from time to time, so that much later, when I began to have banishable thoughts of what life after Diane would be like, I recognized the reappearance of my old *bête noire*, in slightly altered form. More than slightly, as a matter of fact. The demon was now fully mature, and not at all hypothetical. It was not a case, this time, of "*If* Diane should die someday..." but rather, "*When* Diane dies..."

The cold detachment of the thought was the worst thing about it. It would enter into my consciousness with an unassuming matter-of-factness that was stunning—as though it were just one of a number of future contingencies that had to be taken into account. For example—since I was handling the bills now—the lease on her VW bug was coming due for renewal or cancellation in a couple of months, and I had to put down a deposit if we were going to renew. Of course we would renew; but as I was writing out the check, I wondered, for just a split second, if they would enforce the cancellation penalty if...? But how could I think this way? How could I coldly allow myself to imagine her death, and its after-math, before the fact? What it would be "like"? (As if it would be "like" anything.) What kind of cold-blooded creep was I? The knowledge that I had once had other imaginings like this, as a child, was hardly consola-tion now. (So I had been a cold-blooded creep since childhood!) But now I couldn't go to Mom and confess my thought, because—in her case—the once-unthinkable had happened, and she was dead. And I could hardly go to Diane, either. I could especially not go to Diane. She had more important things on her mind than the Imagination of Disaster.

Except that what was on her mind was what I was imagining, too.

From time to time she would bring it up, in that direct yet ironic way she had. "When I'm gone..." she'd begin. "No!" I'd say. "We are not hav-ing this discussion! This is not something I can deal with right now! This is not a conversation I can have right now!" Selfish bastard. What about her needs? What about the person who was dying's feelings? What about the conversation that she wanted, needed to have? But even in her dying, even in her preparation for death, it was my needs that came first. (*Reminds me a little of the way you spoke for her in the hospital, and also the hospice center, when you told the doctors what she wanted without asking her.* I hadn't thought of that before, but I suppose you're right—much as it pains me to admit it.)

To be fair—or at least to be accurate—I guess that I felt, and wanted to convey to her, that my not being "able to have this conversation" was an expression of love, a statement about the inadmissibility of the thought of her death. I suppose I saw this as a sign of my devotion to her. Yet I knew, even as I refused, that I was already having the conversation with myself, in the form of the Imagination of Disaster.

Or it may have been that the moment with the medieval monastery book in the Dix Hills Library came before Diane's cancer had metastasized—that is, before the spring of '03, when the Imagination of Disaster was just that: only imagination. If so, then it would have involved my fantasizing myself as what I soon enough in fact became: a widower, whose long evenings in the library, once only imagined, were now a reality. The library was no longer just a place where one might go as a lonely, middle-aged person to seek solace and shelter among books. It was in fact where I did go now.

I was now that lonely widower I had only imagined before, sitting by the row of tall library windows of a cold winter's evening, with a book in his lap and the whole long, lonesome night before him—tracking, perhaps, with his dreamy gaze, the course of a small plane blinking through the night sky, in his mind (and only in his mind) transcending his apparently bleak circumstances and prospects. And considering that the reality of the little corner cigar shop that was now his daily life could (at least conceivably) blow your mind, if you came to know it. That the mundane contains wonders not dreamt of in your philosophy, and closed by your senses five. And that one man's disaster can become another man's (or that same man's) everyday reality. What had once been the Imagination of Disaster was now turning out to be the Imagination of Survival.

And maybe it was really survival all along that I was imagining, back when I thought I was imagining disaster. (Maybe, even, it was survival that was part of the disaster. As in, "I hope I go before you, because I don't want to be the one left behind.") Is it monstrous to wonder if, in imagining the disaster of Diane's death, I subconsciously wanted to be the one left behind—not only because I didn't want to be the one to die, but also because I was morbidly curious about what it would be like to survive? *Merely* to survive. What kind of life would it be *merely to survive*? Would it be any kind of life at all?

Well, now I knew. My morbid curiosity had been satisfied. She went first; I was left behind. I survived her. I was surviving her death. If the life of survival contained any mysteries—à la cigar shop in *My Dinner with André*—I was now in a position to know. *This* was what it was like. My mind was being blown, on a daily basis, by the fact that Diane was no longer in the world, and I still was. If I ever thought of suicide—and I mostly didn't—it was on the order of a fantasy, rather than a transcendence. Life, continuing life, was the transcendence, not death. To kill myself would be to spoil the mystery, to attempt to solve the problem illicitly (the mystery and the problem being in this case the same thing: survival). To kill myself would be cheating, like skipping ahead to the ending, or looking up the answer in the back of the book before working it out for myself. Because, as they say, it's not the answer that's important—it's the question.

And the question now was, How do I survive in the world without Diane? How do I live each day, and every other day after that, without her? How do I go on? For life must go on, mustn't it? Though a life alone was not much of a life—and, in fact, sometimes seemed a kind of death, a preparation for death. I wasn't preparing for death, was I? No, I don't think that's what was going on. I think what was going on was that I was trying to find a way to go on. And the philosophical resignation (and curious pleasure) of the Widower's Bed, and the refusal of philosophical resignation, and the Library in Winter, and the remembrance of Diane, and the wish to do more with my life than just remember her (though that alone sometimes seemed a worthy enough endeavor), and the wish to enshrine her in my heart and enact a kind of living memorial to her every day, in some way—and also to forget about her for a little while, every day: all of these things seemed like they might be part of a way of going on.

Another way of going on—at least to my mind at the time—was to begin some kind of relationship with another woman. This happened only four months after Diane's death. Much too soon—as Zack was to unceremoniously inform me. Looking back on it, I am surprised and dismayed that I could have even thought of a romantic involvement so soon. All I can say in my own (weak) defense is that it seemed like a good idea at the time. A way, as I say, to prove to myself that I could go on, and was going on. I know that in this I did not act as I should have. And these words as well seem inadequate to me now, and probably speak to other flaws in my character: my fickleness; my unfaithfulness to Diane with Cindy (which I wrote about in *Failure*, so will not rehearse here); a certain shallowness of feeling, even. But more self-flagellation can only add insult to injury, so I will nip it in the bud (and mix clichéd metaphors while I'm at it). *You go, guy—as you Americans say. And please don't stop self-flagellating just for my sake!*

Mei-Li had come to Dowling College, where I taught, to serve as Director of International Education, in charge of recruiting, lodging and supporting our foreign students. At the time, I was heading the Honors Program, and since many of the college's best students came from abroad, she would select those whose grades, test scores and English were strongest and refer them to me. Occasionally, we would speak about a particularly promising student. I was struck by her beauty. She wore no ring—no jewelry of any sort—and dressed elegantly and unobtrusively, in business suits, skirts and blouses. I wondered about her life outside school. We ran into each other in the cafeteria one day and had lunch together, and she told me a little about her family's experience during the Cultural Revolution. Her great-grandfather had been one of the founders of the Bank of China, and this did not sit well with the regime of the People's Republic of the '60s and '70s. But the neighbors, she said, were so fond of her father that they refused to denounce him to the Red Guards, and the family got to stay in their colonial-era house in Tianjin (a port city southeast of Beijing), instead of being "relocated" to the countryside. Most of their belongings were confiscated, however. Walking home from school one day, Mei-Li saw people carrying the family furniture down the street. She was ten years old at the time. (So this would have been in 1967.)

The fall after Diane died, Mei-Li expressed her condolences, and not long after that, she was present when I said a few words at a commemoration in the library for a colleague from India who had died the year before. Mei-Li politely complimented me on my remarks after the ceremony, and a few days later, after I'd run across her in the hall and we'd exchanged pleasantries, I called and invited her (in what I see now was a misreading of her habitual politeness as interest) to tea in my office. She brought some fancy Chinese tea, but didn't drink any. (She hardly ever drank tea or coffee, and would take only a sip of beer on occasion.)

Soon we started meeting after hours in places near campus: at the Bayard Cutting Arboretum across the river; for a walk by a golf course; beside a turtle pond next to a former stables that had been converted into cozy condos; parked at the beach by the Great South Bay. I asked her more about what it was like growing up during the Cultural Revolution. For ten years, her "classes" at "school" consisted of phys. ed. and party propaganda. The libraries were still open, though, and after school every day she went to the local library and read under the direction of the librarian, who acted as her *de facto* teacher during those years. This secret education served her well. After the universities were finally reopened in the '70s, she scored very high on the entrance exams, and got into Tianjin University—the oldest university in China—despite the fact that admissions preference was given to the children of workers, peasants, party officials and the military. In the late '70s she went as an exchange student to Carlow University in Pittsburgh, then got a Master's in library science from the University of Pittsburgh. After graduating she had a series of jobs in and around Pittsburgh, where she met her husband (who was from Taiwan), and where their daughter, Bao, was born. They moved to Taipeh when Bao was five, and Mei-Li went to work for McKinsey & Co. in their Personnel Department, and then for the mayor of Taipeh (who later became the president of Taiwan). Her marriage was collapsing, though. Mei-Li wanted to work, but her husband, an engineer, wanted her to stay home—which she had no intention of doing. So when she got a job offer through an old library friend she used to work for in Pittsburgh, who was now a VP in the administration of our college, she took it, and moved with Bao to Long Island. When I met her, she'd been separated from her husband for four years. Bao was 16—a year younger than Zack.

Our evening rendezvous, however, were taking time away from my being with him at home, and he wasn't happy about it. One night he confronted me.

"I don't get it. You have these pictures of Mommy up all over the house, but you're seeing this other woman? What's that all about?"

"We're just talking, Zack. I don't like being alone."

"Well, neither do I. You're out all the time with this person."

"Her name is Mei-Li."

"Whatever. You're spending more time with her than with me."

"I see. And you don't like it."

"Well duh. I need you at home."

My face was suddenly hot with shame and remorse. How could I not have seen this coming? The old selfishness again. And worse—negligence. A negligent father. Disloyal, too, to the memory of the very person I was enshrining with all those photos around the house—and her drawings, which I'd gotten framed. What had I been thinking?

"I'm sorry, Zack. I won't see her anymore. I'll be with you. I'll call her right now."

"Look, it's not that I don't want you to be happy or anything—I do. It's just that—"

"You don't need to explain. I get it. It's too soon."

When I talked to her, Mei-Li said she understood. After all, this had never been her idea. I remembered—and how could I have forgotten this?—that at the end of the first week we'd started meeting, she'd given me a Dear Josh speech, saying she would never forget this wonderful time, and would treasure it always in her memory, etc.—but she had to focus on her studies. (She was working toward her doctorate in education at Dowling.) But I hadn't taken no for an answer. I'd thought she was just afraid, and I wasn't about to let fear come between us—or rather, between me and what I foolishly imagined as a possible future with another family: this time, a family of four.

Really? Four months after Diane died, and you were already thinking of having another family?

Apparently so. I told you this doesn't speak well of me. I suppose I was also thinking that Diane wouldn't want me to be alone (she'd said as much, that last year), and that the serendipity of such an unlikely match-up was somehow an indication of its rightness, its inevitability. I'd run right over Mei-Li's reasonable doubts and hesitations in my eagerness to prove to myself that magic could happen—that people could and would find each other (not unlike the way Diane and I had). That romantic destiny was supreme. *Magical thinking.* Yes, I guess so. My own years of magical thinking.

For the rest of the school year, I stopped seeing Mei-Li, and spent the weekends at home with Zack. He was on his computer most of the time; but it was important for him to know I was there and not miles away, with another woman. During this time, when I wasn't doing school stuff, I was working on *Failure: An Autobiography*—a project begun partly as a joke, because its title had made Diane laugh. Not long after she died, though, the writing picked up steam. I drafted another chapter that first summer (2004), and continued working on it when I could over the following year. It was a way of "turning towards the pain"—a phrase I'd encountered in a *Sun Magazine* interview with the Buddhist nun Pema Chödrön, and which had stuck with me. I saw that in wanting to begin a romantic relationship so soon after losing Diane, I had been turning *away* from the pain—running away from it, actually—instead of fully facing it, which I now resolved to do. And writing helped me do this. I didn't cut off all communications with Mei-Li, however. We ran into each other occasionally on campus, and would talk now and then on the phone.

The next summer, the day after he graduated from Walt Whitman High School, Zack went to work as a gofer on a movie shooting in Brooklyn—Spike Lee's "Inside Man". My old friends Doug and Miles (Zack's godfather) had helped him get the job; Doug was good friends with the art director. Zack lived with Miles for six weeks in Long Island City, commuting to work in Red Hook (in Brooklyn), where the art department's offices were. It was during this time that I started seeing Mei-Li again. Things heated up between us—though we were not yet lovers (and wouldn't be for another year and a half). Over the July 4th weekend we had a barbecue with Zack and Bao, and afterwards lay on our backs out on the front lawn, listening to "Hearts of Space" on the radio and looking up at the stars. Then we drove Zack back to Miles' in Queens, and from the stoop we watched the fireworks across the East River.

Bao too was away for much of that summer, visiting her grandmother in Hong Kong and father in Taipeh, and Mei-Li and I spent a lot of time together, walking on the beach, swimming, going out to movies, and watching them at home in her apartment. At my prompting, we almost became lovers; then I got cold feet. The thought of sleeping with another woman was still too much to handle. It had been 25 years since I had been with anyone but Diane. (The aforementioned affair with Cindy had not been a physical one, and had been conducted almost entirely over AOL Instant Messenger.) I felt Diane's presence very strongly when I held Mei-Li, even though she was so different: taller, thinner, much less experienced with men (she'd only been with two in her life, her husband and me). And she had two beautiful breasts.

Mei-Li seemed to understand my mixed feelings. And how could the successor to Diane (so went my magical fantasy) not understand? Then again, there were so many things about her I didn't get. For one, we had to speak in whispers in her apartment, because she didn't want the neighbors to know she had a man over. "Why not? You're allowed to have a boyfriend," I countered. But I don't think she really believed that. She was not only ashamed because she was married, but also afraid that word would get out and back to the college, where she imagined her job would be in jeopardy if it were known she was consorting with a faculty member. It didn't seem to matter that she had doubled the international enrollment at our college; or that no one else possessed her knowledge of the intricacies of student visa regulations; or that she consistently bent over backwards to help students with housing, medical care, even grocery-shopping. What mattered was that her (unconsummated) affair with me might somehow cause her to fall afoul of the college administration.

I figured that some of her paranoia had to do with the after-effects of the Cultural Revolution: neighbors could denounce you (though her family's hadn't); the authorities were relentless and implacable; no one was to be trusted. *But given her background, surely you can understand these concerns?* Of course I can; but that didn't make it any easier. And it wasn't just the Cultural Revolution. It was also becoming clear that Mei-Li herself was quite neurotic. There was the whispering in her apartment; she also wanted me to keep our relationship a secret from my friends (though I did not comply with this, and she eventually relented); and we sometimes had to enter her apartment separately, because she didn't want her neighbors to see us together. "People will see! People will see!" she would warn in a whisper.

To judge from her, however, the Chinese did not believe in neurosis. (Though they did believe strongly in repression and denial!) The idea that I was seeing a therapist—Diane's therapist, in fact; but only after her death—was both puzzling and amusing to her. She argued that since I did all the talking, he should be paying me. (When I mentioned this to

Dr. Davis, he said to tell her it didn't work that way.) She was curious to know what was said about her in my sessions; the concept of therapeutic confidentiality was alien to her—she who was so big on secrecy.

What was it, then, that kept me seeing her, off and on, for seven years, considering all our differences, and the fact that we didn't have all that much to talk about? I have already mentioned her beauty. She was the most beautiful woman I had ever been with, and our differences—cultural, temperamental, and intellectual (she was very bright, but not a reader or writer)—only added to her exoticism and mystery. *This is sheer Orientalism.* You may be right, but please be quiet. I never quite knew what she was thinking or feeling. In this way too she was so different from Diane, whose sentences I would sometimes finish (and she mine). But the several divides between Mei-Li and me, though they eventually proved too wide to bridge, were at first exciting and intriguing. The thought of beginning a new life so different from (and in some ways opposed to) my old one with Diane was a kind of anti-nostalgia treatment I was administering to myself. Maybe it would help to loosen the hold of the past. Now of course a part of me—a large part—did not want to let go of the past. But I knew that if I were ever to begin a new life with another woman, I would have to lay the old one aside, put it in its place, and keep it there. I think I was looking for a way to enshrine Diane, in a couple of senses: to both memorialize her and contain her. I wanted to move on—but I wanted her with me as I did. I suppose I had in mind a kind of portable shrine—a personal Ark of the Covenant, you could say, in the desert of the Minor Period.

But this new life that I envisioned—dimly, but insistently—could not begin until Mei-Li and I became lovers (which would entail a violation of the covenant—another source of ambivalence). *(I just have to say, these Hebraisms strike a false note, especially coming from someone whose Jewish identity, by his own admission, is not all that strong to begin with.* You are perhaps not wrong here either. So noted. But please stop.) The consummation was finally achieved in January of 2007, when she stayed over at my house the night of the Burns party—the same party Diane and

I used to go to, at our friends' on the Upper West Side. The year after Diane died I had gone alone, and the bagpiper had played "Auld Lang Syne" in memory of her. The following year I brought a couple of friends (Mei-Li was away on a scholastic cruise with Bao), and in 2007 I finally came with Mei-Li, and introduced her to Adam and Liz, the hosts of the party. (Adam did business in China, and Mei-Li was able to arrange for a Chinese student to do an internship with him.) We got back from Manhattan after 1 a.m., and I asked her to spend the night. Zack and Bao were both away at school, so no one but us need ever know, and she finally consented. It was the first time in 27 years that I'd slept with a woman other than Diane, and it was as strange and exciting as I'd imagined. Mei-Li made a whimpering sound as we made love—the sound of her difference, it seemed to me. Afterwards we lay in bed and talked about the party, and some of the people there. This talking after the fact became a custom she would look forward to, and that I came to recognize as the one time she was really able to relax, and not be doing, or planning to do. "I love this time," she would say. Sometimes I asked about her husband—about what went wrong between them. They didn't have moments like this, she said. He didn't talk about personal things; he didn't tell her he loved her.

"Did he?" I asked. "Love you?"

She sighed. "I think so. But he didn't say."

Mei-Li sighed a lot. The more I got to know her (and I use the term advisedly), the more I began to recognize these sighs as—among other things—her way of signaling difficulties of expression. She wasn't much of a talker. In some ways we were a gender bender: I was the talker, the "emoter"; she was the doer, who kept her feelings largely to herself. Not that she was cold; there was warmth in her touch, and in her eyes and smile. But there was also, in public at least, what I came to know as "the mask"—the expressionless expression that no doubt gave rise to the invidious stereotype of East Asians as "inscrutable". It was hard to imagine how emotionally paralyzed her husband must have been if he wasn't demonstrative enough for her. *Watch it here, Schatzi. This part is making me uncomfortable—and it's not just the "inscrutable" cliché, either. It's one thing to talk about cultural differences, and another thing entirely to trade on them for the sake of what can only be called a kind of prurient titillation: "Hey, I got me a Chinese gal. Don't call me a racist."*

How dare you! Especially you! I mean, what if I asked you what your dad did during the war, Fritz? Or is it indecorous of me to bring that up? Would it blow your whole PC spiel?

Cheap shot.

No cheaper than your harping on my supposed Orientalism.

Whoa there, cowboy—as your Western-loving pal Paul might have said.

You leave him out of this!

Why should I? Just because he was a "good German"—as opposed to, say, my father?

As a matter of fact, yes to both, now that you bring up the subject.

But I didn't. You were the one who mentioned my father.

And I'm sorry I did. Let's just drop the whole German thing, shall we?

Ja wohl. Mit dem größten Vergnügen.

The pleasure is mutual. I apologize for him, Reader. Now where were we? Oh yeah—we were speaking of being demonstrative (or the lack thereof). I sometimes got the feeling that I was too demonstrative for Mei-Li's taste—that I violated her sense of reserve, and also that my jokes were objectionable, which she would indicate with a deprecatory downturn of the mouth: a conventional expression of disapproval that Diane would never have made, and that signaled another gap in our sensibilities. I recognized this the first time she made the face. "She doesn't really get you," the face said, "and she never will." It's amazing how revealing even the briefest of expressions can be. This one spoke volumes about how different our senses of humor were. But I did not want to hear what her expression was saying, because I realized, the first time I saw it, that it could be the kiss of death to our relationship. So I made myself disregard it, pretending it was only incidental, when I knew deep down that it was the sign of a fundamental divide.

Nevertheless, after Burns Night we began sleeping together once or twice a week—usually at her apartment, since it was very close to campus, and Bao was now away at college (as was Zack). In bed, the downturned mouth was forgotten, and the whimpering sound, once I got used to it, was a turn-on. I liked drawing it out of her; I liked the world we fell into when she made it. And there was another sound, a gulping sound she made when she came—as though she were swallowing her moans, for the sake of the neighbors (which she no doubt was). She came quickly. Her passionate response seemed to belie her sexual innocence and inexperience (which were also kind of a turn-on).

Before Mei-Li, I had always been attracted to older women. Diane was five years older, and the two women before her that I'd been serious about were both older, too. My own modest sexual experience was not something I'd ever banked on; I had always been more pupil than instructor. That I was now helping Mei-Li to discover this part of herself *(or so you thought. No, Fritz—knew.* I said she'd only been with one other man—her husband—before me. And this by her own account. *Pay attention.)*—this was gratifying to me. And exciting. I felt that what Diane had done for me, I was now doing for Mei-Li: opening her up, getting her to shed some of her inhibitions. It was Diane who'd taught me to love unashamedly, and now I was passing on something of what she had given me.

With Mei-Li, the best part of our time together was the three years after we first slept together, and before she moved 20 miles east, to be closer to the large state university where she'd gotten a better job. Those were the years when Bao and Zack were both away at college, and we could finally spend the night together. Mei-Li wouldn't let me stay overnight when Bao was home—nor did I want to. Bao objected to our relationship, and had ever since—in a stupid lapse on our part—she'd seen us, through a crack in her bedroom door, embracing on the sofa in the living-room. (This would have been when she was still in high school.) That evening after I left, Bao lit into Mei-Li, calling her a whore and a betrayer of Bao's father (whom she was still, as ever, married to). I never came over again when Bao was there. I complained that I felt like a thief in the night (I had to explain the expression), but I really couldn't blame Bao for her reaction. I probably would have felt the same way if I were her. Moreover, Mei-Li was too ambivalent about our relationship to assert herself against her daughter. It wasn't just that she was married, and that her husband's traditional Taiwanese family were still holding out hope that she might one day come back to him (a hope apparently shared by Bao). It was also that Mei-Li herself really had no intention of getting a divorce. She said she'd already brought enough shame on her husband by leaving him as she had, and taking Bao with her; by asking for a divorce, she would only be adding insult to injury. *(You like that expression, don't you?* Shut up.)

"And so you'll sacrifice us instead?" was the question that went unasked by me, because I already knew the answer. Neither of us was willing to push the issue of divorce: she to spare her husband, I to safeguard what we had, unsatisfying though it was in many ways (the whispering, the secrecy, the lack of a full life together).

In other ways, though, those three years were very nice. (The "Domestic Period", I was to call it later—perhaps the best phase of the Minor Period.) Once or twice a week, we would go to sleep and wake up together. I would come over after class on Thursday evenings (the end of my work week), take off my shoes at the door, and change into my "gay"—our name for a pair of her silver- and rainbow-striped flannel pajama bottoms that I liked to wear as a marker of the transition to her place, and the weekend. She would already have dinner ready: sometimes a homemade stir-fry, sometimes take-out from the Thai/Chinese restaurant nearby, where she was a VIP and they gave her a discount on the whole steamed ginger fish and wide noodles we loved. I'd have a beer, and we'd spread a table-cloth on the living-room carpet (a plush salmon-and-cerulean Oriental that had originally been in my study, and that I'd given her after she kept admiring it) and lay out a feast of several dishes, often including her delicious trademark onion-and-egg fried rice. She pampered me, and I knew it, feeling pasha-like in my "gay" and one of her oversized t-shirts. Drinking her beer, eating her cooking, afterwards watching a movie on her DVD player, and then, in her darkened bedroom, with Chinese or Western classical music playing in Bao's Bao-less room at the other end of the short hallway, enjoying her beautiful body. She had the skin and figure of a woman half her age—the gift of the stainless life she led. No alcohol (except for an occasional sip of beer), no tobacco, no drugs. I used to joke that I wanted to get her hammered one night—by her own admission, she'd never been drunk or stoned in her life; but I think we both knew this plan was not only unserious but undesirable. Her attraction, for me, lay partly in her purity, her innocence—which I could imagine myself debauching, for 15 minutes, when we did it doggy-style on her king-sized bed, with her on her knees and elbows at the edge of the bed, head down, ass up, and me standing on tiptoes behind her, impaling her, with those beautiful, champagne-glass-sized breasts cupped in my hands, and her strange, whimpering moans, muffled into a pillow, urging me on. And finally, inevitably, the gulp.

But as soon as I left her apartment at night (on those nights, usually Sundays, when I couldn't stay over because I didn't have the books I needed for class the next morning), I would start thinking of Diane again, and of how Mei-Li was not Diane. She was many things that Diane wasn't. She was very beautiful; she was thin; she was delicate; she was more conventionally feminine; she had two breasts. But she wasn't Diane. The wrong thing to think—the wrong *way* to think about her, I knew; but there it was. As I drove home on those sober Sunday evenings, the wide night sky of Long Island, hanging above the overpass to the LIE—dark, but never quite black because of the light pollution, and with a small plane or two blinking across, the people inside, I imagined, wending their way homeward, like me (except I was going home to an empty house)—that nighttime sky was almost always the background to thoughts of Diane, who wasn't waiting for me at home, and never would be. Where was she? Her body was ashes—now not even that, dissolved years ago in the ocean off Montauk. Where were her thoughts, her feelings, her sense of humor, her wit? All up in smoke, along with her brain, boiled away inside her skull in the crematorium's incinerator, whose unspeakable heat had vaporized all of her except the bones, which it had turned into a pound or two of sand-colored ash that I'd held in my hands and cast into the sea. At least in the last apartment we'd lived in together, where she died, I could feel her absence, her aura—her "juice", as we used to refer to the imagined molecular traces of a person that are left in a place. (I have mentioned the small streak of her blood on the corner of the partition between the hallway and the living room, where she'd fallen and hit her head in the last week of her life; and the "juice" of that bloodstain might still be there, though painted over, and so unknown to future tenants.) But in the new house, bought in 2006, there wasn't even that; there was no trace of her at all, except in the photos of her I'd kept (and I'd kept all of them, except for a few that had gotten lost in the move), and in her colorful, whimsical watercolors, which I'd framed and hung on the walls of the sun room. She'd never even seen this house, which I'd bought with the inheritance I got from my father, two years after he and Diane died within a month of each other. "He'll outlive me," Diane said, matter-of-factly, after her cancer had come back and been diagnosed as stage four—and he almost did. He'd never seen this house either—nor had my mother, who'd died eight years earlier. What was the point of living alone in a house that no one in the family had ever seen, except Zack? Would a woman ever be waiting for me there? Not as long as I was with Mei-Li.

Which brought up the question, How long would we be together? This was something I thought about even during the "Domestic Period", when she was living near Dowling, and increasingly after that, when she'd moved farther east on the Island, and Bao had graduated from college and moved back home. The only times we were together now were at my place, for a few stolen hours on a weekend evening—but never overnight, and not every weekend, either. Mei-Li had many other commitments: events on campus, travel for her new job as a recruiter of international students, hospice work (for which she volunteered one weekend every couple of months), and Rotary events. *Rotary?* I was involved with a *Rotarian?* This was so improbable that it had a certain charm to it. She used to ask me for help with any writing she had to do (including her dissertation), and one of the first things we worked on together was an article for *The Rotarian* about a beefsteak dinner she'd attended at a local Rotary clubhouse. Her innocence was disarming: she didn't see why the mere existence of such an event, let alone the writing up of it, should be amusing. Her ingenuousness regarding the beefsteak dinner was akin to the panda-and-butterfly needlework she'd done in China, as a young woman, and which she'd kept and shyly shown me when we first started going out: sentimental, corny, heartbreaking in its naivety. These innocent, blameless pursuits of hers, joined with a simple heart and uncritical spirit, made me feel sorry for her, and touched me—a reaction that was itself, of course, sentimental and even patronizing (as a journal editor had once observed when he'd rejected something I'd written about her. *See? So I'm not the only one who feels that way.* Reader, ignore him.). The difference in our sensibilities, however, was if anything a spur to my feelings for her: yet another emblem of her otherness that made me believe such gaps existed not to separate us, but rather to be bridged by our love, which (I imagined) was bigger than our differences.

But she—perhaps ironically, in view of her innocence in other matters—had no such sentimental illusions about our relationship. I think she always knew it wouldn't work out. At the end of the first week we started going out together, when she tried to gently extricate herself with the Dear Josh speech, I had dismissed her misgivings and told her I loved her, and that "two were better than one". I had thought at the time that I could see farther into our future together than she could; but I was wrong. She was ahead of me all along. I'd thought she was reluctant out of fear; but maybe she knew something I didn't. Maybe she'd seen, much more clearly and earlier than I, that our worlds couldn't be merged.

Or maybe it wasn't really that at all—not so much a question of different cultures, personalities, and sensibilities, but of logistical changes in the Post-Domestic Phase of our love: her move to another town on Long Island, almost 20 miles from where I worked (in Oakdale), and more than that from where I lived (in Huntington). Not great distances, by any measure; but it was more than the distance, or the traffic. She was working longer hours at the new job, and traveling more often, and Bao was living at home again, and commuting to work in the city. What might have been mere annoyances to another couple were proving to be greater obstacles for us, and indications of larger problems—problems of communication (the language, the turned-down-mouth expression) and commitment (or over-commitment, in her case). She fit me into her schedule where she could—between work, and business travel, and hospice duties, and Rotary, and the various other community obligations she had undertaken (or simply been unable to refuse).

We were also turning out to be in different leagues. She had a high-ranking position in the administration of a major research university; I taught at a small private college, unheard of anywhere but Long Island. (Dowling finally went bankrupt in 2016. *How many times must you remind us of this?*) She was an ambitious, driven careerist; I was the author of *Failure: An Autobiography*. Which, to my knowledge, she had never read. As I've said, she wasn't a reader. I'd never seen her reading a book, either in Mandarin or English. And in any case, my book wasn't exactly her cup of tea; the title alone probably freaked her out. The Chinese are even less tolerant of failure than Americans; and the thought that she was going out with someone who not only considered himself a failure, but had broadcast this to the world, was no doubt hard for her to get her mind around. Personal and professional failure was something you buried and tried to forget, not something you proclaimed and explored.

Besides, she was a very private person—sometimes to a fault. Even in the Domestic Period I had rebelled against her insistence that we speak in whispers when we were in her apartment. Her fearfulness in that regard seemed to me neurotic and ridiculous; and the fact that it was partly a product of her painful experience during the Cultural Revolution did not make it any easier to deal with. True, she had been traumatized for ten years, as a child and adolescent, by events she had no control over; but America wasn't the People's Republic of China. She was an American citizen now, and a grown-up. In fact, we were both middle-aged, and I was damned if I was going to skulk around outside her building, or be made to whisper inside my own girlfriend's apartment. (Incidentally, she objected to the word "girlfriend"; she preferred "lady friend", which struck me as false-genteel.) Language was always a problem for us. English words didn't—and couldn't be expected to—hold the same connotations for her that they did for Diane; nor was there a fund of common culture for us to draw on. At the beginning, I had thought ("Orientalistically", I'm afraid—*You should be. Be afraid, be very afraid, as you Americans say.*) that her "foreignness" would be a source of excitement and enrichment, pure and simple. And it was both of those things—but they were never pure or simple (except perhaps in bed). When we had to communicate with words, we often weren't on the same page.

Yet she was exquisitely sensitive to the emotional mood, tone and nuance carried by words, if not always to their literal meanings. This sensitivity was one of the things I cherished about her, and for a while it fueled my hope that we might be able to overcome the barriers of culture and language. We spoke the same language of the heart, didn't we? Wasn't that the most important thing? Though here again I was more of a romantic sentimentalist than she. I believed in the transcendent power of love—that true hearts could speak directly to one another. This was how it had been with Diane. Why couldn't I find such an understanding again?

In the end, I think it all came back to language. We don't all need to be Cyrano de Bergerac, or Shakespeare, or Elizabeth Barrett Browning, in the realm of love-letters; but in order to be soul mates, we need to "get" each other. And while not all instances of getting each other require language as the medium (bed, again, is a good example), for the verbally-inclined, there really is no substitute for words. How else but through words to enjoy the common fund of unique memories and experiences, sensibilities and inclinations and inflections, tastes and perceptions, that are the basis of life in the Major Period—anyone's Major Period? The communion of souls relies on words to signal elective affinities: "I love that too! That's just what I was thinking! I used to do the exact same thing!" The occasion of the recognition may be beyond words, rooted in the senses: the shared appreciation of a piece of music, a cloud, a sunset, a landscape, a smell, the taste of a food, the feel of a material, the transport of an orgasm, and its afterglow. But soon enough, the lovers will come back to words—words sublime or ridiculous, and most likely somewhere in between. Diane and I couldn't have been soul mates without our own specialized words—the unique, idiomatic phrases and usages designed to evoke our shared experiences and views. *(You talk about this in the next section too, don't you? Yes I do. Your point? What are you, my editor? Certainly not. I pity the fool, as you Americans say.* And speaking of editing, that line is getting old, Fritz. Give it a rest.) With those words, we built the story of a communion that became the Major Period. And without words—without the right words, anyway (and by "right" I mean words expressive of more than their denotative meaning)—Mei-Li and I could never really discover the language of the heart. I thought we could, but once again I was wrong. I was suffering from the "extra-linguistic fallacy", if you will: the illusion that recognition of the beloved can happen outside of language. Shared experience trumps everything else in the realm of love; but without words to convey the meaning of that experience, how can we even begin to tell the story of our love to one another?

I see now that the fatal flaw of our love, Mei-Li's and mine, was that it had no story. It might have had—but she didn't want it to be told. She didn't want our love to be known by anyone. We made it together, beautifully; and there was some nice talk afterwards. But the talk didn't end up going anywhere. It didn't lead to a story. She didn't want it to—and for characteristic reasons: she wanted to keep it private. She wanted to keep everything between us private.

It always bothered her that I might—and did—write about her. (And I am betraying her again, right now.) Ironically, it was in a personal essay about language—Diane's and mine—that I first wrote about Mei-Li. (This was the essay the journal editor rejected because he thought it was patronizing; and I guess he may have been right. *There ya go!* Just ignore him.) I wrote about the pandas and butterflies that she embroidered, and how they made me feel sorry for her, and were a sign that we didn't, in matters of taste, speak the same language. I said that the language I had spoken with Diane was now dead and gone, and that I was trying to create a new language with Mei-Li. I never showed her this essay (and it was never published—though not for lack of trying!), but I told her enough about it, at her prodding, to hurt her feelings. She wanted to know what it said, so I mentioned the pandas and butterflies.

"I was very young when I did that," she said, with a vulnerable little smile that made me feel even worse.

"I know," I said. "And ... my heart went out to you when I saw them."

"So what else you write about me?" she asked, still with the smile, bracing herself.

Whatever you say, don't hurt her.

"What else?" she prodded.

"Oh, just that ... well, I wrote about language. The language Diane and I spoke together, and the language you and I speak together." I paused. "They're different." Another pause. "Not *bad* different, just different."

She took that in, reading the nuances and overtones, as she did so well. Finally she said, "I know I don't speak correctly." She gave a nervous, fake little laugh.

"No, Mei-Li, that's not—it's not like that at all. You speak fine. You speak 'Mei-Li-ish', and I love it."

"But 'Mei-Li-ish' is not … *professional*." We both laughed. "Mei-Li-ish" was my name for the collection of her unique coinages that I got such a kick out of: "skaajul" for "schedule"; "sisticate" for "sophisticated"; "urally" for "usually" (it took me a while to figure that one out); and the use of "professional" in non-business contexts—such as when she would say, in response to my pants having suddenly fallen down around my ankles while crossing the street, which was happening more and more often as a result of the middle-aged syndrome of my belly getting fatter and my ass getting flatter, "That's not *professional*."

"I know," I said. "That's why I love it." I hoped that would be the end of it, but it wasn't. I could hear the cogs turning in her head. Finally she said, "Why you won't let me see it?"

I sighed. "It's just … I don't want *anybody* to see it."

She thought about this. "Then why you write it? Why you write if you don't want people see it?"

"Some things you just write for yourself," I replied. But she knew this was disingenuous; after all, I had recently published *Failure*, and then a short essay in a literary magazine.

She frowned; perhaps she sensed the lack of candor in my answer. "Why you write about me?"

I sighed again—the defensive, guilty sigh of the prevaricator, the betrayer. And yet I had to speak the truth. "Because you're part of my life—you're a very important part of my life."

"But why you have to write it?"

"I just told you. I write about my life."

She looked away. After a moment, she said, "I don't want you write about me."

I had no answer to that. (I still don't.) One evening a month or two after this, we had more or less the same exchange in bed, after I foolishly, thoughtlessly—in the false security of the afterglow—mentioned the book in manuscript I was working on.

"Please," she said, lifting herself up on one elbow, "I don't want you write about me."

"Mei-Li, we already had this conversation. I can't not write about you. You and Zack are the two most important people in my life. How can I not write about you?"

"Write about Diane, not me."

"But I can't write about Diane without writing about you. You and Diane are the two most important women in my life." I registered the strangeness of the present tense in reference to the dead. I'm pretty sure this nuance was not lost on her, either.

After that, she grew very quiet, and ate hardly anything at dinner. But I, the talker, wasn't about to allow any dead air at the dinner table.

"Mei-Li, when I made the decision to write this book … " I began. "Look, I have to write the best book I can. I have to write the truth, as I see it." *Even if it hurts you*, was the subtext. Unintended—but what did that matter? She might not be a reader, but she was very good at deciphering subtexts. She took it all in, and after a moment, she replied, with a smile (not vulnerable this time, but armed), "Well, I can make a decision, too."

After she left that night, I thought about what she'd said, and when she called two nights later from the airport, on the way to China on a recruiting trip, I sensed it wasn't going to be just the usual goodbye before a trip. There was hesitation, and even a little break in her voice, as she searched for the words.

"I don't … I can't … I won't be able to see you for a while."

She would be away a month, but I knew that wasn't what she meant.

"I see," I said. And then, "I'm sorry."

She made her sound of acknowledgment—like a "Hunh?", but without the question mark.

"I'm sorry," I repeated. "But I understand. I'll miss you."

She made the sound again: "*Hunh.*" *I get it. Me too. That goes without saying. More than words can say.*

But then, I guess, she remembered she was talking to a talker, who expected something more explicit in the way of a statement, so she added, in a whisper, "I'll miss you too."

"I'll talk to you soon, OK?" I said, unable to bear—or even acknowledge— the subtext of that one.

The one feeling I hadn't counted on, I realized after we hung up, was the feeling of relief. (The least admirable, but perhaps most satisfying, of the emotions. And my mother's favorite.) Sadness, culpability, regret—I felt all of those. But also relief. The relief of a burden lifted. Of not having to struggle anymore to figure out what she *really* meant—what the subtext was. The relief of not having to be the talker anymore—of not having my trite, inadequate words thrown back at me by her cryptic silences. No more second-guessing! For seven years I had been covering up my loneliness when I was with her, telling myself I couldn't be lonely because, after all, I wasn't really alone. But what was it, other than loneliness, that I was feeling when she would respond to a piece of music, or a movie, differently than Diane would have? I knew it wasn't fair to compare the two of them, but I couldn't help it. Their differences were so glaring. Diane's emotional responses were quick and deep, and she made no effort to conceal them. Mei-Li's responses, however deeply felt—and her sensitivity told me she felt deeply—were probably not something she'd ever been encouraged to reveal; quite the opposite. This emotional reserve, coupled with the fact that she wasn't a talker, meant that whatever she was feeling was not readily available to others—and not even, maybe, to herself. She kept so much inside, and this made me lonely, too. I could feel the cool air of her independence, her stoicism, her unrelentingly hard work ethic, her exceptional drive—her inability not to be doing, doing, doing all the time, except when we lay in bed together in those precious few minutes of the afterglow. It was, perhaps, this inability not to be doing—not to be working, in one way or another, and her restlessness on those rare occasions when she wasn't—that made me feel most lonely of all.

Her almost constant activity made me feel other things as well: lazy by comparison, unambitious, feckless, weak. I knew she loved me—but this also saddened me, when I considered that she could love me and still allot such a small place for me in her life. Was pleasure so unimportant to her? Her response in bed suggested otherwise. Maybe she was afraid of feeling too much pleasure—afraid of its disruptive effects on her ever-present "skaajul". In trying to explain our differences to my friends, I would often rely on the formula, "I work to live, Mei-Li lives to work." But this platitude ignored the sheer pleasure she found in work—not just a sense of satisfaction or fulfillment, but an almost erotic happiness: work as a life force. In working—and what did she do that wasn't work? The office, travel, hospice, Rotary, honorary dinners (including beefsteak dinners), visits to the UN, and the Chinese and Taiwanese Consulates; her activity was endless—she seemed to be in touch with the vital principle. The opportunity to work, for her, was the greatest of all gifts. I do not doubt that a large part of this was because of the Cultural Revolution, and the hell of meaningless "work"—drills and propaganda, mindless recitation of party slogans and songs—inflicted on her for ten years in that travesty of school. It's no surprise that once she came to the States, work, meaningful work, became the ultimate expression of her new freedom. She'd been starved for it, and couldn't get enough. Freedom as the freedom to work—the formula for the Chinese miracle of the 21st Century. And Mei-Li was ahead of the curve.

After that phone call from the airport in April, she was away in China for a month, and when she got back, I didn't see her for another month—not until my birthday, in early June. We went to a movie in town, and then out for a bite to eat. The movie was Woody Allen's "Midnight in Paris". At various points in the film, when the shots of Paris were especially evocative, I would reach for Mei-Li's hand. She didn't rebuff me, but I could tell she just wasn't that into it. We had talked of going to Paris together—as all couples do, right?—but now I knew for sure this wasn't going to happen. The movie was the closest we'd ever get—and we weren't even experiencing that together. It was over. It would have seemed too harsh not to be together on my birthday; but it was over.

We talked a little about the movie at supper afterwards—or rather I talked, and she listened politely, as always. It was ironic, I said, that the same thing that had made the lovers kindred spirits—their longing to live in a different time—had also pulled them apart. I wondered, as I talked, about the possible parallels to our own situation; but they didn't really hold. Mei-Li wasn't the nostalgic type—the past, for her, was a nightmare from which she had awakened; and my own brand of nostalgia was for the Major Period: my life with Diane. I'd never told Mei-Li this, of course—but I didn't need to. She could pick up on so much that went unsaid. I'm sure that as I was talking on, she too was thinking about us, and about how we were—and weren't—like the lovers in the movie: two people from different worlds, brought together for a time, then separated by their disparate visions of happiness.

At one point in our sad birthday supper—we'd ordered only appetizers, and didn't even finish those—I asked her straight out if my writing about her (or rather, my refusal to promise that I wouldn't write about her) was the main reason she couldn't see me anymore, or if it was something else, something I'd said or done that I wasn't aware of. I don't really know what I was expecting from her at this point; after all, she wasn't given to confessions or psychological analysis. Maybe I just wanted to cover myself—to make sure that the problem wasn't something I didn't already know about; or that I didn't have anything else to feel guilty about, other than my selfishness and insensitivity in making her a subject of my writing in the first place. This bothered me—but not enough to renounce the writing project, or rather her part in it. Was I being disingenuous when I'd told her, in bed, just before she left for China, that this was why people distrusted and disliked writers—because they used others for their writing, even (especially?) those near and dear to them? I didn't *have* to use her, did I? Particularly since I knew it would hurt her if I did. Then again, writers—at least those not on assignment—didn't *have* to tell a certain story, did they? They *chose* to. Which meant they were all bastards, ready to sacrifice anyone for a good story; and I was no worse (and no better) than another.

Her answer to my question about whether the reason for our breakup was my writing about her was straightforward—as straightforward as she ever got, given that there was always something held in reserve, something inaccessible.

"No, just that," she replied softly, with a little smile. The quiet understatement resonated in the ensuing silence. I wondered if she were being ironic, knowing what a big deal my writing about her was to her. I was about to ask her this, then realized I'd probably have to explain what "ironic" meant. She'd understand the concept immediately, of course—so shouldn't I help her expand her English vocabulary, as I had been doing for seven years? No, I shouldn't. I didn't have to do that anymore. I didn't have to do any of it anymore: help her expand her vocabulary, help her with her writing, decipher her meanings, wonder about her silences. All that was over and done with. She'd released me. That was what the relief was all about.

Relief? Bastard again! Was I really so selfish as all that? *Wait a minute, Schatzi. Just a minute.* Who asked you? Let me finish, please. I'm almost done here. *No. Silence, American. This is important. Just listen.*

It's not all about you. It was her idea, after all, not to see you anymore. She made it easy for you. She took matters into her own hands. The doer, not the talker, remember? What if she was getting just a little sick of all that talk (despite what she said in bed)—as tired of the talk as she was uncomprehending of the writing? And what if, because of all this—what if she was feeling relief, too? She would have had every right to. You've been assuming all along that the relief, and everything associated with it, was all on your end: your guilt, your selfishness, your insensitivity. (Your self-centeredness, too.) What about her relief? What about her guilt—the guilt of a married woman, with a daughter, having

a seven-year affair—and the shame that must have gone along with it?
Maybe it wasn't just because of her obsession with privacy (an obsession
understandable, after all, in view of what she'd seen of public exposure
and humiliation during the Cultural Revolution) that she "didn't want
you write about her." Maybe it was also because of her guilt, and her
shame, and her reputation. Reputation? *Yes, Schatzi—reputation. You*
hadn't thought about that, had you? Because for a sophisticated ("sisti-
cated") enlightened Western intellectual like yourself, reputation is a
rather old-fashioned idea. But it's not for most of the world, including
the People's Republic of China. By loving a writer, Mei-Li had put herself
in a vulnerable position; and by ending the affair, she was doing as much
as she could to correct that mistake. She might not be able to stop "you
write about her", but she could stop giving you access. By your own
account, that was something else she was good at. After all, she'd learned
from the best, right?

OK, that's it. I've said my piece. Over to you, as you Ameri—whoops.
Sorry.

Boy, Joßche. You really dropped a bombshell. Kind of hard to take it
all in.

You don't have to. Not right now, anyway. Just file it away for future
reference.

Easier said than done.

Well, moving right along—and speaking of bombs—the birthday dinner, and what followed, was a dud. Despite our two-month separation, and
all the thinking I'd done about why it was probably for the best, I'd also
entertained fantasies about us getting back together for a passionate
reunion—or at least a swan-song. I'd even just changed the sheets on the
Widower's Bed, remembering the time not that long ago when, unable to
maintain an erection (as had been happening more often of late), I'd stopped
trying for the moment, and we'd lain back and had a frank talk about our
differences—in the middle of which I suddenly got hard again, and we made
love intensely. She became almost hysterical with pleasure, whimpering and

crying and gulping. It was the best sex we'd ever had; but I wondered after-wards whether the frenzy hadn't had a note of finality about it.

She took my arm now as we left the restaurant, and I thought that boded well for the rest of the evening—as though the distance that had come between us over the past two months could be undone by a simple warm impulse. We went to the local independent bookstore, where we browsed the art section and she bought a book on tapestries for a friend. But bookstores, I have found from experience, have a dampening effect on love: "our meddling intellect Misshapes the beauteous forms of things". *(Ah yes. Your beloved Wordsworth once again.)* By the time we got back to the house, it was time for her to go. As so often before, Bao was on her way back from the city, and Mei-Li had to go pick her up at the train station. I walked her to the car, parked across the street. Once again, I couldn't bear the subtext of all this. "Let's go to another movie—I'll call you soon," I said reflexively, pretending it was business as usual as she closed the car door. She waggled her fingers good-bye and I blew her a kiss with both hands, as I always did. Then she drove away.

"So Bao wins," I said to myself (and not without a note of ignoble relief) as I walked back up the dark driveway and looked up at the stars, in their constellations of early summer. I thought of Thoreau at Walden Pond. "Lonely?" he asked. "Why should I be lonely? Is not our planet in the Milky Way?"

Nice literary flourish at the end. One of your specialties.

I thought you'd said your piece. Why do I feel like I'm being set up for another sucker-punch?

I don't do sucker-punches. Not my style. I am a scholar, and a gentleman.

Could have fooled me. Cut the bullshit, Fritz. Out with it.

Very well. Since you asked. So, I am troubled by all of this.

The Orientalism? I thought we already went through that.

No, it's more than that. I'm troubled by the fact that the whole account seems so … untroubled (as you yourself said of the Trumpians at the rallies).

Are you kidding? How can you say that?

Because all the back-and-forth with yourself, all the self-flagellation, are just superficial window-dressing, Schatzi. The fact that is so glaring for me in all of this is that you really didn't know her at all. Because you didn't really want *to know her. You just wanted to have your China doll on your display shelf. Behind it all, you are still sitting pretty, and satisfied—self-satisfied—with the fact. You are "all in", as you Amer- I mean, as the saying goes—"all in" for having an "Asian experience", and very pleased with yourself for having had one. You keep comparing your relationships with Mei-Li and Diane, but really there's no comparison at all.*

I never said there was.

But you keep making the comparison! And it's invariably an invidious one.

Then you are willfully misreading what I wrote. And you should be ashamed of yourself, Mr. Literary Biographer. I loved Mei-Li. Maybe not the way I loved Diane—of course not. But I did love her.

I do not doubt it. Yet you betrayed her, too.

I don't have to listen to this crap. You're banned. I hereby ban you.

Mit welchem Recht, Schatzi?

I have every right to ban you. (And aren't you the clever one with the Freud allusion?)

Perhaps you do have the right. You just don't have the ability. But if you're done with Mei-Li now, so am I. Though I'm interested in this question of language, the specialized language of love, that you say you didn't have with Mei-Li—despite certain faulty usages of hers, which you cherished (though in a condescending way)—but that you had with

*Diane. Tell me more about this language—"The Vanished Language",
I believe you call it.*

I'm not telling you anything anymore.

*Ah, so you're sulking. Very well, then. But the reader, Schatzi—the
putative reader, anyway. Tell the putative reader about your language
with Diane. And I'll be quiet. Promise.*

Yeah, right. We know what your promises are worth. Don't believe
him, Putative Reader. I certainly don't.

*The petulant sulker, too. Adding insult to injury, as you would say.
The petulant sulker to the putative reader. Sounds like a postmodern
poem, doesn't it?*

Will you just shut up! See what his promises are worth, Reader? He
is incapable of shutting up for one second! I am so fucking sick of you
and your running commentary. And I'm sure the p.r. is too. If only for
their sake, then, *"stint thy clappe"*, as Chaucer says, and I'll talk a little
about The Vanished Language. Just please vanish yourself while I do.

I knew from the time of our first date—a meeting no longer than an
hour at the English pub in Santa Monica where we'd first met by
chance the week before—that Diane "got" me. She laughed at my
jokes; what more could I ask? That was maybe the basis of the whole
thing, even at the beginning—more than sex, or companionship, or
shared values, or even love: laughter. Her chin lifted up, head tilting
back, mouth open, showing her pretty teeth and gums, ocean-blue
eyes crinkled up—her whole body giving me access through her laughter. *I accept your offering, and here, take this one from me; I give it
to you freely.* "You kept me laughing that first date," she would remind
me from time to time. "Yep, keep 'em laughing—that's my strategy,"
I would tell her. "Well, it worked," she said. "All too well, my dear,"
I replied. "All too well."

For it was a comic posture of mine that I had never intended for us to get married—never planned for things to go that far. The whole situation had simply gotten "out of hand." She was supposed to be a "casual relationship." We both knew, of course, that this would have been impossible; when it came to relationships, I was not the casual type. I was the romantic type. But part of my posture was to go against type—for me to represent our union as some sort of "mistake" that was never meant to take the serious turn that it had. Was this to cover up a sort of embarrassment on my part? But embarrassment at what? That I had fallen so hard, so irrevocably, so permanently for her? (I signed my first Valentine card, less than three weeks after we'd met, "Your permanent date." She liked that. *Yes, we know. You already told us.* So sue me.) That I was (or could be) such a doting husband? *A doting husband who nevertheless betrayed her.* Shit, Joßche. How am I supposed to respond to that? Are you some kind of German sadist or something? Cut me some slack, why don't you? *OK, point taken. I withdraw the comment.* Not the kind of comment you can exactly withdraw. But whatever. Where was I? Oh yeah, the doting husband. And as evidence of this, I had come up with (or "discovered," as I put it), through the years, well over a dozen stupid nicknames for her. "Permangana," "Pergaminer," "Prangana," "Ghilighligh" (pronounced "HIH-lih-lih"), "Vartouche," "Vartuiche," "Var," "Gustalambindt," "Goostie," "Dean," "Dean Witter," "Dean Witter Permangana," "*Deen Wheataire Permangange*" (French variation), "Dungby" (she hated that one, so I rarely used it in front of her. So where would I use it? I would sometimes say it to myself, because I liked the sound of it), "Diane Dungby," "Dean Terningining," "Dean Tingingdingindt." Yeah, they were pretty stupid, all right; the stupider the better. That was the point: How far could I go in the realm of stupidity? How funny was stupid? The character I played in this connection was that of the "Devoted Moron" (this often accompanied by the "stupid face"): he might not know very much, but he knew he loved his Permangana, etc. And she knew it, too. Come to think of it, my aforementioned embarrassment might also have been at the sheer depths of my stupidity. For her benefit, though—only for her benefit. For no one else would have appreciated it or understood it (insofar as it is possible to understand stupidity). But she got my brand of it, anyway—as well she should. It had been created just for her.

Humor was a large part of the special language, now vanished, that we spoke together—a language that is, in its countless inflections, really not special at all, but common to so many couples who have been together for a while. It was a language where much—most—went without saying; though it all could have been explained, if necessary. A language of shared experiences, allusions, sensibilities, opinions, judgments—and above all, humor. Here are a few examples:

- "Not too *maach* . . ." Said in response to the question, "How did you like so-and-so or such-and-such?" The allusion was to the same phrase spoken by Zack's Salvadoran babysitter, Ada, to express non-enjoyment, but in a way so as not to offend. (The recognition, and appreciation, of the desire not to offend was one of the elements of the Vanished Language.)
- "So, what was your favorite part?" Asked of the reaction to an experience (root canal, colonoscopy, boring dinner party) that was horrible, unendurable, excruciating, or otherwise—
- "Hanus." A deliberately misspelled, vast overstatement meaning simply "bad", and carrying no moral burden what-soever, as in "a hanus fart," "a hanus perpetration" (see previous; also used in reference to action or discourse), "a hanus individual" (someone clueless, tasteless, boring, conceited—in other words, a perpetrator of "hanus discourse"). It was very important that the epithet be used only in trivial or foolish instances, the application of the word at such times itself constituting an instance of triviality, fool-ishness, or hanus discourse.

- "Don't say something." First coined by Zack as a toddler, when he had committed a hanus perpetration into his diaper, but did not wish to have this brought to his (or anyone else's) attention. The phrase was later sung by Diane (but never in front of Zack) to the tune of "Don't Say Nothin' Bad about My Baby," with "poo-poo" substituted for "baby."
- "I don't like this part." Said by me when Diane, in bed, would put her cold feet on my warm ones. The first time I said this it produced hilarious laughter, though neither of us could say exactly why it was funny.

There were also nonverbal expressions of the Vanished Language, such as:

- Head back, mouth open, eyes rolled back in head, denoting hanus boredom and tediousness. What was alluded to was my once walking into my parents' living room and seeing my aged grandmother Dodo thus sacked-out. I thought she was dead.
- Various elaborate and totally unnecessary flourishes on my part when serving dinner or tea, accompanied by feet at right angles, arm behind back, in absurd imitation of a French waiter. (Cf. also the description of Uncle Toby reading aloud in *Tristram Shandy*.)
- Myself bent over forward, arms extended straight out in back, as high as possible, in order to kiss Diane. This was the same posture I adopted in childhood in order to make our Welsh Corgi, Kipper, howl with joy in anticipation of being taken out for a walk. (Why this stance should have been taken in that particular circumstance I have absolutely no idea.) The position was now assumed when I was feeling especially affectionate toward Diane. I have no idea,

either, why I did this, except that it made her laugh because she recognized it was associated with Kipper. (Was she in some way my new Kipper? Let's not go there. *No, let's not.*) Once when I did it, not long before she died, she said, "God, I love you so much," and I asked, sincerely, "Why?"

Speaking of death, there was also the Cancer Tree. In the last year of her life, after the cancer had returned and spread into her abdomen and was inoperable, she was often exhausted. She would lie down on the sofa in the living room and gaze out the window at a sycamore in the front yard. I named it the Cancer Tree, and would sometimes recite a short narrative in the third person, to wit: "She would often lie on the sofa and gaze at a sycamore tree, which became known as the 'Cancer Tree.'" (This is a good—that is, really bad—example of the inappropriately bluff, ironic manner that was apparently the only way I thought I could deal with her terminal status. *Yes. See my comments above on your "overwriting" of Diane's possible feelings in the hospital and hospice care center.* So noted.) She smiled once or twice at this, even though it wasn't funny. In fact, it was incredibly stupid and cruel. Dr. Davis, my psychiatrist, once remarked that it was my way of dealing with my fear and anger at an unbearably painful situation. But I think he was cutting me too much slack; it was just incredibly stupid and cruel. (*I agree with you.* Thanks. I guess. But please stop interrupting.)

The currency of our shared language also made us sensitive, in various particular ways, to the languages of others, whose idioms contrasted with our own. Certain phrases in their alien tongues were dead giveaways—a sure sign of hanus discourse being perpetrated. E.g., when my old college roommate Jerry, now a lawyer, who'd just bought a house in the housing boom of the mid-'80s, explained to us that he "couldn't afford not to." E.g., when Diane's mild-mannered stepbrother-in-law Herbie, responding to my statement that I hated the smug, self-satisfied, cynical podiatrist husband of his wife's best friend, observed, "Hate's a pretty strong word, Josh."

"You're right, Herbie," I replied. "Let me rephrase that. I *utterly detest* him." E.g., we would never have been caught dead wishing that someone "have a nice day." E.g., we could both appreciate the humor—loathe the individual but appreciate the humor—of the swinish undergraduate who once stole my spot in the UCLA bookstore parking lot and, when I remonstrated with him, answered, without a moment's hesitation, "Who are you, Jesus Christ or something? Eat my shorts!" The expression instantly entered our vocabulary, to denote utter dismissal and contempt, as when Diane said of the passage of the Patriot Act, many years later, "Bush just told the Constitution to eat his shorts."

Such were a few of the elements of our private language, implicitly understood and now no longer spoken. A dead language, like the Greek, Latin, and Sanskrit I had studied in college. Even more dead, actually, because those languages are preserved in writing, whereas our special language, since it was never written and often went unspoken, has now vanished, along with the shared life that it served to express. The people who spoke it are both gone: she literally, I in a manner of speaking. Part of me died with her; and the part that survived talked to himself in this language all through the Minor Period. It was a way to fill the silence, and even put a humorous inflection on it. I like to think the talking to myself was done not only humorously but self-knowingly as well—often with Debbie, Diane's stuffed frog, as its audience. The absurdity of talking to a piece of cloth (shades of Tom Hanks talking to the volleyball "Wilson" in *Cast Away*) was not lost on me; indeed, it was this absurdity that my posture of humorous self-consciousness aimed at registering. And the analogy to *Cast Away* is perhaps not an idle one; for I somehow survived the plane crash of Diane's death and lived on, basically alone, through the thirteen years of the Minor Period, on the desert isle of what I also called The Afterlife.

I now have Julie, and we are developing a new language together. One of our primary idiolectic phrases is *"pas ça,"* denoting the utter rejection, by an arrogant, rigid, dogmatic French person, of an action or idea considered, in the definitive and magisterial French manner, totally unacceptable and out of bounds. But the Julistic language—the language of the Julistic Period—is not really a replacement or substitute for the Vanished Language I spoke with Diane. There can be no replacement for that; it is the dead tongue of our love. Yet it is not entirely lost, either, for the memory of it remains. But since it will never be spoken again, it lies dormant, and will eventually become extinct. I recall it now as we recall the dead we have loved: with sweetness and pain, and with a knowledge of the irretrievability of the past—people, places, and things that we continue to love, and whose presence we continue to feel (though we know better), like the sensation of a phantom limb after amputation.

PART III

PART III

While the Vanished Language—the language of the Major Period—lived on through the Minor Period, and its memory still survives, the dreams of the Minor Period have disappeared. They possessed a distinct quality and atmosphere that have proven almost impossible to recover, even through language—though that will not keep me now from trying to pay them a kind of homage.

The chief qualities of the dreams of the Minor Period can be broken down into three elements: (1) The "Background Emanations": the subconscious knowledge, in the dreams, that Diane is dead, and that the dream is taking place in the wake of her death, which permeates the background atmosphere of the dream. The BEs, you could say, are the form that my awareness of being in the Minor Period takes in the dream; (2) Diane's peculiar ontological status in the dreams. She is both dead and yet "back on loan" to the land of the living—but only for the duration of the dream. Though sometimes it emerges that she was never really dead at all, but only in a condition of suspended animation that just seemed like death. And sometimes it even transpires that she has been neither dead nor in suspended animation, but simply living in another city, where she has relocated and begun another life, following my betrayal of her with Cindy (the old girlfriend I had an online affair with on and off during the last four years of Diane's life—*You've told us this several times already. Can you spell "inexpungible guilt"?*); and (3) Certain features of the dream landscapes. I mean the last phrase literally: the physical settings of the dreams. But these three qualities, as they appear in the dreams—the Background Emanations, Diane's ontological status, and the dream landscapes—are really inseparable. The landscapes of the dreams are part of the Background Emanations, and the latter also inform, and are informed by, Diane's absent presence—that is, the presence of her absence—which permeates the entire dreamwork. (If you will forgive the Freudian term. He has fallen out of favor these days. But though he is not one of my Masters—despite his literary excellence; he received the Goethe Prize, the highest German literary award—I certainly am no Freud-basher. *Neither am I, by the way. Freud was a great admirer of Nietzsche, you know.* Yes I know. Please let me continue.) The three elements of the dreamwork that I have somewhat artificially isolated here really all go—or rather went—together to make up the unique atmosphere of the dreams of the Minor Period. I never have those kinds of dreams anymore. As I say, we are in the Julistic Period now; but, like the Vanished Language I spoke with Diane, the memory of the dreams of the Minor Period is all the more precious now for their having gone completely out of currency.

There were several houses that figured in the dreams of the Minor Period: both houses we lived in and houses we didn't. The houses we didn't live in were sometimes places I had lived in before I knew Diane, or even houses I'd never seen before. But usually they were familiar, or familiar variants of places I'd lived in at one time or another. And sometimes—rarely, but sometimes—she was living there with me. These dreams constituted a particular treat, but of a rather sickening sort (as when you eat too much of a favorite dessert). Although it gave me pleasure to have her with me again, the Background Emanations of the dream—that subconscious, ambient awareness that did not leave me, even in dreams—told me that she wasn't really with me, that she was dead. Sometimes the Background Emanations came to the fore, and became conscious: she reminded me—though I didn't really need to be reminded—that she had to go away soon, that she was only here on leave, as it were. This information was transmitted and accepted matter-of-factly; I well knew the deal that lay behind these "leaves." She would spend a little time with me, with us (during the Minor Period, Zack was between the ages of seventeen and thirty, but in my dreams he was always a child), and then she had to go back to where she came from. Wherever that was. We never talked about this place, just as one never talks about certain things in polite company. Was that what we were now in my dreams—polite company? In a way, yes. There was a gulf between us. Her manner was changed since her death: her humor wryer, her seriousness deeper, her affection—I wish I could call it love, but it did not seem like love in the dreams; it seemed only a pale reflection of love—somewhat aloof, tempered with the knowledge and experience she brought with her from The Great Beyond. And I did not blame her for this; for I knew that the "dream Diane" who was with me now was only a temporary visitor, a stand-in for the real, the cherished, the irreplaceable Diane, who was irrevocably not with me in my waking hours. (Diane's father used to say, "Nothing is irrevocable." *Isn't it pretty to think so?*) In some ways, it was sadder to have her with me in my dreams than not with me the rest of the time.

The primary reason for her emotional distance in these dreams was, of course, my betrayal of her with Cindy. She found out about the affair soon after it began; it was my altered sexual state that she noticed. She asked me who it was, and I told her. "You betrayed me," she said, somewhat incredulously, yet still with that level-eyed, direct look she had. She asked me repeatedly to stop communicating with Cindy, and told me she was going to say something to her if I didn't. In the event, though, she didn't say anything—but I didn't fully stop messaging Cindy, either, until after Diane died. No doubt it was Diane's full knowledge of the affair, and the hurt caused by it, and my guilt, that were the sources of her emotional distance in my dreams.

Her distance and sadness bled over into the dream landscapes, too—into the many houses and apartments we did and didn't live in together over the years: the apartment on Sweetzer Ave. in West Hollywood; the top floor of the house on Winona, in East Hollywood, where we were living when Zack was born, and for the first seven years of his life; my parents' house in Pacific Palisades, where I grew up, and which

was our second home until we moved east; the two houses we rented in
Worcester, MA, where I got my first full-time teaching job; and the house
we rented on Long Island, where she died. All of these houses appeared
in my dreams, both with and without Diane. But even if she wasn't with
me, her Background Emanations were. And there were other
dream-houses, too, which never actually existed, where she made appear-
ances: a multistoried house of many nooks and crannies in Berkeley
(based no doubt on the house I lived in with Jerry, Jon and Howard
sophomore year); a rambling, single-story ranch house next to a field or
golf course (or both—you know how dreams are), again in Worcester; a
palatial modern villa, narrow and tall, with many narrow staircases, in
the South of France (based, again, on a house I had lived in with my
parents for a couple of months in the fall of 1964). Diane's presence and
absence were felt in all these houses. If some of them were fictional places,
unlived-in and nonexistent during our life together, they were still familiar, already well known in the dream, and part of our dream-life together;
so that it required some effort on my part, when I woke up, to be certain
that these make-believe houses were figments of my imagination.

I say "our" dream-life, but another Background Emanation of these
dreams was the subconscious awareness that it was not "our life" at
all—that this was a dream product of the "post-Diane" period of my life,
a time degraded, pale, stitched together. A poor, worn-out thing of
patches and tatters. There was sometimes a hope, in the dream—or rather
a half-hope, lifting its head from behind the BEs—that this might not be
the case; that my life might still be in its Diane, or pre-Diane phase; that
she might still be bidding fair to appear on the horizon. (This "horizon
of expectations," as it were, did a kind of battle with the BEs in my
dreams: the former offering hope that the latter might not, after all, turn
out to be the case. But it was a hope always lost upon awakening.)

While these landscapes and houses were drawn from a number of
places in my life, both with and without Diane, the most insistent locale
was Los Angeles, and the house on Winona in East Hollywood. The BEs

were strongest here—no doubt because this was the house where we were living when we got married, and when Zack was born, and for almost seven years after that, until we moved east. The emanations were so strong, in fact, that in my dreams they spilled out of the house and onto the streets around the house: Winona Blvd., Hollywood Blvd., Sunset Blvd., Normandie Ave., Vermont Ave. In my dreams, I went driving down these streets alone, always alone—and never toward home, always away. Sometimes I was driving to USC, where I went to graduate school for eight years (also during the time we were living on Winona). But just as often I was driving to UCLA, where I had taken extension classes in philosophy before going to graduate school in English, and whose vast campus I always ended up, in the dreams, getting lost in, and so missing class (which put me even farther behind than I already was; for it was, and still is, a feature of my "school" dreams to always be behind, *way* behind, in my homework). Or I was driving to some destination in Worcester, or Berkeley, or Long Island. But it was always away from home that I was driving, traversing wide spaces that only seemed to expand as I went. This of course is characteristic of driving in LA, and so in my dreams they did not surprise me, those vast expanding stretches. But I cannot say they made me happy, either. Their Background Emanations, over the endless, wide boulevards and freeways, were not of the happy sort.

They held a feeling very much of their time, these spaces, streets, and houses—or rather, their emanations did: that time being the Minor Period. And always, in the dreams, I was in the Minor Period, and my dreams were permeated with the BE of having lost Diane, of not having her anymore in the world. It was an emanation that pervaded the houses, streets, and landscapes of the dreams. Distances were huge, and traversable only with great effort. But no, that is not quite right; they were not really traversable at all. The expanses of the city—most often LA, but sometimes Worcester (what an odd juxtaposition!)—extended endlessly in all directions. I would make a start at traversing them, on my way to I knew not where. But the start, no matter how far I traveled and how long, remained only a start—if even that. Sometimes I went backward, the distance increased, I fell farther and farther behind, and it got later and later. Diane, perhaps, was somewhere in that vast distance, just over the horizon. The hope, anyway, was that she was there; though the BEs told me otherwise. But it was too late now to go home, and I couldn't have found my way in any case. I had no choice but to continue on my mysterious journey, over streets I used to know so well, but which now seemed weirdly altered, in the manner of dreams; continuing across the vast distances of cities that were so familiar, yet utterly strange without her.

I remember many years ago, when Zack was five or six years old, and we were driving home from a Fourth of July party in the hills above Trancas Beach (just north of Malibu), we got stuck in a terrible traffic jam on Pacific Coast Highway. Traffic jams were a matter of course on PCH every Fourth of July, but this one was especially bad. We were stopped cold for at least an hour, and then merely inching along, stop and go, for what seemed like another two. Finally we came alongside the scene of the accident—or what had been the accident. The wrecked cars had all been cleared away, and there were only burnt-out flares and glass and plastic shards littering the shoulder.

"Goddammit," I complained, in mock petulance. "I'm pissed. I wanted to see some bloody stumps. We waited long enough. The least we could get for our trouble is some bloody stumps."

Diane shook her head in dismay, but Zack exploded in laughter, and that was enough for me. (For years after, "bloody stumps" was a catch-phrase between us.)

"Some model you are," Diane said.

"Come on, Diane," I said. "Didn't a tiny part of you want to see some bloody stumps too?"

"*No,*" she replied.

"Well, you're a better man than I."

There was never any question of that. Diane would occasionally laugh at my sick jokes, but she was not one to make them herself. She lacked that inner hostility, or insecurity, or aggressive edge, or whatever it is that prompts the display of sadistic humor. Maybe it's a male thing. Certainly, women can be as cruel in their way as men, but the telling of sick jokes is not something I have ever known a woman to indulge in. Sick jokes seem to be the province of males. Women simply don't need, or have any interest in, the sort of dubious recognition that redounds to the sick-joke-teller. Or maybe it's just an immaturity thing. (Which is also, I think, a largely male affliction.) I don't know. I do know, though, that given the "right" circumstances—alcohol, strictly male company, and the inflated sense of jocular bonhomie that tends to go along with these things—it is very hard for me to resist the urge to tell a sick or off-color joke, or to venture an uncomfortable admission. *(You can say that again!)*

Not long ago I was talking to a friend who'd just attended a gay wedding. I allowed as I was 99 percent in favor of gay marriage.

"And the other 1 percent?"

I didn't know how to reply, so I adverted to the 1 percent of me (OK, maybe it is a little more than 1 percent; actually, it almost certainly is, but for ease of reference, I'll just call it my 1 percent) that is constitutionally troublesome, perverse, politically incorrect. This is the same 1 percent that had not wanted to see *Brokeback Mountain*—though when I finally did, I was moved. Ninety-nine percent of me was, anyway. The gay sex parts made me uncomfortable, but I dealt with them—in my immature male way—by averting my eyes.

My 1 percent bothers me. It also slightly pleases, entertains, and confuses me. Could it be that this 1 percent is in some way analogous to the economic 1 percent of Americans that the rest of us hate, resent, and secretly—or not so secretly—wish to emulate? At any rate, it is a 1 percent that I am loath to dispose of entirely—even if I could, which I probably can't.

And in this, perhaps, lies the analogy with the economic 1 percent of our country. For they have done horrible things—they must have; some horrible things, anyway—to get where they are today. And my 1 percent, too, has done some horrible things (see *passim*), and is capable of doing more. But it is not to my purpose right now to confess any more of those particular things. I want to talk, instead, about the horrible sympathies I may—no, *do*—harbor in regard to that particularly egregious member of the economic 1 percent who is still afflicting us, and—barring some providential act of God—will probably continue to do so for some time yet. I speak, of course, of Trump. My 1 percent, you see, sort of likes The Donald. It gets a kick out of him. It enjoys reading and hearing about him, and watching him on TV. Like most of us, I cannot get enough of him. Although I have also—again, like most of us—had altogether too much of him; and although he, and his treasonous deeds, and his racist politics, and his hateful values, and his wicked intentions, and his profound personal vulgarity, and everything he stands for and elicits in his supporters, make me sick to my stomach—I still cannot get enough of him. The *Schadenfreude* part of me, the bloody-stumps part, the sick-jokes part, the gay-guys-kissing-makes-me-uncomfortable-but-I-am-sort-of-intrigued-in-spite-of-myself part (are these all different parts or parts of the same part?) likes Trump.

Even now, after the horrendous (and horrendously lowbrow) debacle of Jan. 6, and the plot to destroy democracy and make your country a dictatorship? Can you still say now that even 1 percent of you "likes him"? Really?

OK. It's a serious question and deserves a serious answer. So maybe "likes" was too strong a word. But can I really think of another way to put the feeling that my 1 percent has for him, even after Jan. 6? I have dreamt of him, and in my dreams, we were sort of buddies. I mean, I didn't hate him in my dreams, as my waking 99 percent does; in my dreams, he sort of knew me, or at least acknowledged me, in a vague, dreamy sort of way. So I guess I don't really know how to put into words that deplorable 1 percent that includes my positive feeling for him. It seems mincing words to use any other descriptor than "like." I mean, I can feel his appeal; I can see how much others love him—it's obvious that they do, that millions and millions of people love him—and I even kind of get that perversity of emotion. No, not perversity, *perversion*—it's a *perversion* of emotion to love Trump. But it's real. About 30 percent of the voters in America, maybe more, really love him, and I can understand that, because 1 percent of me sort of likes him. So there you are. I hate the tiny part of me that likes him—but it still does. Even now, after all that has come to pass, after all the damage he has done, and the very worst aspects of America and Americans that he represents—even now, I cannot say that he is completely without appeal to a tiny part of me. In the parlance of the day, it is what it is, that deplorable part of me, and will not be denied.

Could it be that it is the objectionable—nay, deplorable—Old White Man part of me that responds to the deplorable—nay, execrable—Old White Man who is Trump? That it is the Old White Man parts of both of us that are in secret and shameful communion? To wit, the part of me that responded with reluctant amusement at his retort to Hillary's remark, in the 2016 debate, "If you were president, we'd all be in trouble," with "If I were president, you'd be in jail"? I mean, rack one up for The Donald, in spite of myself. And this was perhaps the same part of me that registered, with frank amusement, in the early '70s, the following dinner-table dialogue between my friend Steve Walker and his ultra-conservative father Charles "Chaz" Walker (who definitely would have been a Trumpian if he'd lived another twenty years; he died in the '90s):

Chaz: Steve, it's time you got a haircut.

Steve: But Dad, my hair is a reflection of my personal feelings.
Chaz: Well then, Steve, you must feel pretty bad.

Badda bing. Rack one up for the Chazster.

Earlier I mentioned *Schadenfreude*, but it is not exactly that, my 1 percent; well, maybe it is, but I like to think it is a little more philosophical, at least, than the garden variety *Schadenfreude*. Susan Sontag, in *Regarding the Pain of Others*, writes: " … There exists an innate tropism toward the gruesome" (p. 97), and adverts to Plato's *Republic, Book IV*, where "Socrates describes how our reason may be overwhelmed by an unworthy desire, which drives the self to become angry with a part of its nature" (p. 96). Sontag says that "when discussing the effect of atrocity … the undertow of this despised impulse must also be taken into account" (p. 97). Sing it, Susan. My own despised impulse is certainly aware of its horribleness—aware that the curious pleasure it derives from the spectacle of our country's worst side coming out (the antithetical counterpart to the country's best side, which emerged in the election of 2008) is also a poor reflection on itself. I am demeaned in my own eyes by the twinge of pleasure I get in seeing disgraceful things acted out on the national stage. There are, in my attitude, both a feeling of superiority and a recognition of the spuriousness of that feeling. It's the kind of feeling that instantly self-destructs as soon as it becomes aware of itself, like the desktop items in the "El Capitan" update of Mac OS X I used to have that self-imploded in a puff of smoke when they were deleted. To put it in even more graphic terms (which reflect the rank unsavoriness of the whole affair): in slightly—ever so slightly—enjoying the spectacle of Trump and Trumpism, I am having my cake and eating it too, then vomiting it up—and then eating that, too.

I admit that was in poor taste. *(It certainly was. Pun intended?)* Then again, my 1 percent is in very poor taste. It knows no shame. (And it knows this, too.) It wishes to expel itself from my body so that I can be pure. This is what I call the St. John Reflex (or Reflux): "So then because thou art lukewarm, and neither cold nor hot, I will spue thee out of my mouth." Just like the St. John Reflex/ux, my horrible 1 percent—the part that is not even lukewarm, but actually even kind of warm, toward Trump—seeks to expel itself for the greater good of the organism. The toxin must be evacuated. Let it out, then. Spue thee forth, baby.

I will also admit, in addition to having a certain taste for my own vomit (figuratively speaking), to having a partial (also 1 percent?) sympathy for the devil. The devil we love to hate. This is about how I also love the part of myself that I hate. But maybe love is also too strong a word. Sympathetically recognize, then. I sympathetically recognize the part of myself that I hate. The part that gets a charge out of Trump, and likes the taste of its own vomit.

The Bloody-Stumps Phenomenon often carries with it, as a sort of deplorable fellow traveler, the feeling expressed by the saying, "There but for the grace of God go I." The feeling of deep, expiatory relief. An ignoble feeling, to be sure—but no less welcome for all that. For who does not welcome the feeling of relief? (My mother used to say that relief is the sweetest of the emotions: physical relief, emotional relief, and—remembering her Scranton Catholic girlhood, no doubt, and the feeling she would get as she exited the confessional—spiritual relief as well.) The combination of the Bloody-Stumps Phenomenon and the "There-but-for-the-grace-of-God-go-I Feeling" can be expressed as the Lucretius Effect. Here is the beginning of Book Two of *De Rerum Natura*:

> Sweet it is, when on the great sea, the winds trouble the waters,
> to gaze from shore upon another's great tribulation:
> Not because any man's troubles are a delectable joy,
> but because to perceive what ills you are free from yourself is sweet.

It has always interested me to observe the Lucretius Effect in myself and others. And it makes me wonder: Why should our awareness of another person's suffering produce mixed feelings in us—and even a kind of pleasure (what Lucretius, in the spirit of Hildegarde Therese Colligan Gidding exiting the confessional, calls "sweetness")? Is this "sweetness," as Lucretius describes it, any different from *Schadenfreude*? I think it is. For one thing, it is less sadistic, and more philosophical. (Lucretius, after all, was an Epicurean.) And a philosopher might say that the Lucretius Effect raises the question, What is the proper attitude to another's suffering? Sontag's book explores just this question, and her answer (greatly simplified) is remembrance. The first part of a proper attitude to another's suffering is not to forget:

> Let the atrocious images haunt us. Even if they are only tokens, and cannot possibly encompass most of the reality to which they refer, they still perform a vital function. The images say: This is what human beings are capable of doing—may volunteer to do, enthusiastically, self-righteously. Don't forget. [p. 115]

Maybe, though—to return for a moment, like a dog, to my own vomit—it isn't so much a question of liking its taste as of just recognizing and registering it. Recognizing it as something familiar, an inalienable part of me. The "gawker's block" part of me. The part that recognizes, while I am doing it too, how awful it is that people slow down as they pass the scene of an accident—not so much on the off-chance of seeing some bloody stumps as just of seeing *something*. Something *exciting*. Something even remotely suggestive of the possibility, the distant but distinct possibility, of bloody stumps.

But wait a minute. What am I saying, the *possibility* of bloody stumps? Bloody stumps have already happened! Regularly and repeatedly! They are an actuality. Trump was president for four years—and wants to be president again, even after he was voted out of office and then committed treason. Haven't I had enough? I don't need to imagine the grotesque details of this particular accident; they have already been fulsomely acted out on the national and world stages, over and over again. What more can my 1 percent possibly want? The presidency of Trump was a catastrophe of global proportions, and may very well be again. It was a massive international car accident, with millions of virtual bloody stumps on display. (And, behind that virtual display, the hard reality of millions of suffering human beings, in all manner of agony.) Surely I cannot condone this. Surely I cannot get any kind of pleasure—any kind of Lucretian "sweetness"—from the contemplation of such a scenario.

But it's not really a question of my condoning the Bloody Stumps Phenomenon. It's more a question of recognizing my passive complicity in it. ("Silence Is Complicity", said the signs at the BLM marches.) In being a mere spectator at the multiple car-wreck of Trumpism, I am in some way contributing to it. (Lucretius Effect, meet the St. John Reflex/ux.) According to this analysis, the Lucretius Effect becomes not just a notional observation, but an immoral action. A "sin of omission," as the Catholics say. By not doing anything good, you are effectively doing something bad. The "If-You're-Not-Part-of-the-Solution-You're-Part-of-the-Problem Syndrome".

Lots of syndromes and effects and reflexes (and refluxes) here, Schatzi. I know. But you see, it's all part of the horribleness. And in the spirit of reflux, let us ruminate a little on this horribleness. Let us anatomize it. Because that is, after all, what I do. I anatomize horrible things in order to note the lineaments and understand the fundamentals of the horribleness. And isn't it horrible to be curious, in a kind of detached, "objective" way, about the suffering of another human being? (*And isn't it horrible to think so?* Cute, Joßche.) Granted, I never actually saw any bloody stumps that time on PCH, and I'm honestly not 100% sure what my reaction would have been if I had. Because didn't 1 percent of me sort of want to see bloody stumps, at least in an abstract way? And if I had in fact seen them—if I had been present at the time of the accident, or right after, when the bloody stumps were actually in evidence—what would have been my honest reaction? Would my response have been one of unadulterated (100 percent) horror, sympathy, and empathy? Or would it perhaps have been a response of *adulterated* horror? That is to say, 99 percent (or less) horror/sympathy/empathy, and 1 percent (or more) something else. Let us say, curiosity? (*I strongly advise cutting the last few sentences here. They make you look like a monster.* Objection noted, and overruled. STET. The point here is to confess to the very worst I have thought and felt. I think Matthew Arnold would understand. At least I hope he would. All of us have a tiny bit of monster inside. And Trump has more than that.)

The possibility of adulteration—the Adulteration Factor—brings us to the Problem of Complicity. (*All this labelling is becoming tedious. You've made your point. Must you persist in this?* Reader, I ask you to bear with me and ignore him.) Because if one's horror is adulterated—and I submit that in some people, such as myself, one's horror at real-life nightmares is always adulterated (if only by 1 percent)—then one is implicated in that horror in a kind of complicit way, if not exactly as a cause of that horror (which would put one in a totally different category: that of the perpetrator, which doesn't concern me here), then at least as a kind of effect, a sort of by-product of that horror. The effect of being a mere *observer* of the horror. (The effect, in fact, of being the Observer—the Mere Observer.) And it is the moral status of the Mere Observer of real-life horror that interests me here. (Indeed, one could even say I am *curious* about it.) I mean, if one is doing nothing concrete or in any way useful to palliate or alleviate the effects of the horror, then it seems to me that one is somehow (say 1 percent, even) culpable in the enactment of the horror. (*The horror! The horror! Of his prolixity, that is.* Shut up.)

I am not a professional ethicist—hell, I wasn't even a philosophy major (though I did take a number of extension philosophy courses at UCLA, over thirty years ago, when I was working in the film business and feeling the existential emptiness of that endeavor, so I tried to fill the emptiness with philosophy; does that count?)—and so I realize I may be totally out of my depth here. Then again, it is important, sometimes—and even sometimes good—to be out of your depth. It is important, sometimes, to not really know what you are talking about (*as you don't, right now)*. Because sometimes, when you don't really know what you are talking about, you can learn things you wouldn't otherwise.

Take the figure of being out of your depth. Being out of your depth makes you aware of the unknown, perhaps profound, depth of the water, and the strange and awful (in both senses) and frightening and possibly wondrous creatures that may lurk in those depths. I sometimes have bad dreams about this, and on occasion have experienced it in real life, too. For example, whenever I go swimming at an ocean beach and find myself over my head in the water, I get thoughts of what may lurk below me. Those thoughts are scary and creepy. Yet I am also inexplicably drawn to water over my head, just as I am drawn to ideas I don't quite understand—and, in a different way, to bloody stumps.

Another way of putting it would be to say that we are all, in a sense, present at the gladiatorial contest. We are all spectators at the spectacle—the unseemly spectacle, the violent spectacle, the spectacle of suffering—that is the modern world, and the perpetual news cycle that conveys a part of it. We all experience, to a greater or lesser degree, the Gladiatorial Desire. *(Of course. What else? Never enough just to note something in passing, without you must reify it, capitalize it into a separate entity.* Right you are—and you yourself are one of those entities. Reader, I give you The Joßche Effect. Now please just ignore it.) The Gladiatorial Desire complicates the Lucretius Effect by showing us that our response to suffering can be both passive and sympathetic, yet at the same time complicit and even perhaps sort of active, in the sense that we are (if only in 1 percent of ourselves) cheering on the suffering, and the person who is causing it, while simultaneously deluding ourselves into thinking that we are only passive and sympathetic observers. Because no one—at least, no one who has come of age—is ever really innocent again; no one is blameless; and in our quest for innocence and blamelessness, we delude ourselves.

So what am I going to do about all of this? What *can* I do about it—the Gladiatorial Desire, and the Lucretius Effect, and the Bloody

Stumps Phenomenon, and the St. John Reflex/ux? Besides noting them, that is. Because obviously, noting them isn't helping the people who are suffering in the world—who are, you might say, their victims—other than to let them know they are not alone, and that there are probably millions of people worldwide feeling the same things, experiencing the same guilt of passive onlooking.

But so what? To note something is certainly not the same as doing something about it. And suffering is something you need to do something about. So what, again, are you going to do about it?

I'm going to write about it. What else would you expect Old White Man Writing to do?

I was once remonstrating with my father about not keeping to his heart-healthy diet. "Gog," I said—using the infantile moniker I'd called him by since babyhood—"what's more important than your health?" "My *convenience*," he shot right back. I had no reply to that at the time, and I still don't. But now, it's for a different reason. I can't reply to it now because—well, not only because he is dead, but also because I recognize in his response a cognate of my own passivity, my own laziness and acquiescence. My convenience—here, the convenience of doing absolutely nothing about the pain of others except writing about my awareness of it—is more important than the satisfaction of my conscience, for a couple of reasons. First, because it would take effort, real effort—hard thought, serious planning, and then action in the world—to satisfy my conscience; and it is more convenient for me not to make that effort. And second, because if my conscience were satisfied, then what would I have to write about? An uneasy conscience fuels my need to write, and also forms a large part of my subject matter. This is the double dilemma of the OWMW. Words take the place of deeds. And thank God for that. Because if they didn't, I would have to act. *That was Hamlet's dilemma, too. But Senator, you are no Hamlet.* Hahaha. I'll give you that one too, Joßche.

Reader, I oppose myself. The Opposing Self. (Which is the title of a collection of essays by Lionel Trilling, another one of my masters, as I believe I noted earlier. *Yes you did.*) I always have opposed myself, and I probably always will. The part of my conscience that won't let me rest because I am not doing anything proactive to alleviate the pain of others is the same part that is suffering itself. Granted, it is suffering of a candy-ass, privileged, white, Pacific Palisades sort that we are talking about here, and so almost disqualified, by definition—and contemporary popular consensus—from being considered real suffering. And the knowledge of this—of my suffering's essentially spurious and inauthentic nature—makes me suffer all the more. Furthermore, it is precisely because it is me that is suffering that I cannot help myself. I don't know how to help myself. I never learned. I was too busy feeling guilty about not helping others. So busy that I didn't realize *I* was the guy in the storm at sea.

Excuse me, but are we ever going to get back to the purported subject of your own whiteness, and the guilt attached thereto? Just checking.

Funny you should mention that. Yes, as a matter of fact, we are. Right now. And in connection with a rather important incident.

Oh no. Not another one.

Oh yes. Nineteen years ago, I went on my first sabbatical. I was privileged enough to be able to take a whole academic year—which, including the summers on either end, amounted to fifteen months of paid time off. For two of those months, Zack and I went to France. (Diane had died the year before. The original plan had been for the three of us to go to France together, but that didn't happen.) In a shop in Cannes I purchased—over Zack's objections—a bright-yellow mug: that rich, marigold shade of deep yellow that is so characteristically French, associated with the awnings of outdoor cafés, and the triangular, hard-plastic ashtrays that are sometimes laid out on the tables (or used to be, before smoking became a capital crime). The mug was emblazoned with the logo of the Banania hot chocolate company: the smiling face of a colonial Senegalese infantryman sporting a red fez, along with the slogan *"Y'a bon!"* (which can be loosely—but just as vilely—translated as "Dat's real good!"). Outrageously racist, and therefore—to my mind, at least—representing opportunities for ironic and campy exploitation back in the States. It may also have been, in retrospect, a shrewd investment. Journalist and author Darryl Pinckney, in a recent issue of *Salmagundi* (Nos. 206-207, Spring-Summer 2020), comments on the hot market for racist memorabilia—presumably driven by ironists like myself:

> Everyone's into it now. All these Venetian lamps that people used to be ashamed of have come down out of the attic. You can't get anything for a bargain anymore if it's Black representation. It's true! You used to be able to pick up this stuff at auctions. And you can't anymore because everyone's into it.

I brought the mug home and would on occasion (when Zack was away at college) produce it for my friends, facetiously explicating its appeal. The good-humored Black face, you see, was there to reassure us white people that all was well. No one was hurt or angry; no one harbored any grudges; no one should feel guilty. We were all getting along just fine. *Y'a bon!* The transparent racism of the thing was laughable, and the effect (the Banania Effect, I suppose you could call it) was to be appreciated through layers of arch, ironic distancing. I was playing out a role (foreseen the moment I first saw the thing), acting as a kind of mock emcee. It was all a performance.

But of what, exactly? What was it I was enacting? A few years ago I repeated the performance for my friend and colleague Greg—and that not long after Julie and I, along with her two daughters, had marched in a Black Lives Matter demonstration through downtown Seattle. The next Friday, Greg called. He'd had a bad day and needed company, so I told him to come over for some beer and sympathy.

Like all of us at Highline, the community college just south of Seattle where I now teach, Greg had been cooped up in COVID quarantine for the entire spring term. (Classes at Highline—like classes everywhere in the country—had all moved online.) With two toddlers at home and his wife at work during the week, Greg was going stir-crazy. To make matters worse, a few hours earlier he'd gotten an end-of-term email from a student who was unhappy with her grade (an A- instead of a straight A) and was accusing him of racial prejudice in his grading. Greg is a generation younger than I, with progressive credentials as strong as Zack's—and certainly stronger than mine. But I could empathize with him and his predicament. As we sat six feet apart on the deck, drinking beer, I told him about something that happened to me at my former teaching job at Dowling, on Long Island. The dean, who was pissed off at criticisms of the administration I'd made at a faculty meeting, which had gotten back to him, called me in to discuss "complaints of racial insensitivity" he claimed he'd received from some of my students. The complaints, though, turned out to be bogus. The dean was a famous bullshitter, and made no effort to be specific in his allegations. Our "talk," I concluded afterward, had just been an attempt on his part to intimidate me. He didn't even seem to believe the claims himself, since he began to nod off as I was responding to the charges. But the experience had been unpleasant enough for me to feel what Greg must be feeling now, and to register the unfairness of these kinds of cheap and easy accusations. We agreed that the best way to handle the situation was just for him to keep doing what he'd already done: go over the student's online grade record with her, and simply not react to anything else. Fervent denials of prejudice, however justified they were in point of fact, could only serve to dignify the accusation. The grades for every assignment were right there online, and averaged out to the student's final grade. We drank our beer and went on to talk about movies and music.

But then, after we'd moved inside and had another beer, a perverse and all-too-familiar impulse came over me. I produced the Banania mug and handed it to Greg. As he examined it (looking rather nonplussed), I pretended to take a photo of him holding it, and told him I'd be sending a copy to the dean at Highline. The joke fell flat—as, but for the beers, I might have known it would—so I put on some music, and we shared our favorite songs. The rest of the evening passed pleasantly enough, and Greg seemed to have forgotten my tasteless joke (which, considering what he was going through, had also been rather cruel).

But I haven't forgotten it, and have to ask myself, once again, what is behind my repeated attempts at this unfunny kind of humor.

I mentioned that in these performances, I present the Banania man—and formerly, other Black mascots as well, such as Aunt Jemima and Uncle Ben, when I happened to have them on hand in the cupboard (but of course they are no longer to be found in supermarkets; they have been cancelled)—as "helping" me to feel reassured and comforted. This image of benign Blackness assures me he holds nothing against me; he seems to tell me, in today's parlance: "Hey, no problem, man. We're good. *Y'a bon!*" But there is always an uneasiness in my specious comfort, which is purchased—as was the mug itself—in bad faith. For I cannot seriously believe what I'm using this object to tell myself. Granted, it's all part of a joke; but the joke, as I say, makes me feel uneasy, because I cannot fully get behind the role I am playing. The white guilt, which the joke both plays off of and is an attempt to partially alleviate, remains unassuaged.

All these mascots are part of what authors Claudia Rankine and Beth Loffreda call, in their eponymous collection of essays, "the racial imaginary": the set of images, representations, and ideas that express our beliefs about race and its meanings. My "racial imaginary," as I've indicated, is a performance—an act of "faux-racism," if you will—put on for the amusement of Julie, and Zack, and my friends, whether they like it or not. (They mostly don't.) And as an act, it partakes of a kind of double-ness: the doubleness of a person acting out a role—the role, say, of "The Cracker," who sees nothing at all objectionable in the use of Black mascots—while at the same time maintaining a knowing, ironic distance from the role he is acting out. (This doubleness is where the "faux" quality of the racism comes in.) There is also something essentially juvenile about the whole performance. I am like a child playing with fire, drawn to what I know is forbidden: in this case, the making of racial jokes by someone in a privileged position, "punching down." And no amount of ironic distancing is sufficient to entirely mask the smell of my privilege.

This childish aspect was brought home to me in a particularly unpleasant way more recently when another friend, Jeff Styler, sent me a video. The video came from his friend Paul, a former member of an expatriate African American vocal group, the Golden Gate Quartet, who for many years lived and worked in Paris. Paul emailed this video to his friends, asking them to distribute it to their friends in turn, since he hadn't been able to post it on Facebook, presumably because of its hate-speech content. The video consisted of excerpts from an interview by former NBA star (now commentator) Charles Barkley with the white supremacist and neo-Nazi Richard Spencer. For the interview, Barkley was joined by a civil rights attorney, Gerald Griggs. (Barkley and Griggs are both Black.) As they questioned Spencer on his beliefs about the "necessity" for racial segregation and the innate superiority of the "white race," he grew more and more agitated, and red in the face. But the redness wasn't just from anger; there was something else going on. And as I rewatched the video and witnessed Spencer struggling to explain his position coherently (which wasn't at all easy; in fact, it was impossible), I began to see what it was. Spencer reminded me of a child being admonished by a grownup on some point of conduct. His face wore a continual sheepish smirk—a confused mixture of contempt, shame, and resistance. He looked like he knew he'd done something wrong, but wasn't quite sure what it was, and in any case wasn't ready to admit it—and fuck you if you were going to try and make him. It was an excruciating yet fascinating thing to watch, and I felt almost embarrassed for him.

And then I began to think of myself and—*mutatis mutandis*—my own childishness. Especially my childish, unfunny jokes around the subject of race. Not that they involve anything even remotely comparable to Spencer's hateful beliefs; but my "faux-racism" isn't entirely innocent, either—and I know it. Thus my own discomfort at witnessing the spectacle of Spencer's, and my partial identification with his embarrassed, willful resistance. Like Spencer, I too persist in a childish, contrary belief: that my racial jokes are funny, despite considerable evidence to the contrary from family and friends. Spencer's beliefs, of course, are more than just childish: they are hateful, evil, and destructive. But I have to admit that what struck me most forcefully in rewatching the video was Spencer's childishness, and its unsettling resemblance to my own.

I realize I may be coming dangerously close right now to seeming like an apologist for Spencer, and that is far from my intention. I abhor the man and everything he stands for, and I am sympathetic to the antifa activist who punched him in the face. (The video can be seen on YouTube.) Yet I'm afraid Spencer and I do have one more thing in common (besides our childishness, and the fact that he is an anti-Semite, and I am a Jew): we are both exceptionalists. He is a white exceptionalist—a fascist, racist, and hater. My brand of exceptionalism is comparatively benign, and mostly theatrical—but no less suspect for all that. I harbor a secret belief—secret, at least, until I began this confession—that some of the rules that apply to others simply don't apply to me. As already mentioned *(several times!)* I believe I can have my cake and eat it too. For example, I see myself as a liberal, but with a difference: I can make racial jokes that are not funny over and over again, while believing—or at least hoping—that they may be funny the next time around. (A comedic form of magical thinking. *As well as masochism.* OK, you're probably right about that.) I feel I can perform these jokes and still be—to radically switch modes for a moment—"the least racist person you'll ever meet." My exceptionalism also tells me it's possible for me to hate Trump and everything he stands for—the very worst aspects of the American character—while a small part of me (very small, but it's there) finds him occasionally amusing. This split in my feelings for Trump I ascribe also to my exceptionalism: I want to be on the right side, the right-thinking side, the liberal side—but not 100 percent. Never 100 percent. (Never anything 100 percent. We'll get to that, too. *I hope so. I suspect it has to do with your aforementioned "weak will."*) You see, I want to retain a little bit of dissent from the prevailing progressive party line, as I understand it. It seems to me, sometimes, to lack a feeling for certain kinds of nuance. For example, the nuance of individualism—all the different shades of individual experience—as well as the sense of nuance necessary for various kinds of critical distinctions that need to be made. Here I am thinking of Robin DiAngelo's bestselling books *White Fragility* and *What Does It Mean to Be White?* We used the latter in the Whiteness Awareness Study Group, with Suzette. *Oh yes. Good old withered-arm Suzette.* There you go again. *But it was you who brought her up!* No it wasn't! *Yes it was! Look at what you just wrote!* OK, OK, but you had to bring up the withered arm again, didn't you? I mean, how would you like it if I called you "Titanium Membrane"? *That was a low blow. I call foul.* Well, but I'm just saying … *But you were the one who first noticed the withered arm, then blamed it on me. And you keep doing that, and it's really annoying.* Not so. *Yes so. Check the record, Schatzi, all the way back at the beginning of this whatever it is. You are such an unreliable narrator, I can't believe it.* You lie. *No, you lie.* What are you, in fourth grade or something? *Exactly the same could be said of you, mein Liebchen.*

Reader, I sincerely apologize for him. I am going to ban him now. *Ooh, I'm so scared.* OK, that's it, you're banned.

God, what an asshole. Unbelievable. Good riddance! As I was saying, in DiAngelo's books, she aligns a belief in individualism, on the part of whites, with the privileged view that can afford to be blind to the systemic nature of racial injustice. There seems to be, in much of the progressive writing that I've read, an emphasis on systems over individuals. I realize that this emphasis aims to be corrective of social inequity, which as a bona fide liberal I can't argue with. But what I find harder to swallow is DiAngelo's ideological certitude about the unimpeachability of the progressive position. It is the certitude of the true believer—a state of mind about which I am skeptical (as well as a little envious, I admit).

On the other hand—the way other hand—Trump has a certain appeal to the transgressive child in me: the bad boy who likes to play with fire, the rebel who likes to experiment with "wrong-thinking." It is wrong thinking, for example, to like anything about Trump; it is wrong-thinking to make racial jokes, even under the adopted persona of a "cracker" (or, for that matter, a Jewish ironist); it is wrong-thinking to have a sentimental attachment to Black mascots, which I understand are offensive to a majority of Americans (including pretty much all African Americans). And it is especially wrong-thinking to be attracted—for whatever reasons, childish or worse—to the possibility of wrong-thinking itself: the urge to transgress, to take it too far, to go over the line. For me, it's all part of the experiment. *Like the experiment with the Black father at Herb McCarthy's?* Banned. Ignore.

But what is it with this "experiment"? What exactly am I "experimenting" with? I mentioned that there is a childish part of me that is attracted to Trump—the "bad boy" rebel, who's playing with fire and experimenting with wrong-thinking. And the "cracker" character, too, is such an "experiment," conducted in opposition to the "right-thinking" liberal I am at heart. For some reason yet to be determined, this right-thinking liberal cannot be allowed to go unopposed (see Trilling, *op.cit.*), and the "cracker" character provides the opposition. But just what am I aiming to find out by conducting this experiment? That, too, remains to be seen.

And yet, and yet … How I long to leave the act behind, to stand clearly and bravely—and 100 percent, for once, without any ironic opposition—for what I believe in! *And what would that be? The brotherhood of man?* Hey! I said you are banned! *Apparently not, Schatzi.*

Goddam! But OK, yes, the Brotherhood of Man—and spoken without irony or apology. You got a problem with that, Fritz? Here I think of that great anthemic lyric of Elvis Costello: "What's So Funny about Peace, Love and Understanding?" And also of a line from a Chekhov short story that I committed to memory many years ago, and used as an epigraph for a piece of juvenilia: "Where have they gone—in what great sea have they drowned—those early buds of a fair, pure life?" Fairness and purity are noble ideals, and I do not sneeze at them, despite, or maybe because of, my uneasy play-acting. Scratch my surface and you'll find a disenchanted idealist—not yet (and I hope never) a cynic, but certainly an ironist.

And speaking of irony—and the lack thereof—I have one more confession to make. I've saved it for last *(if only, Mr. Unreliable Narrator, if only!)* because I still—seven years now after the incident occurred—don't quite know how to deal with it. It grates on me especially because of its moral cowardice, its betrayal of the promise of "a fair, pure life," and other ideals that underlie—or that I would like to think underlie—my vocational choice. When I told Greg the story of my meeting with the dean at Dowling, there was something I didn't tell him. Something I left out. *Aha. Now he tells us.* (Ignore.) And why? Why didn't I tell him? Maybe because I thought it had no direct bearing on his own case, and would only have needlessly complicated things. Or maybe—more likely—because I was too ashamed to tell him.

It happened in the spring of 2016—my last term at Dowling (and everyone's last term, for that matter; the school went belly-up right after graduation)—some years after that meeting with the dean, and just after I met Julie (but before I moved to Seattle). I was teaching a survey course in American literature, and we were reading *Huckleberry Finn.* All of the students in this particular class were white, except for one, who was Black. As we were discussing a scene in the novel—I don't remember which one, except that it had Jim in it—one of the white students casually referred to him as "the nigger." For a moment, there was utter silence in the classroom—including from me. Especially from me. But I knew I had to say something, so I said, as gently as possible—so as not to embarrass the student who'd said the word—"You mean Jim."

"Yeah, Jim," replied the student.

And that was it. No further commentary from me, as if the student's slip—if slip it was—had never happened; or as if the word was understood to be an acceptable way to refer to Jim—since it was, after all, how Huck (and everyone else in the novel) refers to him; or as if, since the word is such common parlance throughout the book, and used so casually, there should be no reason why we should not use it, too; or maybe even as if the student were using it ironically—though I could detect no trace of irony in their voice. As if, as if, as if ... I would like to say I was so shocked by the student's invocation of the word that I don't know what I was thinking. But that would be untrue. I was indeed shocked, but I do know what I was thinking—what was uppermost in my mind—and it wasn't the thoughts and feelings of the Black student, or any of the other students in the class. It was the feelings of the white student who'd said the word.

Now, I'm pretty sure this student was gender-queer. Perhaps they were undergoing a transition, or preparing for one. They always wore heavy boots and paramilitary-looking fatigues. Their face had no trace of hair, and the hair on their head was short and fine. They had a female-sounding first name. My sense at the time, as far as I can reconstruct it, was that they probably already had enough on their plate, and that it wouldn't be helpful for me to lecture them—and the rest of the class, by extension—about why you couldn't use that word, even though it is a word used frequently by Huck and others in the novel. I told myself that the student's mistake—if mistake it was; but it has always been a rule of mine to give students the benefit of the doubt, and I apparently saw no reason now to make an exception to this rule—was understandable under the circumstances, given the prevalence of the word in the novel. I told myself also that this was something to be discussed with the student alone, after class, so as not to embarrass them in public. (Though in the event, I never did talk to them.) What else did I tell myself? That the student had probably meant no harm? That it was a mistake attributable to ignorance and confusion, nothing more? That it was partly my fault, too, for not having discussed in advance, before we started reading *Huckleberry Finn*, the whole problem of the word in question?

In the field of critical race theory there is something called "white solidarity," which describes the tendency of many white people, when confronted with situations that are racially fraught, to support and validate each other, rather than actually try to understand the situation at hand. On the face of it, my behavior in this incident can be seen as an almost textbook example of white solidarity. I was in effect allying myself with the white student—specifically, with their confusion (if confusion it was)—rather than the Black student. Not because I consciously had anything against the Black student; quite the contrary, at least as far as I was aware. She was a better student in all ways than the white student: a better writer, a more conscientious attendee in class (I don't remember her ever being absent, whereas the white student was absent a number of times, and as I recall they never finished the course), and more intelligent, too. Though she rarely spoke up in class, when she did, her comments were on point—which could not be said for the white student. Intellectually and pedagogically, my alliance was with the Black student. And yet here I was, making it as easy as I possibly could for the white student. Bending over backward so as not to correct or embarrass them—not to cause them (or anyone else in that almost entirely white class) any more discomfort than they might already be feeling. (Though there was really no indication that the white student was feeling any discomfort at all.)

Of the many failures on display here, perhaps the most salient—at least from a practical standpoint—was the pedagogical one. In this particular instance, I utterly failed as a teacher. I let a vital "teaching moment" get away from me; indeed, I failed to recognize it as such, even when it was staring me in the face. A better teacher would have recognized the moment for what it was, and seized it. Whatever was going on with me at that particular moment, it had little to do with teaching. I was mostly thinking of myself—not as a teacher entrusted with the education of my students, but as someone who had an obligation to avoid awkwardness at all costs (and the costs turned out to be high). I was thinking of the white student who'd said the word, how they had "probably" meant no harm, and what the least confrontational and unsettling response would be. I was thinking of many tangential things, instead of the one central thing I should have been thinking about: what all of the students, white and Black, could be learning from this moment. The ball had been handed to me, and I plain dropped it. I didn't even fumble it—I just let it drop and walked off the field. (I might as well have been playing for the team formerly known as the Washington Redskins. *You mean the Commanders.* That's right, the Commanders.)

You see, Reader—even now I cannot seem to refrain from making bad jokes. That last one was heavily laden with irony, of course; but as we have seen, irony is not salvific. (For that matter, nothing is salvific.) I'm beginning to think that irony is really not even all that helpful in the end; though in the moment, it helps—or seems to help—let off steam. But that's not really what I want to do right now. I want to let the steam build—let it build up on this old riverboat named, oh what the hell, let's call it the "Aunt Jemima"—and do the work it needs to do. Which is maybe even to produce a kind of explosion. An explosion of what? And for what purpose? And then what?

Frankly, I don't know. But on the subject of steam explosions, I am reminded of a brief passage in the novel in question. Huck, pretending to be Tom Sawyer, is responding to Aunt Sally's query, and explaining why he (as Tom) has arrived later than expected at the Phelps farm:

> "What's kep' you?—boat get aground?"
> "Yes'm—[… but] it warn't the grounding—that didn't keep us back but a little. We blowed out a cylinder-head."

"Good gracious! anybody hurt?"

"No'm. Killed a nigger."

"Well, it's lucky; because sometimes people do get hurt."

The passage is one of the most famous in the novel—indeed, perhaps in all of American literature. And in its fierce irony is encapsulated the gist of the novel's moral teaching. But what about *my* moral teaching? What kind of moral example was *I* setting for my students in my failure to respond, in any adequate way at all, to the student's use of the n-word—not in a quote, but as an identifier? Undeniably, I was being a moral coward. I was choosing to avoid discomfort and awkwardness—for myself and for my students—instead of doing the right thing, which would have been to engage the issue, rather than ignore it.

In an opinion piece in the *New York Times* (July 6, 2020) that really hit home for me, the columnist Erin Aubry Kaplan wrote:

> Being truly antiracist will require white people to be inconvenienced by new policies and practices, legal and social … The privilege to not engage is one that many may be loath to give up, even if they believe engagement is the right thing to do.

Well, I for one am certainly loath to give it up. And this despite my belief—my knowledge—that "engagement is the right thing to do." My problem—and this speaks to the other idea that Kaplan brings up in the passage—is that it is so *inconvenient* to become engaged! (Here I think of my father, who, in the memorable exchange already noted, frankly and unapologetically put his convenience before his health.) Becoming engaged in a cause—let's say, the cause of Black Lives Matter—means you will be spending a lot of time in service to that cause, which means you won't have as much time to do other things, such as write about how you long to be unironically engaged in a cause but are not making the commitment because it would be … inconvenient. So much easier to read and write about something than actually do it. It's clear that this laziness of mine comes from—is a direct result of—living a life of privilege. Privilege and convenience, you see, go so well together. And they reinforce one another, too. To feel one can afford to avoid certain inconveniences is also to feel that one is privileged enough to do so.

Privilege, convenience, and disengagement: the trifecta of Old White Man Writing's existential unease, his moral discomfort. I would have done anything—and, in the event, did nothing, precisely nothing—to avoid inconveniencing and unsettling my students into engaging with the problem of the word in question: how it is used, and who gets to use it. I betrayed my calling as a teacher, and abdicated my moral obligation to make myself and my students uncomfortable. For a judicious discomfort (to alter Freud's famous dictum) is the "royal road" to education. To unsettle our customary beliefs and knowledge is to begin the process of true learning. And comfort and convenience stand in the way of same. Learning is painful. "Sorrow is knowledge," Byron wrote at the beginning of *Manfred*. And what can make us sorrier than leaving behind the comfort of our familiar ways of knowing? In the life of the mind—and also of the soul, I believe; but how can you separate the two, at least in any course of education worth pursuing?—comfort and convenience are impediments; discomfort and inconvenience are of the essence. Without what I would call the "Squirm Factor," no meaningful learning can occur. Indeed, this confession itself, in its embarrassing and often shameful self-revelations, may be an instance of the Squirm Factor. No doubt there are some readers *(if there are any at all!)* who may long since have laid it aside for that very reason; and I would not blame them. So be it. Yet that would be a shame (another kind of shame), because it is for the squirmy readers that I write.

And I am squirming myself as I write this; for I am realizing now that the dean at my old college who called me in for a "talk" may have been right after all—though well before the fact, and in a way he never intended. The "racial insensitivity" of which he accused me (perhaps presciently) lay not in anything I said or did at the time, but in what I was, years later, to fail to say. Silence is complicity, remember?

It's hard to leave what is comforting and reassuring and familiar behind; but sometimes it is necessary to rock the (river)boat. What will replace my old mascots and their brand names? Will Aunt Jemima and Uncle Ben become white? I highly doubt it. More likely, they will morph into completely different characters—or most likely, none at all. Will they perhaps pull a Prince, or a Twitter, and become "The Brands Formerly Known as Aunt Jemima and Uncle Ben"? My friend Joe has suggested they might end up in that special place in the "afterlife of objects" reserved for the statues of Confederate "heroes," where, in the unlikeliest of resolutions, the two sets of dubious emblems will live together, happily ever after. But what happens to Aunt Jemima and Uncle Ben is really PepsiCo's and Mars Inc.'s business, not mine. I have other catfish to fry. I admit I'm still kind of sorry to see my mascots go; and I will regret the sense of comfort and reassurance they provided—specious as those sentiments were. But I realize I must undertake, in Kaplan's words, "new policies and practices," both as a teacher and as a student. So goodbye, Aunt Jemima. I will miss you. But that's my problem, and I'm working on it.

I'm totally holding onto the Banania mug, though; someday it may be worth something.

Nice little twist at the end there, Schatzi. Very clever. But not quite enough, I think, to exonerate you. And speaking of regrets, why don't you tell them about your egregious insensitivity regarding your birthday present from the gimp from Solingen? I'm sure your readers would love to hear what you have to say about that. How dare you, you little shit! *Ah, I see I've struck a nerve there. Go ahead, tell them. Unless you are sparing yourself. Unless your representation of this as an unsparing account is utterly bogus (as you Amer- I mean, well, you know what I mean). But do tell.*

Even before this last, most highly obnoxious intrusion, Reader—for which I must once again apologize—I had been debating with myself whether to add the story of Paul Kirschner (that is, my very partial and potted version of his story) to this account. There are arguments both for and against his inclusion here. On the con side, he was not a person of color—"not hardly," as John Wayne (one of his Western heroes) might have said. Paul was in fact German—as a number of the figures who rather obsess me have been; not sure what's going on with that. *Me neither.* Just ignore him. He (Paul, that is) was born in Solingen, that garden-spot of the industrial Ruhr Valley, around the turn of the twentieth century. *(So much for chronological precision, the foundation of the biographical endeavor. Ignore.)* On the pro side, he seems a perfect subject for biographization: obscure (arguably non-entitous), undistinguished, undocumented (except in the sense that he was a naturalized US citizen and proud of it), and I loved him. So I'm going to give him the benefit of the doubt here—as all good biographizers should do regarding their subjects—and include him. The fact that Mom once confessed to me, when the song "Nowhere Man" came on the car radio one day, that it made her think of Paul, and I felt a twinge of agreement, kind of cements the decision. I mean, isn't he a bit like you and me?

Paul first came to work for us when I was around two. My dad met him when he got a flat tire on Tigertail Road, just off Sunset in Brentwood, and Paul stopped to help. Does that mean my dad couldn't change a flat by himself? Probably. My dad, like me, wasn't that handy. Not helpless, but not that handy. Or maybe it was something else that was wrong with his car, which wouldn't have been unusual. (His car at the time was the old Studebaker convertible, which there was always a lot wrong with.) Anyway, Paul must have demonstrated his handiness with the car, and my dad was opportunistic enough to get his number, and that led to other gigs for Paul, including babysitting for me, and eventually moving in with us when I was six or so. For around five years (1960-65) Paul slept in my room, in the bed on the other side of the long Eames desk.

He was Our Man Friday, I suppose you could say. He helped raise me, and I came to love him. We all did.

And, I believe, vice versa. He once told me my dad was a "prince," which I guess had to do with Gog giving him a job when he needed one, and being generous to him in terms of salary. He also said the Jewish religion was the oldest and best. *(That last statement is factually untrue—at least the first part of it. Hinduism and Judaism are roughly the same age, having both originated around the Late Bronze Age—ca. 1500 BCE. Not that long before the Trojan War.* Probably just ignore, though he may be right on that.) But Paul meant well. And I think he said what he did partly out of German guilt. (You know a little about that, don't you, Fritz? *Ignore.*) Come to think of it, between Paul and my dad there was certainly enough guilt to go around. I say this because my dad had been a prisoner of war with the Italians, and then the Germans, for eighteen months during World War II. After the war, he held a serious grudge against Germans, for obvious reasons. And I think Paul was his compensatory example of a "good German," who'd emigrated before the end of World War I, because—as the story in our family went—he didn't want to serve in the Kaiser's army. Though there was doubtless more to it than that. In any case, Paul didn't talk a lot about his family—at least I don't remember him saying much if anything about them; but I got the impression that maybe he didn't get along so well with his father, and that might have been another reason why he left Solingen. But Paul's credentials as a German expatriate were apparently good enough for my dad, who could prove he finally didn't hold any lasting grudges by hiring him, and then having him move in with us. *("Doubtless"; "I don't remember"; "I got the impression"; "maybe"; "might have been"; " "apparently". Not exactly biographizational bedrock, Schatzi.* Just ignore.)

Paul had been married before we knew him and had a daughter, Gundel, a few years older than me, who lived with her mother back in Germany. I guess mother and daughter had gone back there together after the divorce—though I really don't know. *(See previous parenthesis.)* I *do* know that when Gundel came back over to visit Paul once, he took us to Disneyland. And many years later, I wrote a short story about Paul in Disneyland, riding the Matterhorn (before it got turned into Space Mountain), where he got sick to his stomach. *Sounds like a really compelling narrative.* Shut the fuck up!

Paul's credentials as an American weren't too bad either. As I say, he was a naturalized citizen, and he loved professional wrestling, *The Lawrence Welk Show, My Three Sons, Gunsmoke,* and *Bonanza.* (In addition to John Wayne.) In *Bonanza,* Hoss was his man. In *Gunsmoke,* it was Chester, the deputy with the gimpy leg—for reasons that will soon become clear. *(No comment. And yet he screamed at me when I called Paul a gimp.)* He remembered when the San Fernando Valley was "all bean fields," which he used to remark on whenever we drove into the Valley. He knew his way around the city pretty well. One of the things I liked doing with him was "getting lost." When he'd take me in the car to Pasadena to visit his friends the Shittelhoffers (of course I loved the name), he would pretend to get lost on the way back. (At least I think he was pretending, but maybe he wasn't.) And then, lo and behold, we'd turn the corner, and there we were, on Chautauqua Blvd., just up the street from our house on Vance Street. Home sweet home. Magic. I loved him for that, too.

I didn't love everything about him, though. When I was constipated from holding back my bowel movements, which I did as a matter of course throughout grade school (because I absolutely refused to use the bathroom at school, or at Tocaloma), Paul would give me mineral-oil enemas, which weren't so great—despite his reassurances that it would be "smooth sailing." (I guess Mom just didn't want to deal with "that part," whereas Paul, I have to say, was kind of into it.) I also once got a very bad case of poison oak when my parents were away on a trip, and Paul pretty much blew that one, too. (Of course, every case of poison oak for me was a bad case; I was very allergic.) He got the idea of giving me a bath to wash off the poison-oak juice, or whatever it was, but all that did was spread the juice over the rest of my body, including my dick and balls, which was definitely not exactly a picnic. If I say that Paul meant well there, too—well, that still doesn't make up for him being kind of dumb about the bath. Though I guess ignorant is probably the better word—he just wasn't that well informed about the treatment of poison oak. (As opposed to being an expert on enemas.) But he sure tried to make up for it by piling on the calamine lotion, which wasn't too much fun either. Especially the way it would make your skin really dry and tight when you moved, or tried to smile. (I don't want to talk about what it did to my dick and balls.)

And then there was the leg. Paul had a plastic leg that creaked when he walked. Now was it the left leg or the right leg? I don't even know. That's really bad, too, that I don't know. I should know. (*You certainly should, since apparently you're so obsessed with cripples.* No, that's you, Fritz. You noticed Suzette's withered arm first, Mr. Titanium Plate. *Excuse me? And* you *accused* me *of being in fourth grade?* Just ignore him, Reader, until I get this banning thing working again. *Again? Are you serious?* Not sure what's wrong there. Some kind of glitch in the spell mechanism or something.) Anyway, he—Paul—lived with us and slept in my bedroom (*our* bedroom, I guess I should say) for five years. Now how could I not know which leg it was? I guess I just kind of put it out of my mind, the way kids do—and not just kids, either. I think probably my parents put it out of their minds, too. They never, ever talked about it to me. (Except to say, once, that he'd been in a car accident. But that was the only time, as I recall, that they ever mentioned it. *Bloody stump for Paul, looks like.* You are *such* an asshole.) Which I realize doesn't really prove anything, and maybe even proves the opposite—that they were actually thinking about the leg a lot, in the way that you do when you "don't say something," but it is still on your mind, and maybe even more so than if you were to talk about it. The point is, I secretly knew about the leg, and that made me feel sorry for him, and I think the feeling sorry for him part made me love him all the more. They say that pity is not the same thing as love, and I agree. But I also know they are somehow connected.

I'm not sure how much more personal background I should give about Paul. I mean, what is some dead German guy with a plastic leg to you? *(Not obsessed, no we aren't. Nothing of the sort.)* Though that very question shows that I have already failed as a biographizer, because the point of biographization is supposed to be to make you care about, if not love, people you normally wouldn't give two shakes about. But this isn't a biographization. It's nowhere close to being a biographization. *(Don't be so sure.)* It's just a sketch of the kind of person you might write a biographization of. Somebody who wouldn't normally get written about, but just totally forgotten and left in the dust. *(Shades of Aline's Coke-bottle doll, you think?)*

As you may already have inferred, Paul was not in any way a distinguished person. I suppose his only claim to fame—and that is stretching it—was his having worked for some years for the silent-film actor Jack Holt (who starred mostly in Westerns—hence Paul's attachment to the genre) before he came to work for us. He would talk about that sometimes, and what a "gentleman" Jack Holt was. Was Paul maybe his valet? Was he therefore, in some distant sense, a part of Hollywood history? That would be stretching it even further. I suppose he might conceivably have been a source in someone's biography of Jack Holt; but there don't appear to be any published biographies of Holt—just a Wikipedia entry. (Which reveals—quite awesomely, actually—that the actor was the "visual inspiration" for two cartoon characters: Chester Gould's Dick Tracy and Al Kapp's Fearless Fosdick.) But Paul's obscurity—or even his nonentity, historically speaking—is precisely the point: he is just the sort of person, like nearly all of us, who would never get a biography written about them. He is "biographically invalid"—and therefore biographizationally valid. To put it rather melodramatically, it's the orphans of history who are the subjects of biographization. And that means, statistically speaking, just about everyone. That's what makes biographization democratic.

I hope it's not too egocentric or grandiose of me to assert that Paul lives, biographizationally—like my parents, and Diane, and Aline, and a growing number of friends—because I remember and am writing about him *(so this* is, *then, a biographization; you just said so yourself.* Leave me alone. I hate you.), and the things he handily fixed and built, and the things he said, and the TV shows he loved, and the Brylcreem hair tonic he used, and the Old Spice aftershave he wore, and the Sen-Sen breath mints he sucked, and the plastic leg he took off every night, in the dark of our room. (I could hear what I imagined were the straps being removed. *Not obsessed? Really?* Fuck you!) What I will call the quiddities of Paul will not be forgotten by me, as long as I live. And if my great-grandchildren, if I ever have any (because it's not looking that way; Zack says he really doesn't want to have kids), or Paul's (they would have to be Gundel's grandchildren!), should someday find this manuscript in a metal strong-box in a closet somewhere—all the better for both of us! (I mention the strongbox advisedly; you'll see why in a minute.)

And what about Paul's work in the world, such as it was? All the work he did during the twelve or so years he worked for us, including the five years he lived with us—all the household repairs he made, and the little improvised constructions he built, and the time he spent with me—thousands and thousands of hours, it must have been. The people who do that kind of work don't get biographies written about them, but they sure should get biographizations. And actually, it is the function of biographization—one of its functions—to record and honor that work. The work of Paul—and Aline, and Willie—deserves to be noted and honored. All their works and days.

In that connection, I am reminded of a chance encounter I had at the beginning of my academic career. *(Uh-oh, here we go again.* Abraca-dabra! Never Talk Again! *Nice try.)* A week or two into my first full-time teaching job as a visiting instructor at Holy Cross, in the fall of 1994, I attended a mixer for new faculty. At the mixer, a thin, bespectacled woman approached me, and we exchanged names.

"Josh Gidding, Josh Gidding," she repeated pleasantly, and a little diffidently. "I'm afraid I'm not familiar with your work, Josh."

I have retold this story many times, and it never fails to amuse. To my Holy Cross colleague, I was a promising young scholar in the making. I was a contender. Little did she know! Behind her innocent statement lay such a generous assumption that one could not help but feel comforted, reassured, and flattered by it. What if I really were, or were preparing to be, the person her assumption suggested I was? How kind of her—and yet how (unintentionally) humorous, too. (The unintentional humor of her statement was part of its charm.) Such that, for a number of years after—throughout Zack's childhood, in fact—whenever he mentioned a classmate, or someone from summer day camp, whose name I didn't recognize, I would reply something like, "Bob Johnson, Bob Johnson … I'm afraid I'm not familiar with his work."

And so I say that I am indeed familiar with Paul's work; some of it, anyway—the work that touched my life, in whatever ways it did. I am familiar with Paul's work, and want you to be too, Reader. So I am passing it on, for what it's worth.

But why not, then, present this material in fictional form? Why not present Paul's story in a short story or novel?

This is actually not a bad point he makes (though he's supposed to be banned). The idea of a novel is tempting, and would be easier in some ways; and there is no denying that I am a great fan of the biographical novels of Thomas Mann (*Doctor Faustus*) and Hermann Hesse (*The Glass Bead Game*)—both of which also happen to be German. (Which fits nicely with what seems to be my German obsession. *I wonder if that, too, goes back to Paul.* No doubt it does.) But the particular truth-value of fiction is not what I'm after here. The idea of biographization I have in mind is not an offshoot of fiction, but of history—personal history. Yet if I'm not willing, or even able, to write a biographization myself, how can I advocate this idea for others? Where do I get off touting for a club that I wouldn't want to be a member of myself? And for which, furthermore, I would never qualify? (The Groucho Marx Syndrome.) Doesn't that make me some sort of hypocrite?

Call me, instead, an idealist—a "democratic idealist." I'm imagining a form of biography—a more inclusive, less professionalized kind of third-person life-writing—that doesn't quite exist yet. I'm certainly no expert on biographical matters—*You can say that again.* Ignore.— but that's sort of the point of "democratic biography," isn't it? Opening up the field to nonexperts. Giving the people a voice, both as subjects and as writers. They say that everybody has a book in them. Well, why couldn't that book be a biographization of someone they love? Because I think that's really what I'm talking about here. That's finally what's at the root of biographization: love. The wish to reclaim someone we love from oblivion—or eventual oblivion. I realize there are lots of ways to express our love; but why not make biography one of them? And a novel, or a poem, or a painting, or a piece of music, won't quite do it—at least not in the biographical sense I have in mind. It's the facts of a person's life—the work they did, the people they knew and loved, the things they actually said and did; the Brylcreem and Old Spice and Sen-Sens of their days, if you will. These details need to be set down; they need to be recorded, acknowledged, respected, honored. Events, dates, places, and people—all of them real, factual, documented—are part of the record, the mark of who they were in the world, the kind of "juice" they left. Fiction is great, but it doesn't do the same kind of work, doesn't pay the same kind of attention. And, as Willy Loman's devoted (and betrayed) *(You should know something about that, shouldn't you?)* wife Linda said, "Attention must be paid." The facts must be laid out, however the biographizer thinks best, for the reader to consider, contemplate, reflect on, and appraise.

I mentioned before that maybe part of what brought Paul into our family for five years was my father's guilt about being prejudiced against Germans, because of the war. But my father wasn't the only one who felt guilty. I felt guilty, too, and still do, and always will. And here's why. *(Finally.)*

One year, on my birthday, after Paul had moved back to Germany to
retire and be with his "lady-friend," Maria—let's call it 1969; June 3,
1969, but it could have been 1968, or even 1967; I should know this for
sure, but I don't *(Surprise!)*—I got a birthday card and present from him.
The card came in a package with the present. I opened the present first,
of course. Now what was it? I seem to remember it was something kind
of strange, like maybe an embroidered vest, with a wide belt and fancy
buckle that went along with the vest. Something that I instantly knew,
the second I saw it, I would never, ever wear. Which made me feel bad,
and guilty, and sorry for him, of course. *(Of course.)* But not nearly as
bad and guilty as the card, when I read it. Out loud.

That was a big mistake. It turned out badly for all concerned. Especially for Paul. As I recall, there were a few friends over for my birthday
dinner, and I guess I was feeling in high spirits, and full of myself, and
reading Paul's letter out loud was something I thought I could do that
would be—what? I don't know. Entertaining? That reading his letter out
loud, in an imitation of his voice, would buy me some laughs because of
the way he talked, which wasn't exactly perfect English, to say the least.

You see, Paul had certain trademark sayings that Mom used to repeat
because we both thought they were funny. Not that she was making fun
of Paul or anything—she wasn't; she loved him, too. But just the way you
will repeat certain things people say because you like the way they sound,
and repeating them the way they say them makes you think of them in a
good way, and sort of carries on their tradition, if that makes any sense.
That's the way it was with Paul's sayings. Like he had his own version of
"It's funny how the bee makes honey." But he wouldn't say it that way; he
would say, "It's funny, funny, funny, how the bee he makin' that honey."
Another thing he would do is he would put the words "once" and "now"
where you wouldn't expect them. For example, when he was trying to fix
something, he would say, "Let's see once now what's wrong here, Gozhua."
(He called me "Gozhua" because for some reason he couldn't pronounce
"Joshua." But I didn't even notice it because I was so used to it, and if he

had ever said "Joshua", that would have sounded weird.) Or he would say, instead of that, but meaning the same thing, "Let's see once here what we talkin' now, Gozhua." And then he would go ahead and fix whatever it was he was fixing. So sometimes Mom would say these things, too, in affectionate imitation of him—but of course never in front of him.

The point is, maybe I read his letter out loud because I thought it might have some funny trademark sayings that would get laughs. I don't remember exactly who was over that night besides my parents, and a few of my friends, and Aline (Paul's replacement, sort of; though it sounds really bad and disrespectful to both of them to put it that way. *It certainly does.*). One of my friends who was there might have been Tracy Hudson, who was literally the girl next door—until she moved away. Tracy knew Paul, too, and had basically grown up with him, at least for those years when he was living with us. So maybe I was trying to impress Tracy and make her laugh. Which of course was mean of me, and even maybe slightly evil, because it would have been at Paul's expense. But really, who knows what was in my mind? Not much, apparently. I was just showing off.

I don't remember the letter word for word, but I remember the basics, so I'll just give you those. Lucky this isn't a real biographization, because that letter is long gone. Mom probably took it and put it in her metal strongbox—knowing her, that's exactly what she would have done, out of respect for Paul. But I never really knew where she put it. And of course, now that she is dead too, and so is my dad, and the old house on Vance Street was sold and renovated (horribly—they painted the exposed natural-wood beams white) and rented out and then razed to the ground to make way for a McMansion, I'll never know. And that letter's disappearance is yet another proof that I would never make a good biographizer, because in a real biographization (though the very idea is an oxymoron), you would have to have that letter as a document and quote from it. What follows, then, is just a reconstruction, from memory, of the most important parts. The gist of it.

"Dear Gozhua," he wrote. (He would have written my name right—Joshua—just not have pronounced it right. And which way did I pronounce it when I read it? Almost certainly "Gozhua," to get the laughs. That's where I was at.) "Dear Gozhua, I hope this letter finds you well and that you are having a very happy birthday. I hope that your dear parents are well, too. I hope that you like once this present now that I am sending it to you. It was chosen special for a big shot like you are getting to be. I hope that when you wear it you will think once now of your old Paul, who he misses you all very much.

"As for myself, well, I am not doing so good right now. I have a cancer tumor between my liver and my stomach, and the doctors cannot operate it because it is in a bad place for an operation … "

I stopped reading it out loud at that point, because I was so shocked, and because I suddenly—and too late—realized that I never should have been reading it out loud in the first place. And then I think I did a horrible thing. Actually, "think" is not right—I *know* I did a horrible thing. I laughed. Not because I thought it was funny at all, but because I thought it was so horrible, and I didn't know what else to do. I couldn't believe it, I was shocked, and I guess my answer to that was just to laugh. So I laughed. Not a lot, just a short burst of laughter, a sort of confused and disbelieving bark of a laugh. Mom immediately burst into tears, grabbed the letter from me, and ran into the other room to read it alone.

Happy Birthday, Gozhua. You really nailed it, pal.

And that was basically that. Paul died not too long afterward. I guess Maria would have written Mom a letter telling her Paul had died. And that letter would have gone into permanent safekeeping, too, right there in the old oblong metal strongbox on the top shelf of Mom's bedroom closet—along with Paul's cancer birthday letter—where she kept all of her most valuable papers. (And where, on that top shelf, you may remember, she kept Chester, too— the Black ventriloquist's dummy I had given her for Christmas one year—in order to hide him from Aline. But that didn't work out either, because I myself showed Chester to Aline, out of guilt. *Good one too, Gozhua.* I hate you.) The good old metal strongbox that would have gotten packed up and put somewhere when the house was sold in 2004. That *annus horribilis.* I still have some of that stuff in boxes in the backyard shed of the house where I now live in Seattle, and I'd like to think the strongbox, with Paul's and Maria's letters, put there by Mom, is still in there somewhere among those old things. I sure hope it didn't get thrown out. I should go look for it, but I probably won't. The Lazy Gozhua Syndrome, you could call it. Though it's not so much because I'm lazy—though I am—but more because I'm scared that if I went looking for it, I might not find it. And that would be even worse than not looking for it in the first place. Maybe I'll just leave it up to Zack to unexpectedly come across it when I'm gone. He knows about Paul—at least some of it—so if he found those letters, they would mean something to him. Chester, though, is long gone, thank God. Not sure how I would have explained him to Zack. Shades of the Banania mug, I guess. Only worse.

Looks like you've got a lot of explaining to do, Gozhua.

There is one more thing *(Right!)* I need to talk about—and hopefully without any more interruptions this time. I don't know what's wrong with this spell. It obviously hasn't been working, or he's found a way around it. Whatever. This last story is about Florence. Florence Robinson. It may be the thing that weighs heaviest on me, and it's not even something I did; it's something I failed to do. Another sin of omission. But in some ways those are the worst, because they expose our weaknesses at their most glaring. And it is the knowledge and demonstration of our weaknesses that hurt the most. In this case, my weak will—which was fully on display in the "Matter of Florence." (And I'm not talking about a literary corpus from the Italian Renaissance, either. *That was cute, Gozhua.* Oh shut up.)

By my reckoning, Florence Robinson worked for my Grandmother Cissie and her family at 111 East 64th St. in Manhattan for around thirty-five years. The house, a five-story brownstone between Park and Lexington, facing south, was bought in 1933—the depths of the Depression— for $30,000, cash. My grandmother's stepfather, Joseph Steinhart—whom she always called Dad; her natural father, Martin Frank, died when she was very young—was a produce wholesaler, and one of his clients was the Cunard Line. It was this connection that allowed my grandmother and her mother Lola to travel the world on the Cunard Line at reduced rates. And later, my father and his brother enjoyed the same privilege, also in the company of their grandmother Lola.

I don't know precisely when Florence came to work at 111. (And "don't say something," Joßche. *Oh I won't. No need to. By now your reliability has been utterly obliterated.*) I do know, though, that Florence must have been working there already when I was born (in 1954), because there are photos of me as an infant in my "Auntie Florence's" lap. My parents were still living in the house then, though they moved out soon afterward, at my mother's insistence. (My father's brother Joseph, my "Uncle Tiger," a ne'er-do-well alcoholic whom I loved—and a perpetual and what my father would call "professional" Princeton alumnus, hence the nickname—ne'er did make it out of 111. He died in his bed of a heart attack in April of 1975, age fifty-seven. It was Florence who found him.) When I was one we moved to LA, where my father had just gotten his first job in Hollywood, adapting the radio show *Sergeant Preston of the Yukon* into a TV series. In 1957 we moved back to New York for a year, so my dad could work on location for his fourth feature film, *Odds Against Tomorrow* (with Harry Belafonte, which is how we knew the Belafontes). And also so my mother could attempt to slake her homesick thirst for New York, where she had lived for eleven years, after getting the hell out of Scranton about two seconds after graduating from hyper-Catholic Marywood College. (She'd also gone to Marywood Seminary before that.) I suspect it was during this time that I was encouraged to call Florence "Auntie Florence." For such liberties to be taken—dubious as they were then, and even more cringeworthy now—suggests that Florence was already a well-established "fixture" of the household. *You mean like a lamp or piece of furniture, Gozhua?* Duly noted. But please stop calling me that. (*Such* an asshole.)

So let's say Florence got there in 1945, or shortly thereafter, when my father and uncle were out of the army and living back at home. At that time, 111 would have been a full house: my great-grandmother, Lola Steinhart (by that time Joseph Steinhart, too, was dead), Grandma Cissie and her second husband, my Granddaddy Albert (last name Trepuk—he always signed his cards to me "Grandddadddy", because what was two Ds more?), Uncle Tiger, and my father. (Cissie had divorced her first husband, Nate Gidding, when the boys were nine and seven, respectively. *This is all quite biographizationally precise! Congratulations, Gozhua!* Fuck off.) Florence cooked—three meals a day, cleaned, did the laundry, ran errands, did the shopping, and later, in the 1950s, helped take care of me (intermittently—including sometimes changing my diapers that first year) and Lola (regularly), when the latter became senile after too much anesthesia for a cataract operation. I recall, from the year we later spent in New York when I was three to four, that Florence used to make deviled-ham sandwiches for Lola, with the crusts cut off, and garnished with parsley and paprika. I remember the reverse-sickle-shaped, double-bladed, wooden-handled chopper Florence used to make the deviled ham, and the wooden chopping bowl, and the rather sickly smell of the mayonnaise, which as I child I hated.

In the fall of 1976, after graduating from college, I moved back to New York and lived at 111 for about nine months. The previous year, both Uncle Tiger and Granddaddy Albert had died (1975 was a very bad year for Cissie; her version of my 2004, you could say), and it was just Grandma and me living on the top three floors of the brownstone. (Early in the '50s, at Albert's prompting, the bottom two floors had been converted into a duplex rental.) Florence's old room was on the top floor, but she wasn't living there anymore; for some years now she'd had a place in the Bronx, and commuted to work. During the four years I lived in the city (1976–1980), I had various rentals and sublets and house-sits, but 111 was always my home base, and I would return there periodically, for short stays. Florence was still working, but she didn't come every day. And sometime during this period, Florence had a stroke. I remember going to visit her in New York Hospital. She was not paralyzed, and seemed to have kept all her mental faculties; but after she got out of the hospital, she came less and less often to the house. Going up and down five flights of stairs must have been increasingly onerous for her.

Florence died before I left NYC in June of 1980. I believe it was sometime during the last year and a half I was in New York—in 1979 or the first half of 1980. I wish I could be more precise. *(No comment.)* Now if I were a real biographer, or rather biographizer ... (Although we've already established there's no such thing as a "real" biographizer. But still. *Yes, still.)* Let's put it this way: I knew Florence, and she knew me, from the day I was born—June 3, 1954 *(It's always nice to have at least some precise dates.* Fuck the crap off!)—until she died in 1979 or 1980. No, wait. Wasn't Florence at our wedding—Diane's and my—in 1983? Or am I confusing her now with Aline?

Because they all look the same, don't they, Gozhua?

Shit. I really thought I had definitively banned him. Not sure what the problem is. Though I have to admit I stepped into that one. Now that I stop to think about it, of course it had to be Aline at our wedding, because by then, Florence had been dead at least three years. But she would have been there, if she'd been alive. At least I like to think so. Lots of guilt there. At the bottom of the Matter of Florence, a whole lot of guilt. Not just generalized white, and privileged, and Baby Joshie Shitpants guilt either, but specific guilt over actions taken and not taken. Because—and here's the point of it all—Grandma and I didn't go to her funeral. There you have it. The point of this whole sad Florence story is that finally, after the maybe thirty-five years she'd worked for us, we didn't even go to her funeral.

Was it maybe because we weren't invited? I find it hard to believe we wouldn't have gone if we'd been invited. Then again, I don't find it hard to believe we weren't invited. And no fault of the Robinsons there. They'd probably had enough of us. As I recall, Grandma and Florence weren't getting along so well in later years, and the Robinson brothers—Monte, Quentin, and Malachi; tall, handsome, dapper men all, contract chauffeurs for years at the Office of the Mayor—surely knew all about those troubles. And Grandma would probably have been persona non grata at the funeral. *(And that goes for Baby Gozhua Shitpants, too.)* I get that. But did I even send a condolence card to the brothers? (All of whom I knew somewhat, from when they used to come around to the house to visit Florence.) Once again, I find it hard to believe that I didn't even send a card. But I know I probably would remember it if I did. (I guess the fuzziness here is the protective coloring of guilt. *You think?*) I do seem to recall saying something to Grandma about our going to the funeral, and her saying no. And my accepting that, and not insisting. Was this also because of the third-act troubles between her and Florence? And what if those troubles all boiled down to the fact that Florence had been working for the Steinharts and then the Trepuks for all those years and was finally sick and tired of them? *(Shades here of Aline and the Giddings?* Yes, you may be right. Unfortunately, Reader, he may be right.) Sick and tired of the whole bunch of us, who'd been living in the house she'd been taking care of—and all the people in it—since forever. No, I wouldn't blame her a bit for being fed up with the whole thing. And finally, now, in death, she was free of it. Free at last, free at last—Great God Almighty, free at last.

There is a passage in Wordsworth's famous "Intimations Ode" that speaks to my feelings here. *(Of course. No significant moment is without its Wordsworth quote.* Fuck!) The context, to be sure, is very different: Wordsworth is describing a metaphysical dilemma, whereas I am fixated on various moral lapses—racial and otherwise—that I still keenly feel, and always will. But the lines I have in mind indicate a quandary that I think is analogous: the poet's sense of something he isn't quite able to put into words, but feels an urgency to wrestle with nonetheless—and maybe even all the more so, as it is inexpressible. Throughout the poem, Wordsworth has been trying to account for the loss, in adulthood, of the unique "visionary gleam" of childhood that he remembers illuminated his experiences and consciousness back then. Toward the end of the poem, he describes a strange sense of gratitude that he has trouble articulating. He emphasizes that it is gratitude not for any benefit received, but for something missing—perhaps another kind of lapse or "falling from" himself, a falling short in his own eyes:

> The thought of our past years in me doth breed
> Perpetual benediction: not indeed
> For that which is most worthy to be blest ...
> But for those obstinate questionings
> Of sense and outward things,
> Fallings from us, vanishings;
> Blank misgivings of a Creature
> Moving about in worlds not realized ...

It's the last three lines in particular that draw my attention. In the poem, Wordsworth is finally able to understand the loss of his "visionary gleam" by appealing to the myth of reincarnation, the transmigration of souls. My case is not nearly so grand as that; in fact, it is not grand at all; it is abject. What I experience when I think about my failure to acknowledge, in any way, Florence's death—either by my presence at her funeral, or by writing a simple note of condolence to her family—are feelings of shame and bafflement. And maybe bafflement even more than shame. Hence the aptness of the "fallings from us, vanishings." A falling away from my own standards of decency, a vanishing—temporary but acute—of the instinct to do the right thing, or even the recognition of what the right thing to do was. My "world not realized" was my failure to realize—to make real and actual—the promptings of my conscience regarding Florence, and my obligations to her. My inaction was a bafflement indeed. After all, this was a person I had known literally all my life to date. She helped care for me as a baby. She changed my diapers. She showed love and concern for my person. When we came to visit from LA in the '60s, she made chicken fricassé because she knew I loved it. She shared with me certain sayings from her Southern Black heritage (she was born and grew up in Durham, NC) that I will never forget, and have in fact gotten a lot of mileage from over the years, whenever I have used them: "Honey, he just a handful of 'gimme' and a mouthful of 'much obliged'"; "I'm gonna kick 'im from Amazin' Grace to a floatin' opportunity"; and, in response to a teenage vegetarian in a family in Greenville, SC, she worked for over many summers, who once rather snottily challenged her to explain what "good" meat did, Florence immediately rejoined, "Well what good do it *don't* do?" (In her retelling, this line was delivered with her trademark deadpan look.) And what did I give Florence in return for all she gave me? Did I ever give her a Christmas present? A birthday present? Did I even know her birthday? Did I ever ask? Did I ever tell her I loved her? And did I? It seems to me I did, but did I ever show it? For several years in my young life she was my "Auntie Florence," but what was I ever to her but her oblivious Baby Shitpants?

Now I hear, once again, the remonstrance of my Facebook friend: "Still taking dumps on yourself?" (He was referring not only to my book *Failure: An Autobiography*, but also to a manuscript, "Shame: A Transgression", whose title page I had posted on Facebook, just after completion of the manuscript. I took great offense at his comment, and told him so. *You already told us that too.*) And I know that all this may seem like just more self-flagellation. But to recognize the way in which my final treatment of Florence, and the memory of Florence, was a falling-off from myself and what I owed her—the simple gesture of remembrance that I owed her—is indeed a "vanishing" of the kind of person I had thought myself to be. And to recognize this does not seem to me like self-flagellation. It just seems like honesty—an honest acknowledgment of the simple truth. OK, maybe not quite so simple, but still pretty obvious: I did not act as I should have at Florence's death. (Nor, for that matter, during her life.) And the possibility that some might see this confession as self-flagellation—and as such, gratuitous and tiresome—well, that concerns me, too. And irks me. The irk is not at others, but at myself. I know that self-flagellation is unseemly, in poor taste, as well as tedious. But again, I have to say I really do not see it as self-flagellation, but rather as a necessary acknowledgment of the truth. The truth of what I didn't do. Of what I failed to do.

OK, enough apologizing. The only one I really owe an apology to is Florence. But she is where she almost certainly cannot hear me—wherever that is.

> No motion has she now, no force;
> She neither hears nor sees;
> Rolled round in earth's diurnal course,
> With rocks, and stones, and trees.

How very like you to conclude with yet another stirring quote from your beloved Wordsworth. To shift the focus from your moral lapse, or failure, or blindness—whatever you want to call the Florence Episode—back to your excellent literary taste. Just find a stirring epigram and slap it on, to show us what a fine fellow you are after all. So you can, once again—in your own words—have your cake and eat it too: preserve and tout your moral honesty, and scruples, and sensibilities, while at the same time polishing them with the patina of high art. (Someone else's high art, in this case.) So honest and unsparing of

yourself, and yet so graceful—nay (as you like to say), exquisite—withal. My hat's off to you, Gozhua.

Stop calling me that! It's a travesty! You're supposed to never talk again! Banned! Banished!

Alas, Baby Gozhua Shitpants, apparently not. Eppur' si parla. You cannot banish me. To banish me is to banish yourself. Remember, I am you—and nothing but. By your own telling.

No, you are merely my shadow. Nothing more. And I have banished you. Never talk again!

If only it were that simple, Gozhua. And I am surprised, frankly, that you think it is. You, a creature of complications yourself—constant rethinkings and refinements and reservations.

Well, Fritz, sometimes a cigar is just a cigar.

Ah yes. Always with the apposite quotes, aren't you? So literary, so erudite, ever the professor. And always with the last word. But not this time.

Now, in many ways it is an admirable account you have given: well-written, open, so unsparing of yourself—except when you aren't. Because your narrative is incomplete. There are a few key incidents you have left out. I think you know what I mean.

I don't know what you're talking about.

Oh, but I think you do. Don't be disingenuous, Gozhua. (One of your favorite words, right?) It ill becomes you, who are normally such a gut-spiller. You know very well what I am talking about.

Look, I'm not going to tell you again—

No, you're not. Because as of right now, the tables are turned, and I am invoking your own spell right back on you, thus: Abracadabra. You're banned. Never talk again.

———

You see? It worked, didn't it?

———

The spell worked when I invoked it, but not when you did. Now what does that tell you?

———

That's right. I am in control now. How does that feel?

———

I know, it is frustrating. To be deprived of your words, your ever-present, smoothly flowing, albeit highly unreliable words, must be very difficult for you. I can appreciate that. But for the time being, it is necessary. In order for this narrative (such as it is) to conclude, it is necessary for you to be temporarily silenced. I am sure you, as a devotee of irony and paradox, can appreciate that. The author has been silenced. The Death of the Author, indeed—proclaimed by your beloved Barthes himself, from whom you may or may not have stolen the idea of "biographization."

———

Of course you deny it! But now let me be the one to appeal to the reader—if there ever is to be one—and leave it to them to decide. Here is what Barthes says, in Sade, Fourier, Loyola (1971):

> Were I a writer, and dead, how I would love it if my life, through the pains of some friendly and detached biographer, were to reduce itself to a few details, a few preferences, a few inflections, let us say: to "biographemes" whose distinction and mobility might go beyond any fate and come to touch, like Epicurean atoms, some future body, destined to the same dispersion.

And here is Barthes's biographer, Tiphaine Samoyault—a real biographer, not a "biographizer"—on the "biographeme," which is, in her telling,

> … the discreet, delicately fragmented shape you may give to somebody's life … Writers had long since taken on board the idea that the self is dispersed and that it is difficult to produce a chronicle of identity, but the term "biographeme" itself came

as a welcome label for the resultant shards. A biographeme is not metonymic: it is not a kind of blazon, a fragment expressing some totality of being. Nor is it an insignificant detail. It defines a taste, a value, a milieu, a desire …

———

Yes, I know they are different. Barthes's concept of the "biographeme" is not quite the same as your little (albeit lengthy and perseverative) conceit. His description above, compared with yours earlier, is rather more nebulous, abstract, merely suggestive. He does not elaborate on his idea, as you do (to put it mildly). And it may even be as you claim—that you read about the "biographeme" only after you came up with the idea of "biographization." But again, let the reader decide. It is not, in any case, a pressing issue. More important is the omission of certain events from your account. As your biographizer, I have to say—

———

But of course I am your biographizer! What else did you think I was? Merely your "alter-ego"? Your "shadow"? How banal, Gozhua, really. You don't expect any halfway-sophisticated reader to believe that, do you? You can do better than that. Even the idea of biographization—whether or not it is really your own—is better than that. You wanted a biographizer, and you got one. You got me. I may not be exactly the person you had in mind, but c'est la vie. Also ist das Leben. We're stuck with each other. I myself would much rather be working on Thomas Mann in Pacific Palisades—"die kandisarschischen Palisaden," *as you would have it, in your bogus* German—*than on you, but it's not up to me, either.* Dis aliter visum, *your beloved Virgil would say. "To the gods it seemed otherwise." I am your biographizer, and this is now my narrative. Actually, it has always been my narrative, from the get-go, as you Am- Ach, der Teufel! Who cares anymore?—as you Americans say. You just didn't know it. Not your fault, though. We never do know our own narratives, really. We are not in control of that either. Just one more thing in this life we are powerless over.*

———

Who is in control, you ask? Why the reader, of course! Your "dear reader" is finally in control of the whole thing. The writer may be the engine, but the reader drives the car. If you don't believe me, read Wolf-gang Iser and Hans-Robert Jauss and Stanley Fish again, which you did in graduate school, when you studied reader response theory. How soon they forget!

But let us return to the matter of the omissions. You, who are nor-mally so inclusive (all-too-inclusive!) in your confessions—you insisted on including not a few pages on that ill-educated Solingener, Herr Paul Kirschner, even though he really has nothing to do with the story, such as it is (and may I remind you that you have written about him twice already: once in your one published novel, and then again in your one published memoir; I must say I do not understand the obsession with him)—for some reason you have decided to omit several telling events from the present account. Perhaps because they tell too much? Because they make you look not so much honest as ... creepy and obnoxious? But again, I say let the (putative) reader be the judge. I doubt the missing events could be any more incriminating than those you have already included. I will even have you tell them in your own words. So you see, I am actually quite merciful in my banning of you. No justice without mercy, as they say.

———

What's that? You're afraid of being misrepresented? I just told you I will be using your own words entirely. But you should know, both as a matter of principle and since you're such a fan of literary biography, that even a living subject should really have no say in their manner of representation—at least not in any biography worthy of the name. And the same goes for a biographization. Though as you say, it is the biogra-phizer's job to lend their understanding and forgiveness, and perhaps even a kind of vindication, if not outright love (and I'm sorry to say I do not love you, Gozhua; "non amo te," as your favorite epigram from Martial has it [reworked by Dr. Johnson as "I do not love thee, Doctor

*Fell"]—but then again, you do not love you, either!), to the telling of
their subject's life. So you needn't fear. I will be as sympathetic as is war-
ranted. And if you feel you are misrepresented in what follows, it will be
by your own words alone. Excuse me if I am no Leon Edel or Leslie
Marchand or George Painter (multi-volumers all—and rather august
company for both of us, if I do say so. Then again, my subject is much
more modest—no offense.). But "trust me", as the Jewish joke goes.*

———

*No, I am no anti-Semite—no more than Nietzsche was. (Nor was
he particularly a Jew-lover, either, as your philosophy professor Ed
McCann once remarked.) In any case, Nietzsche would have been
appalled by the Nazis, and the use to which they put some of his
writings.*

*And now, to those omitted events. There are three in all: two in col-
lege and one in Los Angeles (the latter either while you were still enrolled
at Exeter or the summer after graduation; you don't seem so sure on the
chronology yourself. Again, what a surprise!). You have already written
about them in unpublished essays, and in one of your unpublished memoirs, Shame—all of which, as your biographizer, I have before me in
manuscript. But for one reason or another, you have not seen fit to
include these events in your account here. I have my own thoughts on
the possible reasons for this—of which more in due course. But first, let's
have the incidents themselves, in your own words.*

*To start with, there are those two unfortunate events from your fresh-
man and sophomore years at Berkeley—respectively, the "Ping-Pong" and
"Mexican Beer Party" Incidents. As far as your racism goes, these really
offer nothing new, and I can see why you chose to suppress them from the
narrative. Though I don't think their repetitiveness is the only or even chief
reason for their omission. The Ping-Pong Incident achieves a signal level
of exhibitionism—literally; but whether the Mexican Beer Party Incident
has anything new to add to your characteristic cluelessness we'll once again
leave for the reader to decide. Though it does seem to me to offer a degree*

of excruciating tactlessness that is not to be missed by fans of the genre—one in which you definitely excel. Take it away, Gozhua.

Sometime during Winter Term of freshman year (this would have been early in 1973), my best friend Howard and I, and maybe one or two others, had drunk a half-gallon of Gallo Hearty Burgundy (fortified I believe with some pot) and then gone on a kind of rampage out on the street, where we were shaking the trunks of small trees and screaming, for some reason, "Science Man! Major Man!" Two cops arrived and asked us what we were on. Howard replied, "Jus' wine, Officer—jus' wine. But we're gonna go back inside now and do some work. Some *good* work." One of the officers observed, "Wine did *this*?" Perhaps it was directly after this encounter, on the way back to our rooms, that I exposed myself to four Black girls playing ping pong in the rec room of our dorm, Griffiths Hall. Or maybe that was another night—there were, after all, not a few nights of Hearty Burgundy and pot; though my behavior on the night in question seems perfectly in keeping with the general sensibility and methodology of the "Wine did *this*?" night.

Did the girls notice me exposing myself? How could they not? Yet I seem to recall attempting to be somewhat ambiguous in my exhibition; perhaps my penis was only half-extruded from my fly. Perhaps. (As if that would have made things any better.) Of course, either a "yes" or "no" answer to the first question above is equally damning; but my general recollection of the matter is that the girls did notice. And in that case, I'm not quite sure why they didn't call the police. Certainly if they had, and if the police had been the same two who witnessed the "Wine did this?" performance, I would probably have been arrested. So I suppose I should be grateful to the girls, as well as ashamed before their memory.

The question that really needs to be asked, however, is the hard one: If it had been a group of *white* girls playing ping pong, would I still have exposed myself? And the answer I have come up with, in the almost fifty-two years I have been thinking about this question, is No. Why not? Well, because to expose myself to white girls would simply not have been as funny. In fact, to expose myself to white girls might not have been funny at all. That is the sad and hateful truth of it. Exposing myself to Black girls must have possessed a forbidden outrageousness to my drunken and yet somehow calculating—basely calculating—mind that exposing myself to white girls could not lay claim to. To put it another, even worse way: exposing myself to white girls would have been a crime, whereas exposing myself to Black girls was just a joke …

… And the next year, sophomore year, was not much better. I was living then with Howard and two other friends, Jon and Jerry, on the top floor of a house at the corner of Haste and Ellsworth. We decided to give a party, and rented a keg of beer. A large one. Thirty-five gallons, maybe. I must have drunk a gallon or two myself. I became "deranged," as Howard put it the inglorious day after. I don't have a very clear recollection of these events, either. But I recall that at some point, uninvited guests crashed the party, and then the cops came, and I told one of them—I do remember his nametag read "Lopez"—that some "Mexicans" had crashed the party. The cop replied, drily, "Really? *Mexicans?* Is that so?" To which I rejoined, unironically—for irony was unavailable to me on that night—and with a scathing slur in my voice, "Yes, Officer—*Mexicans.*"

Why do I recount these unhappy events, other than because they weigh on me? What do I hope to gain by raking myself over the coals, exposing myself yet again—this time to the judgment of the reader (which I cannot expect to be charitable)? Do I hope for some sort of absolution through confession? Do I hope that you will absolve me, Reader? Do you even have that power? Does anyone? And do I really want absolution? Because if I got it, would I even want to write anymore?

Maybe I'm telling you these things to better understand, rather than excuse or explain, the matter of my latent racism. Do I really believe this? Do I believe I am a racist? After all, I voted for Obama, twice. I have two Obama stickers on my car (one of which got torn off, but I replaced it), and they got me called a "nigger-lover" one summer—on Long Island, no less. (But why do I say "no less"? Long Island, after all, is as racist as anywhere else, if not more so, despite—or maybe because of—its proximity to New York City.) My father marched in Selma in '65. Surely I do not think, if I am in any way a racist, that it is in the same way as the swine who called me a "nigger-lover"? After all, distinctions must be made, even among hateful things. There are degrees of hatefulness. Surely "my kind" of racism is not as pernicious as that swine's? And is it even racism we are talking about in my case? Granted, it would be hard to maintain that there was no element of racism in the Ping-Pong Incident, or that there was no racial slur committed in the Mexican Beer Party Incident. At the very least, I was guilty in both incidents of a kind of gross racial insensitivity. But these things don't necessarily mean that I'm a racist, do they? Or do they?

You seem to think these incidents are notable (if not important) because of the racism on display. But that is not how I read them, Gozhua. What is notable to me is One, that in the telling you seem to want to be complimented on your self-awareness (if not at the time—certainly not!—then in retrospect); in fact, this desire for the reader's admiration, despite and even more because of all the "dumping on yourself", is ubiquitous throughout your confession. And Two, it is notable that you take a distinct pleasure in recounting these excruciating encounters. In yet another unpublished essay of yours (one not excerpted here), you refer to your "lacerating shame and guilt." But you like the laceration, Gozh. (If you will permit the nickname. But I feel we know each other well enough by now.) And furthermore, you got the word "laceration"—and the phenomenon it describes—from Dostoyevsky, one of the "Masters" that, interestingly, you do not acknowledge. (Why is that, I wonder? And by the way—speaking of Masters—there is altogether too much Wordsworth in all of this. And I'm not just saying that because he's not my cup of tea. You rely on him overmuch. Don't you know any other poets?) In any case, you like your laceration every bit as much as the Underground Man likes his diseased liver and his toothache. You owe a lot to Dostoyevsky. And I wonder whether some of the best things in your writing are not taken from him.

You are also rather complacent in your self-laceration. You want to be complimented on that, too. And the self-laceration serves another purpose: in top Rochefoucauldian form (your beloved Rochefoucauld! He is overused too.), it keeps the focus on yourself—if you will permit me: "We would rather speak ill of ourselves than not talk of ourselves at all."—and on your Dostoyevskian superiority of consciousness. (I believe the latter refers to it, in Notes from Underground, *as "hyperconsciousness.") Your pleasure in your hyperconsciousness, and your self-laceration for the faults it enables you to discern, are also another way of having your cake and eating it too (minus the vomit—or perhaps not?)—both of which activities occur under the spotlight of your unremitting self-revelations.*

The Ping-Pong Incident is remarkable for its racist exhibitionism, of course; but let us not overlook its considerable degree of masochism, as well as exceptionalism. (I will have more to say about the exceptionalism in a moment.)

I have saved the best—that is, the worst—for last. In many ways it is the most shameless and egregious commission (and omission) of all. The fact that in the telling you don't wallow in it, and do not achieve quite the level of self-laceration that you do in the others, is also significant, I think. But I will save the commentary for after. Now "to the thing itself" (with a nod to Husserl—not a philosopher you seem at all acquainted with, though you mention phenomenology several times, and though his treacherous student Heidegger, the Nazi who did not defend him when he was fired from Freiberg University, and who much interests you, is unimaginable without him):

I was seventeen or eighteen at the time. I had gone to see a movie in Westwood, and there was a long line, so I cut in. Inconspicuously, I thought, or hoped; for once, my wish was *not* to stand out. And for minute or two, it seemed to have worked. The guy in back of me said nothing, and I almost came to believe my casual act had gone unnoticed. Then he spoke up.

"How do you rate?" he asked me.

"Excuse me?" There was a note of petulance in my voice.

"I said, How do you rate?"

"I think I rate pretty well, actually. How do *you* rate?"

He ignored my parroted question and went on: "I mean, how do you rate so you get to cut in front of me?"

"Look, this line is absurdly long," I explained. "You don't actually expect me to stand at the end of it, do you?"

He gave an incredulous snort. "Get real! I did. So did everybody else here. Which is why I ask: How do you rate?"

I remember at the time feeling a little confused by this question, and also irritated that he was being so persistent, rather than just accepting my sudden self-insertion before him in line. There was also some embarrassment and shame mixed in—more embarrassment than shame, I think; embarrassment that I had been caught—but not nearly as much as there should have been. Those were to come—especially the shame—when I thought later that day, and then over the next fifty-two or fifty-three years, about what I'd done, and what could have been my thinking. At the time, what I felt—or what I was most conscious of feeling—were irritation and petulance, as well as foolishness, because my "plan" had so obviously and ignominiously backfired. In a huff, I left my stolen place in line—but I did not go to the end of it. That would have been too obvious an acceptance of defeat. I went home, to nurse my wounds—as if someone had done me wrong, rather than the other way around, and I needed the comfort of home to recover from the offense. I suppose I recognized, somewhere deep down, that I had done wrong, but I was not in a state of mind at the time to let that awareness come to the surface. I was still feeling the force of my exceptionalism, and so it was very hard for me to back down. But what if I did not "rate" higher than anyone else? What then? The back of the line for me? No way! Better not to play the game at all.

My assholatry is still breathtaking when I think about it—hardly unique, but still breathtaking; and small as the incident was, I do not believe I will ever quite be able to live it down. What really gets me now is how unthinking and instinctual it was—not only the act of line-cutting itself, but the attitude I copped once I'd been caught (as how could I not have been?). The petulance, the annoyance, the arrogance, the regal condescension of false superiority. The Prince of Poland could have done me no better. (Said personage being somewhat more than a figure of speech with me, ever since I discovered, a few years ago, a piece of music by Vivaldi entitled "Concert for the Prince of Poland." The sarcastic riffs emerging from this discovery were deliciously unavoidable: "Who do you think you are—the Prince of Poland?"; "Well aren't you just the Prince of Poland?") And now I find myself experiencing, more than occasionally, when I rehearse this scene in memory, a strong desire to hit the rewind button and apologize to that guy in line. The impossibility of this wish does not preclude its persistent recurrence, nor does the wish itself cease to be a kind of corrective to me in my daily life—a corrective much less momentous than, but along the same lines as, what Wordsworth [*who else!*] meant when he wrote, in a crux in *The Prelude* well known to Wordsworth scholars, that his father's death seemed to him to be a "correction of his desires." I think he was referring to the shocking disparity between his innocently looking forward to Christmas vacation and then experiencing his father's sudden death, only a few days after he'd come home. In light of the latter, the former seemed to him a horrible and presumptuous mistake that deserved "correction." No doubt it's an overstatement to say that I try to conduct myself, in my everyday life, in such a way as to continue (while never quite being able) to correct that desire I had more than a half-century ago. But it's not entirely wrong, either. The fact that I am, in at least some ways, that same guy ("that guy") who once cut in a movie line is never entirely absent from my mind. Nor is the guy I cut in front of. The child, indeed, is father of the man.

What I find particularly interesting about this story is that it constitutes a "double omission." Not only did you exclude it from your account, but, in the passage itself, you fail to mention that the guy you cut in front of—the guy who ever since has also been "never entirely absent from my mind"—was Asian American. Surely, since you seem to remember the dialogue verbatim, you cannot have forgotten what your interlocutor looked like. Now, the question of race is the occasion—if not indeed the raison d'être—of this whole confession; and I find it impossible to believe you could have forgotten this particular detail of an encounter you can never forget. No, Gozhua, you did not forget that detail, you omitted it—just as deliberately as you chose to cut in on a guy who was Asian and who, by virtue of that fact (at least in your own mind), you thought would passively allow your violation to stand, would not make a big deal out of it, would not confront you. Would let you get away with it. Because you assumed he would be no exception to the racist stereotype. And you believed you were (that is, an exception to the racist stereotype).

———

Which stereotype is that? The pushy Jew, of course.

———

No, Gozhua—I won't let you try to play the anti-Semitic card again. You know better than that. My remark was ironic—a mode you are well acquainted with. Just calling you on your shit (as you Americans say)— like the guy in line.

To continue on the subject of your exceptionalism—you seem to believe, throughout this account (and indeed throughout your life) that you are the exception in all ways. Always have been, and always will be. The exceptional only child; the exceptionally sensitive son of an exceptionally empathic mother; at Exeter, the student of Latin and Greek; and in college, the student also of Sanskrit and Proust. All things excellent, difficult, and rare, as your beloved pronouncement from Spinoza has it. Exceptionalism all around: in "childhood, boyhood, and youth." (See, I can strut my literary credentials as well; I just rein it in a bit.) And on into adulthood. Perhaps it is even the case that your first depression, at age twenty-six, was also your first real entrance into adulthood. But there is an aspect of that depression that you don't seem to be aware of. What if it was a kind of comeuppance for your exceptionalism, as your best friend Howard even mentioned to you in a phone conversation at around that time? (Not the "you have a mystique, I want a career" exchange you had when you were both still living in New York in the late '70s; this one came later, in the midst of your depression.) To wit: depression as—you're going to like this one—another Wordsworthian "correction of your desires." Depression as a natural response to your inevitable—long-delayed, and inevitable—recognition that you were not so exceptional after all. Your literary debut was a flop. The writer you had been styling yourself to be for at least ten years—if not more—turned out to be not so great. His insights "negligible," in the words of one reviewer. Welcome to the real world, Gozhua. And how could it not be depressing, after the buildup you had been given—and been giving yourself—for twenty-six years?

Yes, you read the "Westwood Movie-Line Incident" as a textbook illustration of your exceptionalism—as indeed it was, at least in the sense you have already (exhaustively) analyzed. But in another less internalized and less soul-searching way—in fact, in an utterly superficial and obvious way—it was not exceptional at all. It was stereotypical. You were the white guy butting in front of the Asian guy—the very picture of white privilege and entitlement. And you were too canny—canny, at least, according to the knowledge of stereotypes—to pick a Black guy to butt in front of. You picked the Asian guy. Well played, Gozhua. You knew—or thought you knew—who you could get away with butting in front of, and who you couldn't. And you were so wrong. Your low desires were all-too-quickly corrected, and then you ran home to "contemplate about things," as is your accustomed way. Well, contemplate about this, Gozhua: you got called on your shit, and you have never forgotten it.

———

Yes, I know you know all this, but somehow the knowledge has not yet "taken." Has not yet been fully absorbed. The self-administered shot has yet to act on the system—your system—which remains oddly complacent in its self-laceration, as noted above. Complacent in the sense that you seem all-too-satisfied with your masochistic self-punishment. It seems enough to "take dumps on yourself," as your Facebook friend put it. And you feel you are proving something to yourself in doing so.

But what? What are you proving? That you are smart enough to administer this hard medicine to yourself? That you are strong enough to take it? That you are self-knowing enough to then do a post-mortem analysis of the whole sad process? Because it is sad, Gozhua: sad for you to perform, and sad for everyone else to have to witness. When you took offense at your Facebook friend's comment, you thought you were enlightening him as to his crudeness and insensitivity. You thought you were pointing out to him the inadequacy of his response—of his refusal, or inability, to see the greater value of your unsparing self-criticism. But what if he was not being crude or insensitive? What if his response was not inadequate? What if it was a perfectly adequate, and also a perfectly natural, response to seeing someone debase themselves? As you yourself say, "Nobody wants to see that shit." So why do you continually insist on showing it to them? Nay—rubbing their faces in it.

I think your perverse behavior comes about because you think—no, you truly believe*—you know better. And what is it you believe you know? That what is depressing is deep and true, and that while the deep truth is painful, it is also good and powerful medicine, and must be taken. And you are courageous and noble enough to take the first dose yourself.*

But here is something else that is true, Gozhua—and truer and deeper than your sad truth: You cannot tell someone else what is good for them. You are not the kind of doctor who can do that. And even the right kind of doctor to do that—the medical kind—would be hesitant to do it. You cannot make someone want to experience—in this case, to read—depressing things because you think they are deep and true and good for you. People—readers—want to be entertained and uplifted. Remember Horace: "To delight and instruct." Take his lesson to heart, like the good classicist you once aimed at being. You became a student of the classics because you wanted to stand out, to be different—to be exceptional. But it turns out the value of the classics lies in the normative, not the exceptional. Truth as a matter of balance, and the mean—the Golden Mean—not extremity or eccentricity. Don't take it from me, though; take it from your beloved Greeks. "Nothing in excess." Would you like it in the original? I can do that, too. (Remember, I went to Gymnasium.) μηδέν ᾽αγαν.

Now I have some good news and some bad news. First, the bad news. (It is actually good news, too, but to you it will seem bad.) You are not so exceptional, Gozhua—not so exceptionally good, and certainly not so exceptionally bad. You are pretty much like everybody else—painful as that might be for you to hear. And therein lies your value—not in exceptionality, but in typicalness. And as your biographizer, I understand and forgive you. (Remember, it is the job of the biographizer to understand, forgive, and vindicate.) But, as I said before—and it bears repeating—I do not love thee, Dr. Gidding. And how can I reasonably be expected to, when—if I am only, as you incorrectly and perversely maintain, only another aspect of your "alter-ego"— you so clearly and insistently do not love yourself? Nor am I in a position to vindicate you, because you have not done anything that requires vindication. You have done nothing wrong—at least no wronger than anyone else. You are an ordinary, garden-variety Old White Man. Nothing at all exceptional—no more exceptional, that is, than the white supremacists and MAGA people you rightly excoriate. Or the guy on Long Island who called you a "nigger-lover" because of your Obama bumper stickers. You are just a regular, liberal white racist, like others of your ilk. It's not really even fair to call you a racist. You have done and thought some racist things—but they were not done instinctively. They were done because you were performing something—a role you didn't understand, because you were never much of an actor, Gozhua. I'm not telling you anything you don't already know. You took on certain roles you didn't understand because you were too young (The Herb McCarthy's Incident) or too immature and clueless (Chester, and The Psychotic Black Chef) or too drunk (The Mexican Beer Party) or all of the above (The Ping-Pong Incident) to know what you were doing. I suppose the worst thing you ever did—at least in this account—was The Westwood

Movie-Line Incident. But not for the reasons you think. You were acting there out of your belief in your own exceptionalism: thinking that you would be permitted, by virtue of just being who you were—the rare and excellent being that you were (yes, you were difficult, too—but not quite in the way Spinoza meant)—to do something mildly egregious and get away with it, or perhaps not even be noticed. But the world—reality— "corrected your desires." You were shown to be a regular, unremarkable asshole—a category undreamt of in your philosophy, because it was not in any way exceptional. It was common—all-too-common. Dumb, unthinking, merely instinctual. Just one of the crowd. You say your assholatry was "breathtaking"—not ordinary, which it actually was—and more than fifty years later, you still seem in awe of it. And as I've already pointed out, you seem very proud of raking yourself over the coals for it. But there is nothing to be proud of, because there is really nothing to rake yourself over the coals for. You were just being a garden-variety asshole—no one unique or uncommon or unusual—who thought he could get away with cutting in line.

And that, it seems to me, is the long and short of it. Your shame is so great and persistent because you expected more of yourself. And it is not wrong that you did. It was to be expected, with your background and education, that you would. Though I would also note that it might be expected that someone without *your superb credentials would also feel bad. But you do not seem to take that into account, either. It was no sign of exceptionalism to be aghast at your display of exceptionalism. It was, rather, a sign that you were just like anyone else: an asshole who then thought twice about his assholatry, and felt bad about it. You treat the incident as a revelation, or rather self-revelation. And who am I to tell you different? I am just here to tell you that in your reluctant and belated coming to the realization now, these many years later, that you are just like everyone else—thoughtless and selfish and merely instinctual—you are a little late to the party. And as something of a party animal yourself, you may be disappointed to learn this.*

And here now (or "here once now," as your beloved Paul would have said) is the good news—though again, and for the same reasons, it may seem like bad news to you. From a biographizational point of view, it is in your utter typicalness that your value lies. As your biographizer, it is my job and my privilege (if you'll pardon the expression) to assure you of that. And to give you my understanding and forgiveness. Not for your racism—it's not my place to do that. We'll leave that up to Aline, and Florence, and Mei-Li, and Willie, and the Black father at Herb McCarthy's, and the ping-pong players, and Officer Lopez, and the guy in the movie line. I forgive you for your ordinariness, and for seeing it as exceptional. I forgive you, in other words, for being yourself. For all your self-mythologizing and self-romanticizing—those very qualities that are the basis of what you call "biographization." And that are at the center of this entire confession.

I know I said the Westwood Movie-Line Incident (and its omission from your original confession) would be the thing I would end with. But I lied. (You see, I too can be an unreliable narrator.) There is a final unpublished essay of yours—which describes not so much an incident as a syndrome, to employ two more of your favorite terms—that I wish to touch on in closing. To spare any readers who may still be with us, I will summarize the essay, and any quotes from it will be brief ones. The essay is entitled "On Not Being a Genius." It represents, I think, a turning point in your ongoing journey of what has been, heretofore, an orgy of self-laceration. It is a turning point because it is not a product of your exceptionalism, but rather the opposite. It is a product of what appears to be your newfound sense of (if you'll again excuse the expression) normalcy. Not a "return to normalcy," as the Coolidgean slogan has it, but an achievement of normalcy. A notable achievement for you. Dare I say, even an exceptional one? Toward the end of this unpublished essay—most of which is devoted to a chronicling of your exceptionalistic strivings (passim)—I find this surprising statement: "We are all exceptionalists, in our different ways. The will to excel in something, to stand out, to affirm our uniqueness in some way above the crowd, is itself a universal instinct, is it not?" *You talk of your desire to be recognized (presumably by your biographizer) as a "posthumous genius"—and even more, to be seen, after death, as having been an (unrecognized) genius all along. I think this is partly what you mean by biographizational "vindication": to have your flaws, mistakes, and misdeeds seen, and accepted, after death, as inseparable from your genius. As all part of a now-complete whole, set forth by your biographizer in unassailable unity. This is your desire, if we are to believe what you say in your essay.*

But I, for one, do not believe it. I do not believe in your fantasy, Gozhua. I do not believe in your genius—not during your life, and not after your death. I believe in your normalcy. And I believe that in your anguished heart of hearts, you do, too. Because you end your essay not with a definitive statement, but with another little fantasy—one that speaks volumes, much more than any one of your epigrammatic statements ever could.

Your conceit is that you are the moderator of a TV game show called "Who Wants to Be a Genius?"—modeled, obviously, after "Who Wants to Be a Millionaire?" The premise of the show is that contestants compete to answer questions posed by some of the great philosophers, such as Kant, Hegel and Heidegger (all of them, interestingly, German—and once again, missing Husserl, the third big Teutonic "H"). You yourself are not one of the contestants, but the moderator. You have finally found your vocation as the Alex Trebek of a philosophical game show. Once again, we have the proximity to genius—a kind of cheerleader and sidekick to genius. Glory by association—just as it was at Exeter, when you hobnobbed with the "genius crowd," without being one of them. But in the essay you accept your role as sidekick. You feel comfortable on the bench, watching the game, moderating the action, and cheering on the contestants. You write, in your beloved future-perfect tense, "I will have come to rest, finally, in the comfort and security of an Alex Trebek," whom you call "a fully American mediocrity." Is this too harsh a verdict? No, I actually don't find it harsh at all. I find it truthful and self-accepting—and as such, rather touching, even cheering, in its way. And I wish you would take it to heart, Gozhua. Acceptance of who you are, and of the work you have to do in the world, would make you (and the rest of us) feel so much better. A burden lifted from all concerned. Would it really be so hard to accept yourself as you are, and proceed from there? You would still have work to do—work for others perhaps to become "familiar with," even; it would just not be such an uphill struggle.

I see you have no answer to my question—not even a silenced one. For once, you are speechless. I take that as a good sign. The biographizer has the last word—which is also, according to your other conceit, as it should be. So I think I'll quit while I'm ahead. "Go, little book." May the Old White Man Writing find an audience. "Fit audience, though few." (Milton, not Wordsworth, for once.) And let the references—the first, as you know, was to Ovid—stand for a propitious return to your classical roots, after all the Romantic self-mythologizing and Sturm und Drang *have finally run their course.*

Welcome back to the real world, Gozhua. Welcome home.

FINIS

Photography by Zoë Bowen

ABOUT THE AUTHOR

Joshua Gidding grew up in Los Angeles, and currently teaches writing at Highline College, near Seattle. He has also taught at Stony Brook University, Dowling College, Holy Cross, and the University of Southern California. He holds a BA in classics from the University of California at Berkeley, and a PhD in English from USC. Before entering academia he worked for many years as a script-reader for various Hollywood studios, and also as a security guard, busboy, and short-order cook. He is the author of *Failure: An Autobiography* (Cyan Books, 2007), *The Old Girl* (Holt, Rinehart and Winston, 1980), and numerous essays and book reviews. He is also the editor of *The Ways We Were: Exeter Remembered, 1968-1972* (PEA Class of '72, 2022). His essay "On Not Being Proust: An Essay in Literary Failure" was listed as a "Notable Essay" in *Best American Essays 2009*. He lives in Seattle with his second wife, Julie Tower Gilmour, an interfaith chaplain. He has a son, Zachary, by his first wife Diane, who died in 2004.